Youth, Murder, Spectacle

CULTURAL STUDIES

Series Editors
Janice Radway, Duke University
Richard Johnson, University of Birmingham

Youth, Murder, Spectacle: The Cultural Politics of "Youth in Crisis"   Charles R. Acland

Viewing, Reading, Listening: Audiences and Cultural Reception   edited by Jon Cruz and Justin Lewis

The Madonna Connection: Representational Politics, Subcultural Identities, and Cultural Theory   edited by Cathy Schwichtenberg

Dreaming Identities: Class, Gender, and Generation in 1980s Hollywood Movies   Elizabeth G. Traube

Enlightened Racism: The Cosby Show, *Audiences, and the Myth of the American Dream*   Sut Jhally and Justin Lewis

FORTHCOMING

The Audience and Its Landscape   edited by James Hay, Lawrence Grossberg, and Ellen Wartella

Art and the Committed Eye: Culture, Society, and the Functions of Imagery   Richard Leppert

Girls: The Representation of Femininity in Popular Culture   edited by Elizabeth Ann Kaplan

Boys: The Representation of Masculinity in Popular Culture   edited by Paul Smith

Being Indian and the Politics of Indianness   Gail Valaskakis

Frameworks of Culture and Power: Complexity and Politics in Cultural Studies   Richard Johnson

Youth, Murder, Spectacle

The Cultural Politics of "Youth in Crisis"

Charles R. Acland

WESTVIEW PRESS
Boulder • San Francisco • Oxford

Cultural Studies

Copyright © 1995 by Westview Press, Inc.

Published in 1995 in the United States of America by Westview Press, Inc., 5500 Central Avenue, Boulder, Colorado, 80301-2877, and in the United Kingdom by Westview Press, 36 Lonsdale Road, Summertown, Oxford OX2 7EW

Library of Congress Cataloging-in-Publication Data
Acland, Charles R., 1963–
Youth, murder, spectacle : the cultural politics of "youth in
    crisis" / Charles R. Acland
        p.   cm. — (Cultural studies)
    Includes bibliographical references (p.   ) and index.
ISBN 0-8133-2286-3 (hc). —ISBN 0-8133-2287-1 (pbk.)
    1. Youth in mass media—United States.   2. Violence in mass media—
United States.   3. United States—Popular culture—History—20th
century.   I. Series.
P94.5.Y72A25   1995
303.69083—dc20   94-16491
                                                                                 CIP

Printed and bound in the United States of America

⧝ The paper used in this publication meets the requirements
    of the American National Standard for Permanence of Paper
    for Printed Library Materials z39.48-1984.

10   9   8   7   6   5   4   3   2   1

For my nephew Jeremy

Contents

PART THREE: SPECTACLE

Acknowledgments

Any comprehensive attempt to trace out the development of one's own thought is ultimately doomed to failure and frustration. Many factors intervene, for better or worse, to prod and guide the formation of an argument, a critical stance, or simply an opinion, and all deserve some form of acknowledgment. However, I do not want this to look like one of those CD liner notes in which everything from breakfast cereals to Mary Tyler Moore is given credit for "adding to the groove," though I must admit that the impulse to do so is strong. I have been fortunate to have had outstanding encouragement and assistance from a number of people. The following are but a few of them.

To begin with, James Carey, James Hay, and Paula Treichler all provided insightful and generous advice on this project. I am particularly indebted to Larry Grossberg, who continues to be a significant influence in my intellectual life. His contribution was not only one of debate and recommendation; he was also most consistent in providing me with tactics to organize and develop my thinking. I owe much to Frank Burke, Kevin Dowler, and Kathleen Fleming, all of whom, in various capacities as friends and colleagues, were crucial to my own ability to successfully undertake and complete this project; they even went further by reading drafts! And along this line, immeasurable thanks go to Beth Seaton, who provided support and perceptive commentary when they were most needed.

Sheri Zernentsch, fact checker extraordinaire, contributed a generous amount of energy when this work was in its final stages. Her efficiency and humor helped with the book as well as my sanity. And the people at Westview Press, particularly Gordon Massman, Michelle Asakawa, and Jan Kristiansson, deserve credit for expert editorial advice and overall professionalism.

Many others played multiple roles as dear friends and comrades by offering ideas, examples, counterarguments, and much more; they make for an enviable community, one that I am always grateful to be a part of. In the end, they are the reason for going on. They include Will Straw, Julian Samuel, Jody Berland, Bill Burns, Martin Allor, William Buxton, Blaine Allan, the Department of Film Studies (staff and students) at Queen's University, Barri Cohen, Greg Reid, Cheryl Simon, Nancy Frohlick, Julian Halliday, Mark Fenster, Holly Kruse, Philip Gordon, Keya Ganguly, and Keir Keightley. Much appreciation goes to my parents, Derek and Joan Acland. In so many ways, they have been able to supply a perfect mix of professional assistance and familial support. I am deeply grateful to them, well beyond what is possible to represent here. And finally, Victoria Mallett continues to be a profound personal and intellectual inspiration for me. Her ability to cut through layers of critical cloudiness straight to the quick is a skill worth envying, and I do.

Charles R. Acland

PART ONE

Youth

1

Youth in Crisis

We are simply trying to bring to light the texture of a discourse, the texture being composed not only of what was said, but of all that was needed for it to be said.

—**Philippe Riot, "The Parallel Lives of Pierre Rivière"**

On the occasion of International Youth Year 1980, the General Conference of UNESCO in Belgrade produced a comprehensive report entitled *Youth in the 1980s.* Comparisons with the first UNESCO report on youth, in 1968, are interesting. As the authors point out, the key words of the 1968 report were "confrontation-contestation," "marginalization," "counter-culture," "counter-power," and "youth culture." In contrast, the 1981 report suggests that "the key words in the experience of young people in the coming decade are going to be: 'scarcity,' 'unemployment,' 'underemployment,' 'ill-employment,' 'anxiety,' 'defensiveness,' 'pragmatism' and even 'subsistence' and 'survival'" (UNESCO 1981, 17). The assertive terms of the first report depict an instance of vitality, possibility, and ambition. At that time, a significant population of young people, most pronounced in Europe and North America, had attained a privileged social position economically, politically, demographically, and intellectually. Youths were set to begin deploying those powers for confrontation; this was their arrival on the political scene, making demands of representation and becoming a mobilized social energy. However wary mainstream politics remained, youth was indisputably a significant force to be reckoned with. That moment has passed. The terms chosen by UNESCO to characterize the youth of the then-approaching decade of the 1980s demonstrate a striking prescience. UNESCO predicted correctly that "if the 1960s challenged certain categories of youth in certain parts of the world with a crisis of culture, ideas and institutions, the 1980s will confront a new generation with a concrete, structural crisis of chronic economic uncertainty and even deprivation" (p. 17).

3

This structural crisis of youth in the United States throughout the 1980s escalated rapidly to a point that is now commonly recognized as one of unprecedented social strife and disparity between social factions. And even though some contest the historical uniqueness of this predicament, there is something significant about the broad acceptance of this description; it is now part of popular common sense that something has gone wrong with today's youth. For instance, a joint commission report of the American Medical Association (AMA) and the National Association of State Boards of Education (NASBE), *Code Blue: Uniting for Healthier Youth* (1990), designed to alert teachers and medical professionals to the seriousness of the situation, concludes that "never before ... has one generation of American teenagers been less healthy, less cared-for or less prepared for life than their parents were at the same age" (Lewis 1990, A21). This is a remarkable and alarming assertion. The vigor of the young has traditionally provided higher aspirations for the future. The "next generation" as a rhetorical concept has carried the impression of vision and hope. And yet now, the report claims, for ostensibly the first time in this century, not only does the promise of "a better tomorrow" seem absurd—the young also cannot expect even the same quality of life as their parents.

The AMA-NASBE commission report points out that we are living in a situation in which more that 20 percent of American children live below the poverty line. For African-Americans the figure is 45 percent and for Mexican-Americans, 39. The U.S. Bureau of the Census indicates that youth is the most heavily unemployed segment of the population. Unemployment for white males between sixteen and nineteen is 15.4 percent, and for females it is 13.4 percent; for black males, unemployment reaches 34.5 percent, and for females it is 34.9 percent (U.S. Bureau of the Census 1989, 379). Furthermore, the available jobs are heavily exploitive, mostly part-time with few, if any, benefits. This situation reflects a shift in which the young have become increasingly central to many service industries as a cheap, short-term, unskilled labor force.

Even in the context of indisputable economic strife, the AMA-NASBE commission concludes that something is distinct about the conditions of today's youth. The commission argues that unlike the past, in which physical illness was the primary threat to the young, today the problems are primarily behavioral. Here the commission refers to the high rates of teenage pregnancy, sexually transmitted diseases, alcohol and drug consumption, suicide, alcohol- and drug-related deaths, and violent crime as measures of the threats to contemporary youth. Read through the arenas of sex, drugs, and violent crime—the unholy trinity of misguided youth—we are presumably in a situation in which, despite the opportunities and efforts of concerned citizens, something is failing.

The empirical validity of these measures of a behavioral crisis of youth could be debated at a number of different levels. This is an ever-present problem for the positivist social critic: How do we know that we are measuring what we say we are measuring, and how do we know what the numbers are saying? Arguments must be made to interpret findings, which suggests that conclusions are provisional and to various degrees are sites of contestation. However, the question of the accuracy of sociological measures tells only part of the story. Of crucial importance is the manner in which such conclusions are deployed; the AMA-NASBE document intended to serve a public information function, and its conclusions cannot be seen outside of that purpose. Its audience was supposed to be primarily those who deal with young people in a professional capacity, such as teachers and social workers. Sometimes pointing to the structural impossibilities of unemployment, a failing education system, and limited health services, the AMA-NASBE commission also focuses on parental neglect of the young as a principal impetus of their destructive impulses and actions. While the report provides a description of a social phenomenon, it also tells of the attention paid to that phenomenon, or rather to that set of measures and judgments that purport to indicate the existence of a crisis. Whether or not the situation is historically unique, it is certainly being taken as such.

This is the context in which American youth came under scrutiny in the 1980s. And "youth in crisis" took many forms. Whether it was *The Oprah Winfrey Show* on "Teens in Crisis," Tipper Gore's book *Raising PG Kids in an X-Rated Society* (1987), an NBC prime-time news special entitled "Bad Girls," or a Cinemax documentary called *Why Did Johnny Kill?*, there was definitely a vociferous public debate concerning the nature of contemporary youth. Certainly, after Brenda Spencer fired her semiautomatic rifle at her San Diego high school classmates in 1979, killing and wounding eleven people in total, we have seen no shortage of spectacular youth crimes wash through the popular media. Racist youths in Howard Beach, a largely white section of New York, chased and beat three black youths in December 1986, killing one as he ran into the path of an oncoming car. Sixteen-year-old Cheryl Pierson hired a high school classmate, seventeen-year-old Sean Pica, to kill her father in February 1986. Ronald Lampasi, then sixteen, killed his stepfather and wounded his mother in 1983. He claimed to have been acting out a scenario from the fantasy game Dungeons and Dragons. This was followed by concern about the effects of the game, its relationship to satanism, and a number of other murders and suicide pacts whose inspiration was supposedly found in the confusion between fantasy and reality encouraged by Dungeons and Dragons. Los Angeles gang violence provided images of warlike urban conflict throughout the decade, making the "Bloods," the "Crips," and the "drive-by shooting" household words.

As gang violence appeared to move eastward across the country, young murderers seemed to get younger. Britt Kellum was nine when he killed his older brother in 1985 and thirteen when he killed his younger brother. In Florida in 1986, a five-year-old confessed to deliberately pushing a three-year-old off a five-story balcony. In 1992, Amy Fisher, the "Long Island Lolita," tried to kill her lover's wife, sparking an unprecedented amount of coverage, including three made-for-tv movies. And by the summer of 1993, it seemed that no one was immune to the effects of this tide of youth violence when basketball superstar Michael Jordan's father was killed in North Carolina.

Brenda Spencer is particularly important because she reintroduced into popular consciousness a supremely terrifying aspect of contemporary youth violence: meaninglessness. When asked why she committed such an atrocious crime, she replied simply, "I don't like Mondays. Mondays always get me down." The frankness and banality of this explanation—who, after all, would disagree?—were a terrible contrast to the image of her spraying bullets into a schoolyard. How could sense be made of this? Though there were several key precendents to her youthful nihilism—for instance, the 1950s killer Charles Starkweather, particularly as mythologized in *Badlands* (Terrence Malick, 1974)—Spencer's innovation, as it was popularized, was affectlessness. The Boomtown Rats' hit song "I Don't Like Mondays" gave Spencer and her affectlessness a certain folk hero status, much as broadsheets and songs celebrating criminals had done in previous centuries. The romantic tone of the hit song suggested that the representation of violent youth crime was about to be reinvested as a cultural expression of a displaced generation. What would become fearful throughout the 1980s was, for a brief moment, a weird celebration in popular music.

In 1957, when Pulitzer Prize–winning journalist Benjamin Fine published his study of juvenile crime, *1,000,000 Delinquents*, he began by citing examples of crimes in which teenagers "kill for thrills." The idea of teenage crime as teenage entertainment suggests that if society alleviates boredom, the problem is solved. And, indeed, Fine's book ends with a series of recommendations for "training schools" and organized leisure activity. Brenda Spencer made this approach obsolete. Calls for increased prison sentences and trying of minors as adults more frequently became the focal point of dealing with youth crime. For instance, during the 1980s it was not unusual to see articles like the one in the *Chicago Tribune* entitled "Troubled Teens, Big Business" (Kass 1989b). Inside, the author provided helpful "consumer information" for parents who were shopping around for a psychiatric institution in which to commit a "troubled" teenager. The author suggested, among other things, that "*parents should visit several units themselves to see how children are treated.* They should determine when and why medication, handcuffs, leather straps, four-point restraints and solitary confinement are used to control their children. Does the hospital have specific guidelines on these extreme measures?" (Kass 1989a, 18).

Throughout the 1980s, there was a renewal of old debates, such as the negative influence of rock and roll discussed at the Parents' Music Resource Center hearings, questions of censorship, and toughening of penalties for juvenile offenders, which culminated in debates concerning capital punishment for juveniles. In 1986, the state of Texas executed a murderer who had committed his crime at the age of seventeen, and in 1989 there were twenty-seven juvenile criminals on death row in the United States. The 1980s also witnessed the initiation of contemporary agendas, the most pervasive and powerful of which was the "War on Drugs," which in so many ways modified daily life in America. One unique contribution of this period was the marketing of a home drug-testing unit called DrugAlert. As the final link in the circuit tying domesticity to a national law-and-order campaign, private life became the site of surveillance based upon the presumed activities of the young. As the principal target for the "just say no" campaign, youth were centrally implicated by the War on Drugs as both those who required protection and those who were involved in the criminal activity of drug culture.

Warning labels on food, records and compact disks, art exhibits (see Dubin 1992), and, more recently, television programs constructed a new landscape of everyday danger. It is unclear whether "parental advisories" actually placed additional power into the hands of adults, but such advisories certainly gave the impression of concern and fear about the cultural consumption of the young. The James Bond film *License to Kill* (John Glen, 1988), after the usual cocktail (shaken, not stirred) of torture and mayhem, ended with a surgeon general's warning about the effects of smoking. There were complaints that the impressionable would see Bond's smoking as an endorsement.

As absurd as this may seem (why no warning about reckless driving or hang gliding?), lifestyle politics became an important arena in which a person's ethical and moral makeup could be displayed and evaluated. Fletcher A. Brothers founded Freedom Village to help troubled youths by restoring the centrality of "Christian virtue" to their lives, and he also produced a syndicated television program. On the air, he would repeatedly describe a young person as "a former satanist and heavy metal music fan." The continuum between the two was assumed by many to be obvious; certain demonized cultural forms allowed for generalized claims about vast populations of fans.

While cultural consumption provided evidence of criminality, criminal youth remained a specific and pivotal instance of the crisis. Juvenile delinquency, an invention of the nineteenth century, has been a prominent social concern since its inception. In the present context, violent youth is particularly visible. For instance, despite a 13 percent drop in the death rate of youths, the Office of Disease Prevention and Health Promotion says that there has been an 11 percent increase in violent deaths of youths since the 1960s (Friend 1988, 1). Firearms kill more than 10 percent of people who die before the age of twenty ("Fatal Shootings" 1989, 27). The AMA-NASBE report points out that homicide is the leading cause of death among African-Americans aged fifteen to nineteen. Between 1983 and 1987, according to the FBI, there was a national increase of more than 22 percent for juveniles arrested for homicide and manslaughter with intent; in Philadelphia alone, youths under eighteen arrested on murder charges increased 90 percent in 1988 (Colimore 1989, A1).

As reported in the popular press, every empirical measure seems to indicate yet another crack in the previously tranquil and sheltered, or so it is presumed, life of the young. A June 1989 *Time* magazine feature story entitled "Our Violent Kids," in a rather blatant display of alarm, announces that 88 percent of Americans believe that teenage violence is a bigger problem today than in the past (Toufexis 1989, 52; see Figure 1.1). And yet there is significant evidence that contradicts these taken-for-granted measures of crisis. For instance, despite some increases in violent crimes committed by juveniles in the 1980s, the levels are still far below those of the mid-1970s.[1] The U.S. Congress (1991, 591) confirms this claim in a 1991 comprehensive report on adolescent health: "Although current rates of arrests for serious offenses by U.S. adolescents may seem high, *there is some evidence that the aggregate arrest rates for serious violent offenses and for serious property offenses committed by U.S. adolescents have declined since the mid-1970s.*" The report's authors do not downplay concern for criminal youth, citing an increase in murder and nonnegligent manslaughter offenses committed by those between thirteen and eighteen years of age. But the report points out that "*a large majority of U.S. adolescents commit minor offenses at least once and that a considerable minority of adolescents also commit serious offenses at least once*" and that it is only "*a small subset of adolescent offenders who commit multiple, serious offenses*" (pp. 594–596).

Even though delinquency is still dominated by male youths, the 1980s saw a significant increase in the arrest rates of female youths (p. 597). The aforementioned report indicates that arrest rates for serious offenses in the same period were higher for black adolescents than for their white counterparts and that both groups were higher than other populations, including Native Americans, Asian-Americans and Pacific Islanders (p. 598). The report also cites research that points to combinations of family variables, such as lack of parental supervision, parental rejection, poor parental disciplinary practices, and familial criminal behavior, as the best predictors of juvenile delinquency (p. 603).

These items provide a sketch of the terrain of American delinquency in the 1980s. Patterns of incidence of and involvement in particular crimes are apparent. Without question, there is much to be concerned about, and innovative forms of action are warranted. But these patterns do not indicate uniform increases. Instead, the ample public belief in the increasingly violent nature of American youth must be understood as a *felt crisis*. In a description of the ideological work of new conservatism, Lawrence Grossberg (1992, 284) characterizes an "affective epidemic" as one that consists of a fetishized mobile site that is "invested with values disproportionate to their actual worth," where in addition to ideological meaning, there is a "daily economy of saturated panics." For present purposes, how these observations about youth crime come to form and support the feeling of a crisis of youth is unpredictable. And yet we need to unearth the mechanisms for the construction of "saturated panics."

We can point, as the report tries to do, to all the missing information. Is the increase in female arrest rates due to changes in criminal behavior or to changes in attitudes toward women in general, leading to the police's willingness to charge young women offenders where they would have previously been released? Is the higher instance of African-American violent crime actually a marker of cultural difference, as some would have us believe, or it is representative of differential po-

Figure 1.1 A Time *feature article, 1989.*

licing methods? Or is it an expression of general social despair? If nonnuclear families contribute to a decrease in parental supervision of children, are they then contributing to juvenile crime? Clearly, the move from the "obviousness" of empirical measures to their meaning, to their significance for policy and policing, is always a site of contest. And as these questions suggest, this move toward meaning has particular interest for critics of sexism and racism. A framework is necessary to connect up "evidence" about the world with meanings, solutions, causes, and predictors. When we examine *the work evidence is made to do* we have insight into that framework. In this respect, issues of race, gender, sexuality, class, and, of course, age are at the very core of the project of understanding the emergence of a commonsense crisis of youth.

It is also often the case that youth violence is taken to be symptomatic of other supposed social crises, such as the destruction of the nuclear family, the drug problem, the problems of "inner-city" (read: nonwhite) populations, the plethora of pornography, the failure of public education, and even, as Geraldo Rivera is quick to indicate, the popularity of satanism. The aforementioned *Time* feature article is exemplary. Along with general information about "our violent kids," the article points to "causes" such as "lack of parental supervision, lenient treatment of juvenile offenders, too much sex in movies, television, and advertising." And some popular "remedies" are suggested, such as "tougher criminal penalties, and greater restraints on showing sex and violence on television, in movies, and in rock-music lyrics" (Toufexis 1989, 57). At the point of virtually every measure of social crisis—race relations, drugs, censorship, pornography, gender, sexuality, families, poverty, waning tradition—sits the loosely defined, yet rhetorically forceful, youth. Regardless of the empirical evidence, which is itself contradictory, it is clear that "youth gone wild" is a popularly recognized and increasingly forceful site of social concern in the United States. How is the "truth" of this felt crisis enacted and enforced and to what ends, to whose benefit, to whose disadvantage? How does it become a site around which various political agendas are organized? In brief, how is the "reality" of "youth in crisis" constructed?

From Crime to Common Sense

This book establishes the social operations of youth in crisis as it acts as a repository for social concerns and serves as an impetus for debate. "Youth" is the location of social concern and social desire, fear and pleasure. It is always read through the vectors of class, race, sex, and a multitude of other locations that designate the specificity of cultural activity and identity. Consequently, youth is not just a social category with particular forms of cultural expression and investment; it is also a conjunction point for various discourses with powerful implications for the forms and specificities of the popular at a given moment. By the term *discourse*, I mean the modes of expression that shape what can be said and thought. What we understand of youth is partly dependent upon the ways it is talked about and characterized. Discourses are frameworks of thought, and as such they have material consequences for public policy and daily life. This book examines not only the articulation of the concerns—or discourses—about violent youth but also looks at the cultural work these discursive sites are deployed to do.

Crimes do not occur in isolation. To begin understanding them, we must consider the complex contextual determinations that operate to define the criminal activity. This has been one of the great contributions of feminist criminology.

Since Carol Smart's (1976) groundbreaking work, the field has dealt with a variety of questions, including the "noncriminal" nature of women (the fact that the vast majority of offenders are not women), how women are treated by the criminal justice system (Worrall 1990), sex-specific crimes against women, and the relationship between masculinity and deliquency (Allen 1989).[2] Certainly, after the important critiques of Mark Cousins (1980) and Victoria Greenwood (1981), stressing in different manners the dangers of arguments that reassert a necessary, essential difference between female and male criminal behavior, much room had been opened up for gender and sex-specific studies. It has become part of the terms of analysis that there are gender, racial, and sexual dimensions to criminality, and that this tells us more about the society as a whole than it necessarily does about the individual criminal mind.

This set of interests allows an investigation into the way power relations affect our ideas about and responses to crime and criminality. How is sense made of crime? How do crimes come to be socially meaningful? And why do certain crimes become symbolically important to a society in a given historical moment, initiating an array of cultural activity? The crimes themselves do not speak their reason; that is the function of the broader social apparatus. As something becomes part of cultural knowledge, or even a certain popular cultural "literacy," a whole referential and significatory fabric of forces moves as well.

For example, Deborah Cameron and Elizabeth Frazer (1987) begin with the empirical observation that "sexual" murder is almost entirely committed by men, mostly against women. They investigate the cultural construction of an axis of gender along which men's "lust to kill does not disrupt the social and sexual order" (p. 144). They conclude, "The common denominator is not misogyny, it is a shared construction of masculine sexuality, or even more, broadly, masculinity in general" (p. 167). Similarly, Mike Davis (1988, 39) examines the political and cultural import of Los Angeles gang violence to demonstrate that "the contemporary Gang scare has become an imaginary class relationship, a terrain of pseudo-knowledge and fantasy projection, a talisman." Davis traces the contextual determinants in which "this very real epidemic of youth violence" (p. 38) is shot through with registers of race and class "isolation" that lead to a devastating, yet "reasonable," "political economy of crack" (p. 52).

Both of these analyses are exemplary in their historically and culturally specific approaches to crime. Central to both is a concern with determinants of "crisis" and "order" and the complex discursive machinations that ensue. Davis points out how the crisis of gang violence in Los Angeles operates with respect to the order of racial, ageist, and class struggle. And Cameron and Frazer stress how the "disruption" of murder becomes "naturalized," even romanticized, in culturally specific circumstances. Thus, interest in the social construction and import of crime also involves a question of the distribution of social power. A society is always concerned with normalization, with the organization of its order, to assure the continuation of its structures and distribution of powers. The guiding question of the present study is as follows: How does the social construction of youth crime figure in the establishment, form, and reproduction of what is referred to as social order?

Paul Willis (1977, 174), in his study of the social reproduction of class differences in youth, lays out the problematic relationship between culture and social structure:

> The argument here, then, is that cultural forms cannot be reduced or regarded as the mere epiphenomenal expression of basic structural factors. They are not accidental or open-ended determined variables in the couplet structure/culture. They are part of the necessary circle in which neither term is thinkable alone. It is in the passage through the cultural level that aspects of the real structural relationships of society are transformed into conceptual relationships and back again. The cultural is part of the necessary dialectic of reproduction.

Here Willis characterizes the irreducible relation between the material and the conceptual as that which initiates the transformation and maintenance of social order. For the present purposes, the necessary dialectic of reproduction concerns the distribution of social power according to discourses of sex, gender, race, ethnicity, class, and age. These sites of crises are transformed into new material relations. The result is a new, socially prominent set of ideas about ethnicity, gender, and age. It is in this light that the multiple registers of youth in crisis operate. "Youth in crisis" refers to structures of power between segments of the population, including between men and women, whites and "Others," and youths and adults.

Through various forms of cultural activity, youth in crisis comes to sit at the nexus of many debates. This has to do with the representation of crime, with crime as a measure of crisis, with crisis as it becomes common sense, and with common sense as a political challenge. Put differently, the analysis of the couplet structure/culture reveals the distribution of power for a particular site of social investment. This book, in its analysis of the discourses and representations of youth delinquency, demonstrates the way in which youth in crisis corresponds to an anxiety concerning the reproduction of the social order.

What counts as evidence of social crisis, and what does not? What is meant by social crisis? How can it be described and talked about and to what ends? For instance, one of the frequently deployed measures of the contemporary crisis of youth is the number of days American children attend school, officially 180. An often-noted comparison is with the Japanese system, in which children attend 243 days of the year. As Michael Barrett (1990, 80), a member of the Massachusetts State Senate, puts it, there are two trends borne out by the statistics: "First, compared with their peers in Asian and European countries, American students stand out for how little they work. Second, compared with Asians and Europeans, American students stand out for how poorly they do." Although U.S. public education is in an alarming state, and there are a variety of proofs ranging from drop-out rates to the presence of weapons in the classroom to demonstrate this decline, the number of days in school correlated with test results is a difficult, if not utterly invalid, point of cross-cultural comparison. Furthermore, the implications are open for debate. What is the meaning and possible consequence of this situation, and what has precipitated it? In Barrett's version, the crisis of U.S. education is re-ally a crisis of international competitiveness, with a particular fear of Japanese ex-cellence. And in a similar manner to Ronald Reagan's education czar William Bennett, this crisis of competitiveness is linked to the status of American moral fi-ber. In students and parents the "work ethic," so this argument goes, is disappear-ing, and along with it goes the economic strength of the United States. Thus, the "evidence" of an education crisis is exercised to support an intricate agenda of values concerning familial priority and moral obligation and betrays a xenopho-bic fear of a rising Asian menace. These conclusions, of course, are a far cry from what the number of days in school can reasonably indicate.

The treatment of a perceived crisis indicates the importance of an analysis of the discursively constructed social order. Youth, as it was reconstructed in the 1980s, is a site at which the struggles between order and crisis take place. Part I, "Youth," addresses this issue specifically and focuses on three central themes: the historical construction of ideas about youth, the associated ideas about deviance, and the centrality of "youth" and "deviance" in ideas about social order and cri-sis. Youth is a central component and defining feature of the contemporary American scene and the particular hegemonic project of the New Right. Here the New Right's high estimation of the traditional nuclear family is key.

The historical emergence of the American family unit involved a particular economic organization formed around the male wage earner and unpaid female labor inside the home and a social division of public and private space. As Nancy Theriot (1983) points out, the family was not only fundamental to the capitalist system; it also became invested with that system's ideologies. Even though we are currently living in a situation in which only a minority of family arrangements could be described as nuclear, the ideological import of the idealized family feeds a certain nostalgia for a time of imagined stability and certainty. The New Right's deployment of "profamily" politics, the "naturalness" of which has been, in Theriot's words, "established in the American psyche" (p. 34), is responsible for a good portion of the Right's populist success. Indeed, Michèle Barrett and Mary McIntosh (1991, 26) have written that the "appeal of the natural" in the family's moral framework is perhaps one reason for its persistence.

But as feminist critiques have indicated, the currency of "profamily" politics in the 1980s was, in effect, part of a strategic "backlash" against feminism, to borrow from Susan Faludi's (1991) popular rendition of this period. Importantly, youth in the family, and the "dangers" of alternative approaches to childrearing, was a cen-tral focus. Simply put, a now commonsensical crisis of youth has been articulated in an ideologically central position as an indicator of a national-popular will and as a cry of concern for the apparent shifts in the structures of American society, of which the feminist critique is seen to be one "destablizing" force.

The evidence of this cry of concern can be found in diverse locations, from individual crimes to movies, from newspaper editorials to daytime television talk shows. As a series of texts and reponses to texts, the discourses of a felt crisis of youth circulate in popular culture. Part II, "Murder," examines the representation of a youth crime known as the "preppy murder" in photographs, newspapers, magazines, and the murderer's confession. Part III, "Spectacle," demonstrates the circulation of that representation in disparate locations, in particular daytime television talk shows and youth films. Here I trace connections between popular cultural artifacts to show that even as the initial crime is being left far behind, a general crisis of youth is being established. Fundamental to this analysis is how some events are taken as evidence of something else, as evidence of crisis. This is precisely the politics of spectacle. To begin, I want to introduce some of the main issues involved in cultural studies as they are be taken up in the present study.

An Endless Host of Accidents

I have always been intrigued by grisly true-life murder stories. These stories, which include such "bestsellers" as Shana Alexander's *The Nutcracker* (1985), Jonathan Coleman's *At Mother's Request* (1986), Peter Meyer's *Death of Innocence* (1985), Joe McGinniss's *Fatal Vision* (1983), and Ann Rule's *Small Sacrifices* (1988), are not only exceedingly violent, reveling in the intricate details of murder; they also tend to be about the murderous impulses of stable upper- and middle-class families. The various permutations of the tragedy have been well represented: mothers killing children, children killing grandparents, fathers going berserk and killing everyone. A central recurring theme is that of the traditional family unit destroying itself from the inside, self-obliterating. Fans explain their attraction by alternately arguing for the books' literary standing—often with evocations of Truman Capote's *In Cold Blood* (1965) as the height of the canon—or for their journalistic value, as required reading for any informed citizen of the modern world, where we must admit that reports of such acts of violence are rather commonplace. And yet these two rational explanations do not capture the allure of these events, the abstruse and compelling appeal they hold for their diverse and considerable audiences. In a significant part of popular culture, murder is entertainment.

It is a tired cliché of media criticism that by the time the average North American child finishes high school, he or she will have seen "x" thousand stabbings, shootings, rapes, beatings, and other acts of violence, both fictional and actual.[3] More difficult to capture but equally prevalent are all of those associated forms of exegesis—all the rhetoric and debates concerning violence—that also circulate. Popular representations of violence have been seen as agents of socialization (learning how to respond in a socially appropriate manner), desensitization (learning how not to care), and instruction (learning how to be violent). Even though the truth value of these claims is continually under debate and revision, two general propositions are consistently borne out. First, Americans are a profoundly violent civilian population, with murder and assault rates soaring above those of other Western industrial populations. Second, American popular culture is teeming with depictions of violent acts. The investigation of the lines of determination between these two banal observations has historically been one of the principal motors of communication and sociological study. Rather than suggesting another causal relation, I take these observations as the context and condition of contemporary American existence. This is a starting point to understanding the popular fascination with the atrocious and the inventively horrific and the complexities of popular culture as a whole.

During the last few years of his life, Friedrich Engels tried to resist what he saw as a disturbing drift toward economic determinism by Marxists. He admitted, "Marx and I are ourselves partly to blame for the fact that the younger people sometimes lay more stress on the economic side than is due to it" (Marx and Engels 1978, 762). In a famous letter to Joseph Bloch in 1890, Engels argued for the complexity of forces involved in historical determination: "The *ultimately* determining element in history is the production and reproduction of real life. More than this neither Marx nor I have ever asserted" (p. 760). He began to flesh out the ideological as a focal aspect of the "production and reproduction of real life." He indicated a host of domains in which ideology operates, including juridical, political, philosophical, and religious forms of class discourse and struggle: "There is an interaction of all these elements in which, amid all the endless host of accidents (that is, of things and events, whose inner connection is so remote or so impossible of proof that we can regard it as non-existent, as negligible), the economic movement finally asserts itself as necessary" (p. 760). This was Engels's contention of what Louis Althusser (1977) would later reaffirm as the ever-deferred "last instance" of the economic. Its "necessity" may be finally asserted, but not without the intervention of a series of other determinations.

Engels's statement suggests that historical analysis should avoid the imprecision of the endless host of accidents that occur on the course toward the necessary attestation of the economic. These "accidents" are unpredictable, for, Engels argues, they lack an "inner connection" and are "impossible of proof." Though he insists that the consequence of each accident is negligible, the sum total of their effects is not. In other words, in his plea of caution about economic determinism, Engels insinuates an important dimension to the concept of historical materialism—namely, the contradictory qualities of the social formation, where the rationalist discourse of economic analysis is confounded by other seemingly irrational forces. These forces include all those domains of social contest, such as the judicial, the political, the philosophical, and the cultural as well as the economic. Even in the absence of a singly comprehensible "inner connection," the appraisal of these forces defines the exigencies of social and political analysis.

Althusser's (1977, 117) critique of what he himself admits was "only a letter" takes Engels's argument as the inappropriate construction of an apparent binary between the "necessity" of the economic and the "accident" of other forces. For Althusser, Engels reduces the latter to "microscopic dust" (p. 119) and thus offers little to a model of overdetermination. As cogent as his examination is, Althusser tends to obfuscate the intentions of the letter; Engels wanted to dispel the idea that historical determination was unidimensional. Read accordingly, the "endless host of accidents" is an important early move toward the concept of *relative autonomy*.

It follows that the endless host of accidents of historical determination involves the cultural, political, and philosophical existence of people. The *popular* is that realm in which people live, interact, contest, and acquiesce, in both a haphazard and a routine manner. It is where people meet and, ideally, struggle to assert the democratic tendencies of the social formation. An elusive space of considerable force, the popular and its cultural expressions remain an important but often neglected, or brutally simplified, concept. It is a slippery notion to treat with any degree of precision for it simultaneously defines contradictory impulses. On the one hand, we may be tempted to approach the popular and popular culture as a terrain that has been lost to the "culture industries," to corporate capital, and hence as a contemptuous concept to be handled cautiously. On the other hand, we cannot deny the relations of people that are constructed around popular cultural offerings. It is a domain that articulates, forms, and gives texture to "real lives." To disavow this, to suggest that the experiences and expressions of the popular and popular culture are inauthentic or politically incorrect, is to ignore an important aspect in the fabric of people's daily lives. This paradox is what Stuart Hall (1981, 228) refers to as "the double-stake in popular culture, the double movement of containment and resistance."

The history of the relationship between contemporary thought and popular culture is long and complicated, one that touches many areas of intellectual activity and public debate. Andreas Huyssen (1986, 47) points to the interposition of popular culture in modernism and its designation as modernism's Other: "Mass culture has always been the hidden subtext of the modernist project." Huyssen traces out the manner in which the denigrated realm of mass culture connotatively referenced women, where "the fear of the masses in this age of declining liberalism is always also a fear of woman, a fear of nature out of control, a fear of the unconscious, of sexuality, of the loss of identity and stable ego boundaries in the mass" (p. 52). The masses and their ardor for popular culture became a realm in need of management and regulation by cultural "authorities" and elite experts. Fredric Jameson (1979) demonstrates how modernism's critique of capitalism, lodged in the expressed concern for the cultural well-being of the general public, often harbored "proto-fascistic" impulses in its estimation of the "polluting" effects of the market for cultural products, and by implication the masses, upon the vocation of artists. The force of this conception of the menace of the masses and their cultural predilections is unremitting, often evidenced in contemporary public debate. In fact, in many ways the agenda was set for the postwar generation and was typified by Dwight Macdonald's (1957) assessment of the "spreading ooze of Mass Culture," successfully coupling the images of irrationality, B-grade horror films, and the Red Peril in his manifesto for the dying modern.

As John Caughie (1986, 158) notes, unlike "mass culture," the term *popular culture* "seems to have behind it a memory of the people as agents of their own development, a memory which finds its focus in Britain in certain histories of popular resistance to the advance of capital in the nineteenth century." Caughie points to an important connotative force in this term that is also the source of its theoretical slipperiness: Popular culture has to do with people. It moves, and people are moved by its offerings, in a fashion that connects with daily experience. Even though the means of its production are largely inaccessible to its audiences, popular culture relates to a vast array of social groups in an immediate, material, and often creative way.

Such is the enigma: What is the relationship between people and popular culture? Given the diversity of cultural forms and practices, how is it possible to describe the social formation, and moments of its restructuring, using observations about popular discourse and its material consequences, or what Willis calls the structure/culture couplet? How are we to read the endless host of accidents of historical determination? This is a question of discerning the *correspondences* between local cultural evidence, which is itself a broad and complexly inflected category, and the structure of social totality. In many ways, this has been one of the defining features of cultural studies. Here the concept of *hegemony* is crucial.

Ernesto Laclau and Chantal Mouffe (1985, 7) indicate that in its first applications, hegemony "alludes to a kind of *contingent* intervention required by the crisis or collapse of what would have been a 'normal' historical development." Antonio Gramsci (1971) takes hegemony to mean the process of melding historical fragments into a politically viable entity. But in place of the vanguardist position, Gramsci explores the conditions of the emergence of an articulated alliance of social groups, what he describes as a *historical bloc*.

> Structures and superstructures form an "historical bloc." That is to say the complex, contradictory and discordant *ensemble* of the superstructures is the reflection of the *ensemble* of the social relations of production. From this, one can conclude: that only a totalitarian system of ideologies gives a rational reflection of the contradiction of the structure and represents the existence of the objective conditions for the revolutionising of praxis. (p. 366)

Gramsci uses "totalitarian" to indicate the "totalizing" and the "unified," not a particular mode of despotic rule (see p. 335). Implying that there is no single entity that could be referred to as society—that it has no *essential* "totality"—

Gramsci begins to theorize the *logic of the contingent social,* that is, hegemony. Society, rather than being homogeneous, consists of a network of elements located,
somewhat imprecisely, within a wide array of relations. The social as a stable entity is never realized but instead is the provisional product of *articulation.*

Founded upon the notion of the *relative autonomy* of the elements of the social,
"articulation" describes the overdetermined nature of the social formation, with
emphasis upon historical and cultural contexts. Though there is obviously a degree of "predictability" in the continuance of the social formation, it is not guaranteed to be reproduced in precisely that form in the next moment. As an endless
host of accidents, economic and class relations are not the sole determinants of
the social formation and therefore can not be expected to explain every occasion.
This approach forms the basis of Gramsci's *conjuncturalism.*[4]

Hegemony refers to a particular brand of social formation. It involves drawing
and defining the lines between the state and civil society. This hegemonic activity
takes place in a number of different locations—in law, the market, the family, the
schools—and on a variety of different ideological, cultural, economic, political,
and moral issues. The state should be seen as an agent (though certainly one
among many) with a vested interest in this activity as well as a site at which these
debates and their stakes are struggled over. Popular culture is more than one other
location of this struggle. It is where ideas about the world, and the forms of their
expression, are made, transformed, and circulated. Even though we can speak of
common sense as it is represented in popular culture, critical access to it is mediated and inflected in various ways. Popular culture's essence cannot be pinpointed
and expected to remain static—hence the importance of conjunctural analysis.

Through the work of Gramsci, we now have a way to think about one of the
most tenacious problems for cultural theory: How are we to deal with a state that
is not a homogeneous entity, that does not solely represent the interests of a particular class, and that, though it has exclusive access to the means of legitimated
violence, does not normally use them to establish a coercive tenure on its position
of power? Gramsci has provided a manner in which to conceive of that endless
host of accidents of historical determination.

Given the dispersed and heterogeneous nature of the popular, there is an added
complexity to capturing, in Hall's (1980b, 172) words, " 'the crisis' experienced at
the popular level in the universal, depoliticised, experiential language of popular
morality." Recognizing a cry from below involves more than pointing to class relations. The concept of popular voices needs to be understood as a conditional
description. For what appears to be experientially located in people does not
carry an inherent truth value or democratic potential. There is a popular recognition that the promises and potential of youth do not hold in the manner of the
past. Understanding the politics of this popular concern for youth consists of
reading the articulations between a felt crisis of general societal breakdown and
hegemony. Youth in crisis is a point of conjuncture that, instead of being a hege-

monic crisis, *corresponds exactly to the machinations of hegemony*—that is, a *crisis-in-process.*

Disgust and Desire

The appraisal of a cultural phenomenon involves following traces of cultural forms, activities, and histories that lead in a number of directions. The investigator finds old domains of common sense, remnants of past popular sensibilities, new combinations of discourses, and reverberations of other historical moments and cultural forms all entangled in the phenomenon. Charting these relations means having to detect and follow those traces, which always lead to other texts, other traces. The task, then, can be neverending.

Yet it is reasonable to suggest that some traces reverberate more strongly than others, that some make their presence distinctly felt as *symbolically central.* In *The Politics and Poetics of Transgression* (1986), Peter Stallybrass and Allon White write of the social constitution of the Other and of its importance to the stability of a particular social order. They argue that social order can be read through the way in which a culture "thinks" itself: "The result is a mobile, conflictual fusion of power, fear and desire in the construction of subjectivity: a psychological dependence upon precisely those Others which are being rigorously opposed and excluded at the social level. It is for this reason that what is *socially* peripheral is so frequently *symbolically* central" (p. 5). *Symbolic centrality* means that particular sites are invested with significant connotative force, with substantial potency in the social, even though these same sites may be "outside" the bounds of society and seen as deviant in some way. The composition of these sites, similarly conceived as points of conjuncture, reverberates across the social formation.

It is precisely in this manner that youth in crisis operates. Historically, as a discursive and material domain, youth has been inextricably implicated in the way American culture thinks about itself, at least since the turn of the twentieth century. Furthermore, criminalized youth acts as an Other, distanced, yet inseparable, from the social order. Such demarcations are always dependent upon disgust and desire (p. 191). In an important contribution, one that challenges structuralist method and vulgar ideology critique, Stallybrass and White pay attention to a sort of cross-fertilization. Beyond simple transgressions, they suggest that the social formation involves *hybridization*—the incorporation of the Other as part of the order. In the present instance, while "youth" is Other to the order of the adult world, it is also an object of intense interest, desire, even longing, for the culture as a whole. Youth, then, is simultaneously transgressive and revered.

This is the impetus guiding the analytic movement from a crime and the photographs of that crime to confession, to talk shows, and to youth movies. In these movements resides the historical specificity of youth in crisis. Understanding the operation of popular discourse, and the determinations of symbolic centrality, requires more than looking at texts; attention must be paid to the complex and contradictory discourses that form the distinctiveness of those texts and textures.

It is for this reason that this book is not about "real" youth. Obviously, there exist juvenile criminals, unemployed youths, and young people who in various manners bear the burden, and increasingly so, of the ills and excesses of previous generations. One of the better attempts to capture the contemporary lives of suburban American youth is Donna Gaines's ethnographic study *Teenage Wasteland: Suburbia's Dead End Kids* (1991). This work is in the tradition of the classic of American sociology, William Foote Whyte's *Street Corner Society* (1943). In an attempt to understand the reasons for a suicide pact carried out by four New Jersey teenagers, Gaines immerses herself in a group of that community's youth, going to concerts, hanging out, and listening to them talk about their lives, their concerns, and their understanding of the multiple suicide. Many possible insights notwithstanding, my interest is not at this microlevel analysis. Instead, I am interested in the social construction of a category that is referred to as youth and more precisely in its emergence in this historical moment as youth in crisis. The category "youth" covers many social differences. Yet as a discursive construct, it is given a sort of imaginary unity as though we could speak of American youth in general and as though American youth exists as a unity. This construct excludes certain forms of diversity, often with an imagined white upwardly mobile youth standing in for the United States as a whole. Clearly, this unity is an ideological fiction. Nonetheless, this macrolevel idea circulates and has profound effects upon the imaginary formation of youth as well as the real lives of the young. For, above all, the crisis is a *spectacular* one, having to do with representation and performance. It is good magazine and newspaper copy, it makes for popular reading and moviegoing, and it is the topic of policy debates in public offices. The politics of youth has to do with the politics of spectacle; during the 1980s in the United States, the problems of youth became a spectacular crisis.

Consequently, throughout this book youth has been deliberately left without a precise definition. Youth is an empty signifier that becomes meaningful only in given circumstances, coming to designate certain attributes and qualities. Youth captures all the other ambiguous labels of "adolescent," "young adult," "late adolescent," "juvenile," "minor," and "teenager." The age for these categories changes culturally, through time, across arenas, in different legal jurisdictions. For instance, legal arguments can be made to try juvenile offenders as adults. But there are minimum-age requirements depending on the state. For murder, the minimum age is sixteen in California, Delaware, and Oregon; fifteen in Arkansas, Idaho, and Michigan; fourteen in Alabama, Connecticut, and New Jersey; thirteen in Georgia, Mississippi, and New York; and ten in Indiana and Vermont. For felonies, the minimum age is sixteen in Indiana, fifteen in Georgia, and fourteen in New York. Other mobile designations of the arrival of adult responsibility include legal drinking ages, voting and draft registration age, and sexual age of majority.

There are powerful myths of the inherent traits of youth, partly based on physiological changes. Undoubtedly, younger children are not as "prepared for the world" as older ones. But a whole series of cultural values and presumptions intervenes, linking questions of rights, prohibition, and legal responsibility. In other words, there is a definitional process of determining what being prepared for the world means, what the qualities of the world are, and what measures of preparation are in order. And without a doubt, the world indexed is the *adult economic order*—that is, the social universe of the legally responsible and the economically productive. In this respect, Grossberg (1988a, 51) observes, "youth has no meaning except perhaps its lack of meaning, its energy, its commitment to openness and change, its celebratory relation to the present, and its promise of the future. Youth offers no structure of its own with which it can organise and give permanence to a national identity. That is, youth itself, like America, can only be defined apparently in a forever receding future." In short, the fact that youth comes to mark different things—its relative significatory mobility—is an indication of its discursive constitution and of certain struggles waged in the process of its determination.

Finally, it should not be forgotten that, despite my interest in the circulation of ideas about American youth, the associated violence is deplorable. There is certainly a crisis of youth—of education, of unemployment, of despair—to which a response is admittedly difficult. Cornel West (1988) describes this as a *walking nihilism* that exists in many black communities in the United States. However, with respect to criminal youth, the mechanisms of culture do not stop with the act of violence itself. As a cultural studies analysis shows, the crimes do not stand alone; they occur in particular contexts situated in discursive environments. While there is a materiality to crimes—there are victims and perpetrators—there is no necessary link to the "knowable" in the crime's explanation and resolution. Ultimately, it is worth remembering that justice is not wholly motivated by the crime but by the historically specific and culturally constituted category of the "just."

2

The Wreckage of Body, Mind, and Morals: On Youth, Deviance, and Visibility

Repudiating the virtues of your world, criminals hopelessly agree to organize a forbidden universe. They agree to live in it. The air there is nauseating: they can breathe it.

—Jean Genet, *The Thief's Journal*

By the late 1980s, some schools had begun to install metal detectors to search the student body for concealed weapons. Since then, the policing of students has become a standard news story during the "back to school" period after Labor Day, providing a sure sign that students are returning to something that is self-destructing. During the same period, Illinois police initiated a program of search and seizure of entire high schools. Without notice, police officers would take over a school during the day and comb the premises, and the students, in search of various forms of contraband, such as drugs and weapons. This sort of gross violation of civil rights was based upon "probable cause." It was the very presence of people in school as students that in effect made them suspects. Schools were seen doubly as sites of criminal activity and as arenas in which the state had to flex its coercive muscles in order to teach potential criminals a lesson in law and order.

But more than having any demonstrable consequence, these activities betrayed an escalation of fear on the part of adults. It is no wonder that the image of Principal Joe Clark roaming the halls of a New Jersey high school with a baseball bat turned him into a sort of contemporary folk hero. His "tough love" tactics were re-created in the film *Lean on Me* (John Avildsen, 1989), with Morgan Freeman in the lead role, further popularizing the New Right ideal of a black American getting tough with other black Americans. A new pragmatic model for educators' relations with students emerged: the vigilante.

The realm of education was one of many in which youth were increasingly de-monized and treated accordingly. The front line of the War on Drugs was set up to be the traditional family unit, and parents were encouraged to monitor their own little "criminals within." With generational divisions being drawn in this manner, family surveillance went in both directions; children were rewarded for reporting their parent's own drug use as well. A shifting notion of responsibility accompa-nied these developments. For instance, a Florida woman was convicted of drug trafficking to a minor when her newborn tested positive for cocaine. Though she was later acquitted, other similar cases have been upheld. The 1980s call for harsher treatment of youth criminals in general was matched by similar policing of women, in particular as a public maternal body upon which, it appeared, the entire social good rested.

The "problem of generations," as Bruno Bettelheim (1965, 77) suggests, "is what gives us adults so much trouble, and not the problems of adolescence or youth." Bettelheim, writing about the postwar baby-boomers, says, "In many respects youth has suddenly turned from being the older generation's greatest economic asset into its greatest economic liability" (p. 88). Indeed, "generation" has no fun-damental essence *except* as a problem; as a crisis of value, of economics, or of re-sources, it is always played out between at least two ambiguously defined age groups. And this conflict, of course, is only accented in particular ways by the weight of social demographics. For instance, as the culture sways with the hippolike mass of baby-boomers, an attractive and abundant aggregate, the overrepresentation of that generation's perspectives is a given. In this respect, the youth of the 1980s, without the same numbers, could only expect cultural disen-franchisement.

Generations often become associated colloquially with decades, which in turn are described in sweeping generalities: the "shook-up" decade (Salisbury 1958), the "me" decade, the "greed" decade. So it is a mark of salience that there is such an active name search for the in-between generation that came of age in the 1980s and succeeded the massive baby-boomer generation. One sees the range of birth dates demarcating this group as roughly from 1963 to 1971, though some extend it from 1961 to 1981 (Howe and Strauss 1993). And this generation is given a variety of titles, including "baby-busters" and "twentysomethings." Douglas Coupland (1991) calls them "Generation X," the forgotten, cynical generation of essentially overeducated but underemployed individuals. Coupland's resonant description has often met some bizarre alternatives. For instance, a *Fortune* cover story on what it calls the "Upbeat Generation" finds that "89% of young working Ameri-cans in their 20s are optimistic about their own careers and financial prospects in the next decade" (Deutschmann 1992, 42). To arrive at this conclusion, the author buries the fact that all the people surveyed had already begun their careers at least a year previously, which is an extremely atypical scenario for this demographic.

Nevertheless, the struggle to name and describe this apparently anomalous so-cial grouping points to its importance in the contemporary scene. Generations are discursive constructs, marshaling certain meanings and desires into a single imagined location, rather than statistical truths pure and simple. An amalgam of debates about youth in crisis involves this unnameable Generation X, even though during the 1980s, in which this formation was in process, there was no such term. The marking of X suggests that what was indescribable has been given a semiotic visibility. It is one indication of the movement of youth in crisis toward symbolic centrality in American popular culture and politics.[1]

The *visibility* of youth, under the eye of social investigation, exists in a threefold formation: as an object of the critical gaze, as a cultural concern, and as a social category with particular members, relations, and experiences. The relationships among these three are partially determining and partially antagonistic. But they share some prevalent connotations. Youth is "before maturity," "before responsibility," "before concern," "before the real (adult and economically productive) world," where "before" connotes the incomplete, the existence of potential, and the possibility of failure. "Before" also connotes the visible and present, available for the scrutiny and interest of the general culture, founded upon the presumed "obviousness" of who counts as a member of youth. To invest in youth, in all of its three aforementioned constructs, is to invent imaginary futures, ones that invariably indicate the particular struggles of the present.

The result of the rhetoric of concern for youth, always having to do with "their" own best interests (hence, presumably, all our best interests), is the very particular *ideology of protection*. Youth is a time of substantial surveillance exactly because it is a time when the culture is learned. While youth are being allowed to play with the transgressive, they are being checked and marked. The ideology of protection facilitates strategic interventions by the state and others, the purpose of which, invariably, is to guarantee the smooth reproduction of social relations. With this comes the smooth reproduction of racial and ethnic, gender, and class relations. In other words, at stake here is the reconstitution of particular ideas about social stability and an associated hegemony. This carries assumptions about the safety and security of family life, about gender and racial divisions of labor, about meritocracy, and about careerism. Hence, for instance, the issue of day care becomes a significant battleground between women and the state for definitions of family, "appropriate" childrearing, the role of parents, and the participation of various social institutions in the process. The historical traces of the discourses of youth and the ideology of protection are abundant and far from benign.

Where Michel de Certeau (1984) refers to the "unnameable" discourse of death, youth as the as-yet-unrealized is amply named, and not only in generational terms; it is so present, so "before," so available as a site of cultural investment. Youth suggests the "next," the following moment or movement. To invest in youth is to stake a particular claim on the fluidity of the social. And yet the location of the discourse of the "next" is in the present. The "promises" of the discourse, as such, are never realized; they cannot be because that moment would assure the dispersal of youth.

The in-between stage of youth did not always exist as it does today. Philippe Ariès (1962) has shown that in medieval Europe, the movement from child to adult was instantaneous. "Once he had passed the age of five or seven, the child was immediately absorbed into the world of adults: this concept of a brief childhood lasted for a long time in the lower classes" (p. 329). In the seventeenth century, "by the age of ten, girls were already little women: a precocity due in part to an upbringing which taught girls to behave very early in life like grown-ups" (p. 332). In charting the advent of youth, Ariès emphasizes the development of institutions such as the boarding school and the military academy as a fundamental reconstitution of what it means to enter the world of the adult. In effect, such institutions established a distinct social space for the young male of particular classes, separate from the control of the family. For instance, they organized their own structures of surveillance and discipline to regulate the everyday behavior of inhabitants. Unruliness seems to have been the norm for students during the period leading up to the nineteenth century. Ariès reminds us that "schoolchildren used to be armed" (p. 315) and not just for decorative purposes. Indeed, "in the sixteenth and seventeenth centuries, people situated schoolboys in the same picaresque world as soldiers, valets and beggars" (p. 327). Consequently, with the arrival of the modern youth came an array of ideas about youth, among which their discipline and the enforcement of order were central. By the beginning of the nineteenth century, becoming an adult meant undergoing training.

In concert with Ariès, Frank Musgrove (1964) observes the significance of the ties between modernity and the emergence of the social category of youth. He notes the coincidence of the "inventions" of Jean-Jacques Rousseau's adolescent in 1762 and James Watt's steam engine in 1765 (p. 33). Since then, the two central problems concerning youth have been "how and where to accommodate him in the social structure, and how to make his behaviour accord with the specifications" (p. 33). The experience of social change engendered by modernity is inseparable from the appearance and treatment of youth. As this separate social category began to be taken as "natural," youth connoted change and became a site of both the fears and promises offered by that change.

In the late nineteenth century, adolescence was still a specifically middle- and upper-class phenomenon, a consequence of lower infant mortality rates and sufficient wealth. These and other factors allowed for a greater period of dependency than in the past and in a way that was markedly different for less privileged classes. But, as John Gillis (1974, 133) points out, by the turn of the twentieth century, "adolescence [had been] democratized." The middle-class view that adolescence was a distinct period of life led to a substantial reworking of the social system to deal with the young—rich or poor—differently from adults. This period saw the emergence of parallel institutions of prisons, courts, welfare agencies, protective legislation, and universal education designed to accommodate the specific needs of youth. As David Bakan (1971, 981) writes, at this time "three major social movements developed, all of which conspired to make a social fact out of adolescence:

compulsory (and characteristically public) education, child labor legislation, and special legal procedures for 'juveniles.'" This did not mean that all were treated equally by these institutions; instead, this "democratization" established the criteria of what normal youth was supposed to be like, the model for which was rooted in its middle-class origins. The universalizing tendency of what was a middle-class phenomenon translated into an expectation of failure to meet those standards, particularly for other classes and ethnic groups.

In the United States, the work of G. Stanley Hall in effect laid out the blueprint for the particular connotations of youth that were to become commonsensical. His *Adolescence and Its Psychology and Its Relations to Physiology, Anthropology, Sociology, Sex, Crime, Religion, and Education* (1904) is often considered the first moment to announce the discovery of and draw attention to the "American adolescent" (see Keniston 1971; Doherty 1988). Hall's opus certainly hastened the speed with which the term *adolescent* entered popular lexicon. Hall captured and characterized that in-between age that had previously had no formal classificatory existence. Importantly, his conception of the adolescent involved the inseparable connotations of the time between childhood and adulthood as a period of disturbance and distress.

> The momentum of heredity often seems insufficient to enable the child to achieve this great revolution and come to complete maturity, so that every step of the upward way is strewn with wreckage of body, mind and morals. There is not only arrest, but perversion, at every stage, and hoodlumism, juvenile crime, and secret vice seem not only increasing, but develop in earlier years in every civilized land. Modern life is hard, in many respects increasingly so, on youth. Home, school, church fail to recognize its nature and needs and, perhaps most of all, its perils. (p. xiv)

Thus, in this earliest formulation, adolescence was being conceived of as a time of turbulence; this was the initiation of the linkage between the young and deviance, an association that was not without precedence. From the earliest references to the category of youth, it has been formulated as a social concern. As Gillis (1974) argues, the young have historically been involved in the practices and rituals of "Misrule," of transgressive and socially disruptive behavior. But as captured in the quotation from Hall, in the contemporary context this disruptive trait of youth became tied to the changing social relations of modernity, where traditional institutions seemed inappropriate and unable to deal with the confused, threatened, and threatening adolescent. The shock of the new is equally the shock of the young.

For Hall, "adolescence is a new birth, for the higher and more completely human traits are now born. ... Development is less gradual, more saltatory, suggestive of some ancient period of storm and stress when old moorings were broken and a higher level attained" (p. xiii). In the interest of assuring the attainment of "the higher and more completely human traits," the adolescent became the surveyed. Unlike the parenting and guarding of children, youths require surveillance because they have a significantly disuptive potential. The young are seen as "subhuman"—that is, not in full possession of the characteristics of the "normal" adult—and must therefore be guided through that "ancient period of storm and stress." The narrative of development is imbued with the rhetoric of evolutionism; growth is the movement from the absence of the social, the "primitive," to the presence of the prosocial, the "civilized" adult. Among other things, this narrative allows the organization of cultural difference by providing a visible Other against which the "parent" culture (meant in its multiple and patriarchal senses) emerges. Significant, then, is the particular understanding of the qualities of a "normal" adult, a "normal" adolescent, and what measures—tactics of education, surveillance, and discipline—are presumed to be appropriate to assure the "development" of the young.[2]

And eighty years later it is precisely this commonsensical correlation of youth-as-Other that prompts Dick Hebdige (1988, 17) to begin his essay "Hiding in the Light: Youth Surveillance and Display" with the proposition that "youth is present only when its presence is a problem, or is regarded as a problem." Hebdige continues (pp. 17–18):

> The category "youth" gets mobilised in official documentary discourse, in concerned or outraged editorials and features, or in the supposedly disinterested tracts emanating from the social sciences at those times when young people make their presence felt by going "out of bounds," by resisting through rituals, dressing strangely, striking bizarre attitudes, breaking rules, breaking bottles, windows, heads, issuing rhetorical challenges to the law.

Wherever the young "appears," in their practices or as an object of social and sociological inquiry, they are both troubled and troubling. Hebdige investigates the mobilization and installation of these qualities in the context of certain debates. G. Stanley Hall was right: "Modern life is hard, in many respects increasingly so, on youth." And there is a positivity to this hardship. The "wreckage of body, mind, and morals" provides a site at which the social can be ordered.

Centrally, the discourses of youth and deviance inflect and compose the particular historical emergence of youth-as-problem. It does not directly, or solely, correspond to a particular set of meanings, representations, and debates. Instead, its own particularities are the consequence of a variety of determinations, ones that are not guaranteed to be reproduced precisely in different contexts. And yet the apparent stability of this articulation is such that youth powerfully connotes problem.

The dialectic of youth-in-trouble and troubling-youth, also indicated by Hebdige, generates the conception that when we speak of youth we are always speaking of how youth creates discomfort and of how scrutiny and close public and private consideration are necessary. Though it varies with the cultural milieu, there is a somewhat predictable double articulation of youth. The discomfort worries, troubles, concerns, but it also provides an area for social and cultural lines of difference to be demarcated. Importantly, youth, even delinquent youth, are part of the social and are not outside of it. Youth-as-problem can be seen as a necessary element in the constitution of the adult economic social. The bounds of a culture do not exist solely in terms of the consensual designations of normalcy, as though the deviant is exterior, because the demarcations of inclusion/exclusion are equally central to the composition of the social order. The dialectic is irreducible.

Youth is always dangerous. Youth threatens other youths, parents, anonymous persons, property, and values. As a time when the structures of the adult economic social have not been assimilated entirely, youth poses a threat to the broader cultural environment: the terrifying scenario of William Golding's *Lord of the Flies* (1954) or the chilling universe of apathy in Bret Easton Ellis's *Less Than Zero* (1985). Fortunately for the social order, youth is temporary; a constant, but always just a stage in grander narratives. But even though the dangers of youth need not be realized and acted upon to remain threatening, they remain socially productive. The dangers take many forms, but can be collapsed into a fear of the imperfect replication of the social order. The positivity of youth-as-problem is such that the discourses produce and function in manners crucial to the stability of the social order. The transgressive, or the threat thereof, not only introduces exemplars of the limits of the acceptable and of the necessity for such limits. It also provides the alibi for the superstructural activity of differential surveillance and discipline of youth, white and nonwhite, male and female, deviant and straight.

It is clear that there is much at stake in the category of youth, in its mobilization and organization in different contexts; it is a visible and ready repository of concerns and popular interests. To speak of youth-as-problem is to speak of normative bounds and of the placement of the young within the reach of certain agencies and institutions. Such discursive activity is part of the process of structuring what is to characterize youth, the frontiers of the acceptable, and the valuation of this normativity. Youth is the consequence of the relations of social power and is a concern and feature in the family, education, and leisure and consumption. Youth-as-problem emerges from popular (semiotic and discursive) struggle, a site where the currents and directions of everyday life are organized.

Deviance and Social Control

Given that youth invariably intimates youth-as-problem, it is necessary to discuss the discursive import of the deviant. Throughout years of study, deviance has been conceived of as the result of individual action, a statement of individuality, a sign of a lack of consensus in the community, the natural consequence of culture and society, an indication of a lack of state regulation and enforcement, a social

construction, and a discursive construction. And all of these competing definitions have differing impacts upon the conceptualization of social order.

As with the historical emergence of youth, arguments about the nature of the
social order and crime in the contemporary context are inseparable from those
about modernization and the nature of modernity. Critical work about that
period has circled around assertions concerning (1) the relative instability of traditional social structures; (2) the increasing homogenization of society; (3) the
absence of morals and values appropriate to our new environment of social atomization; (4) the increasing lack of contestation, our "one-dimensional" nature;
and (5) thus the potential for the installment of a totalitarian regime. The "evidence" and implications of these five assertions about modernity, often articulat-
ing correspondences between the mass media and society, are employed to support a number of different positions. For example, one of the more prevalent
arguments pertains to the deracination provoked by modern society and the
threat of totalitarianism. As represented by Émile Durkheim, Max Weber, the
Frankfurt School, and John Dewey, the intellectual response seems to be a re-
sounding agreement upon this consequence of the social atomization engendered
by modernity. This argument, particularly in the 1950s, took some very odd,
though perhaps not completely surprising, forms as seen in the work of culture
critic Dwight Macdonald (1957), censorship "expert" Fredric Wertham (1954),
and "hidden persuader" Vance Packard (1957).

How does deviance figure in the shifting movements that characterize modernity? I suggest that there is a double articulation in which the changes engendered
by modernity are written through the emergence of youth and contemporary
criminality. The intersection of youth and crime is a forceful site, one that is a result of the social and economic conditions of modernity and one that bears modernity's particular set of aspirations, values, and social agendas.

Traditionally, the study of criminal behavior accepted the category of the deviant and the criminal as unproblematic; deviancy was an inherent quality of the
behavior and its consequences. Indeed, what Gillis (1974, 170) refers to as the democratization of the adolescent was equally the democratization of juvenile
crime. Previously associated with class, by the 1890s juvenile delinquency was
seen to be the behavioral consequence of immaturity. Generally speaking, the
field of criminology chiefly concerned the behavior of individuals to the exclusion
of the sociological factors impinging upon the activity of the delinquent. This
positivist approach was used to supplement existing institutions of enforcement
or rehabilitation by providing data measuring the effectiveness of public policies.

One of the early and highly influential sociological approaches to the study of
deviance and social control was Durkheim's functionalist conception of the social
order. In an attempt to comprehend the complex relationship between consensus
and deviance, Durkheim concentrated specifically on the changing social relations set upon by modernity. He believed in the reality of social facts and in the
social scientist's access to them through empirical measures. It is possible to see

him as an early structuralist insofar as he saw the organization of social relations as both constituting and constraining the activities of people: society as a "container" of individuals. This brand of structural-functionalism is at the heart of Durkheim's *The Division of Labor in Society* ([1893] 1947). As a positivist, he focused upon the observable qualities that constitute a society, in how its particular workings and structure produce a collective sense of order specific to that society. In this formulation, deviance, seemingly defined as both the result of a rigid consensus and an indicator of the incomplete nature of the social consensus, provides the social with a negative example against which the boundaries of "acceptable" practice can be marked.

Durkheim's other major contribution to the study of deviance is the concept of anomie, which suggests that deviance will increase in situations of normlessness. This is seen most significantly in Robert K. Merton's *Social Theory and Social Structure* (1957). Modern society in general promotes social atomization through the breaking up of traditional communal ties, such as kinship and religion. The theory of anomie argues that in such times of social upheaval and the relaxing of the influence of the central social institutions of the past, deviant behavior begins to manifest itself amid this confusion. Thus, Durkheim ([1897] 1951) explained suicide as a "rational" response to the changes of modern society, an individual act against the imposed consensus of society.

The question of consensus reverberated through American social science. The first discussions of sociology and communications in the United States were precipitated by questions about the securing of democratic ideals, freedom and equality, and unity of the nation. If this was to be a nation of individuals, how would society be held together? Would the democratic project be possible in the face of pluralism and American particularity? The Chicago School's response was to say that it was through what we shared, the proverbial "social cement," that this unity or community was to be maintained. Here the questions of culture and communication, consensus and community, were intertwined. Furthermore, the Chicago School's interest in the mechanisms of consensus meant that the school's adherents were equally interested in the mechanics of deviance.

As Harold Finestone (1976) points out, Chicago, as New York City's new and rapidly expanding rival at the turn of this century, provided a unique milieu in which to examine the effects of urbanization and mass immigration. Not surprisingly then, juvenile delinquency, as a consequence of rapid social change, was given notable attention. For instance, it was in this context that Jane Addams wrote the highly influential *The Spirit of Youth and the City Streets* (1909). A social reformist interested in the welfare of working-class youth, Addams argued that the "spirit of youth" consisted of an amorphous set of desires, including a need for play, adventure, and idealism. Unfortunately, this spirit was being smothered by rapid urbanization and cultural displacement.

Addams's work in many respects launched what came to be a theory of human or social ecology. This perspective employed a biological metaphor to refer to the

symbiotic nature of social interaction. Disharmony in the social environment occurred when there was some disruption in the presumed natural ecological balance of the social order, usually described as some form of consensus. Robert Park
(1925, 106) wrote, "Delinquency is, in fact, in some sense the measure of the failure of our community organizations to function." Here social disorganization, resulting from conflicting values and goals, produced an "unnatural" situation,
subverting the "proper" role of social institutions—the production of consensus.
This model took the changes of modernity as threats to the natural order and its
presumed consensual arrangement. In this respect, the human ecology perspective represented an inherently conservative rendering of the problem of deviance.
Consensus was taken to be a desirable consequence of social activity and was often assumed to have existed unproblematically prior to modernity. This perspective ignored the question of power in particular formations and therefore could
not apprehend the fact that conflict as much as, if not more than, consensus is apparently an immediate and "natural" result of society.

Deviance at some level always corresponds to a breach of the normative bounds
of the social. But, of course, not all forms of deviance are treated equally. This
prompted Howard Becker (1973) to distinguish between "rule-breakers" and "deviants," where the former do not necessarily become defined as deviant and therefore avoid the severity of cultural censure. This ability to distinguish between
forms of deviance is a constitutive feature of its visibility; deviance can exist only
through the lens of the social. This means that the naturalness of deviance, and its
social effectivity, is drawn into question. In other words, what counts as deviant,
how a behavior comes to be recognized as deviant, and what role this plays in
structuring the social are all questions that address the social construction of the
category of deviance and its effectivity.

For instance, Kai Erikson (1966) investigates the role of deviance identification
and definition in the establishment and maintenance of community normativity.
He writes that "crime (and by extension other forms of deviation) may actually
perform a needed service to society by drawing people together in a common pos-
ture of anger and indignation" (p. 4). Erikson asserts this to explain the fact that
deviance seems to be a necessary consequence of any normative agency or activity—that is, culture or society in general—and that not all deviant acts are truly
threatening to the social group or its community. In other words, they must perform another social function, that of consensus building via negative example.
Culture, then, is the process of boundary construction and preservation: "Deviant
forms of behaviour, by marking the outer edges of group life, give the inner structure its special character and thus supply the framework within which the people
of the group develop an orderly sense of their own cultural identity" (p. 13).

Erikson's approach seems to work well in studies of specific and close communities. However, anything broader would clearly need to consider a more heterogeneous culture where, on the surface, conformity seems not so easy to describe.
The presumed characteristics of a stable community, like those of the human

ecology perspective, are still at the heart of this approach and as such need significant reworking to be appropriate in other cultural contexts. In this respect, Erikson's project becomes somewhat too obsessed with the sociological method of Durkheim. For instance, it is an ambiguous claim that "agencies of control often seem to define their job as that of keeping deviance *within bounds* rather than that of obliterating it" (p. 24). This view implies that there is an acceptable volume of deviance, beyond which extreme measures are taken. The goal is one of deviance stabilization. Although in most circumstances this may be the case, there are moments when the tendency does not appear to be the normalization of deviance but the amplification of public concerns. It is exactly this that Stuart Hall and his colleagues explore in *Policing the Crisis: Mugging, the State and Law and Order* (1978), where, they argue, a general crack in the postwar hegemony was being managed by the "agencies of control" through the constitution of a category of social disturbance—the urban black crime, mugging. Even in functionalist terms, normalization is not the only role to be played.

Arguably, interactionist theory was the first, in Becker's (1973) words, to "demystify deviance." At a basic level, symbolic interactionism sees social reality as formed and framed through a process of social interaction, or communication. Meaning and structure are brought into our social existence, creating cultural bonds and unity within a community. The task of the social analyst is to identify and interpret these human acts of cultural self-expression and definition. Here the blatant empiricism of traditional criminology is discarded, and the "material" is problematized. Instead, a consideration of the social construction of the deviant and its place in the operations of social and cultural normativity is deemed necessary.

This is the domain of labeling theory, sometimes referred to as social reaction, transactional, or deviance theory. How does deviance come into existence in ways that are socially significant? One finds the earliest statement of this perspective in Frank Tannenbaum's *Crime and the Community* (1938, 19–20):

> The process of making the criminal, therefore, is a process of tagging, defining, identifying, segregating, describing, emphasizing, making conscious and self-conscious; it becomes a way of stimulating, suggesting, emphasizing and evoking the very traits that are complained of. If the theory of relation of response to stimulus has any meaning, the entire process of dealing with the young delinquent is mischievous in so far as it identifies him to himself or to the environment as a delinquent person.
>
> The person becomes the thing he is described as being.

The suggestion that there is no inherent criminal quality to delinquents but that people become what they are described as being is central to this perspective. As evidenced by the preceding quotation, Tannenbaum perceptively portrays this process as a string of activities: tagging, defining, stimulating, emphasizing, dealing, and engaging in all those social and cultural activities involved in designating deviance. The deviant is the product of cultural endeavor; indeed, of *performance*. Furthermore, there is a positivity to this cultural enterprise and production, of which the deviant is but one consequence of the interstice of particular discourses. For example, Becker's classic ethnographic project, *Outsiders: Studies in the Sociology of Deviance* (1973), concerns the social constitution of the consensual aspects of being deviant—the inside of the outside. As Becker writes (p. 9):

> Social groups create deviance by making the rules whose infraction constitutes deviance, and by applying those rules to particular people and labeling them as outsiders. From this point of view, deviance is *not* a quality of the act the person commits, but rather a consequence of the application by others of rules and sanctions to an "offender." The deviant is one to whom that label has successfully been applied; deviant behavior is behavior that people so label.

Central to the construction of such a consensus is the visibility of the deviant; the behavior and its perpetrators must be identified and defined as such. The unit of analysis is, as Edwin Lemert (1972, 48) describes, secondary deviation.

> Primary deviation is assumed to arise in a wide variety of social, cultural, and psychological contexts, and at best has only marginal implications for the psychic structure of the individual; it does not lead to symbolic reorganization at the level of self-regarding attitudes and social roles. Secondary deviation is deviant behavior, or social roles based on it, which becomes means of defense, attack or adaptation to the overt and covert problems created by the societal reaction to primary deviation. In effect, the original "causes" of the deviation recede and give way to the central importance of the disapproving, degradational, and isolating reactions of society.

So one of the conditions of "successful labeling," a term whose usage in the literature is an indication of a latent functionalism and tenacious ties to Durkheim, is the presence of what Erikson refers to as the "social audience." It is, as Tannenbaum puts it, a "dramatization of evil," where the definition of certain individuals and behaviors as deviant provides a public sense of the limits or bounds of cultural norms. This model presumes that there are no inherent qualities to behavior or to an individual that indicate deviance. Instead, it is part of a social construction that rests upon the visibility and display of the deviant act. The social is the audience, and the crime is the drama—the *spectacle* of deviance is thus the assurance of its own operational activity. As Richard Quinney (1970, 23) proposes, "The social reality of crime is constructed by the formulation and application of criminal definitions, the development of behavior patterns related to criminal definitions, and the construction of criminal conceptions." This presumes that the deviant activity has visibility or at least that the social drama of deviance is a necessary condition for successful labeling. In this respect, there is an important link between deviance and its social effectivity; and the linchpin is the spectacle.

Labeling theory asks how it is that some come to be identified, and indeed come to see themselves, as deviant. Most significantly, this approach facilitates the examination of the political power involved in the question of marking the normative bounds of culture. The definition of deviance, what it is applied to, and where and how it is to take effect are a particular form of knowledge production and therefore a form of power. One sees early attempts to deal with the structures of power that are constructed around the category of deviance. With the term *agencies of control* Erikson is trying to capture this, as Becker does with *moral entrepreneurs,* whose activities could generally be called superstructural in the construction and maintenance of social and cultural normalcy. Even though this process is much more complex than either author allows, particularly since control is not the only function of these agencies, or the only way existing social relations are reproduced, this is an important moment in the study of deviance. It introduces the possibility of speaking of the relationship deviant behavior has with the broader structure of the social formation allowing for the critical analysis of such concepts as consensus, unity, and community.

As Hall (1982, 63) writes concerning labeling theory, "What was at issue here was the problem of social control, and the role of social control in the maintenance of the social order." The observation that social order needs disciplinization "radically problematized the whole notion of 'consensus'" (p. 63). The construction and continual reworking of the consensus point to the processes and systems by which society expresses and reproduces itself. Here Hall calls attention to the role of mass media, which he sees as not only reactive or reflective but also involved in the complex loop of definition, specification, and legitimation.

As respresented in the collections *The Manufacture of News: Social Problems, Deviance and the Mass Media* (Cohen and Young 1973) and *Deviance and Social Control* (Rock and McIntosh 1974), there was a period of dialogue between British cultural studies and radical criminology that led to a new approach to deviance.[3] In particular, the contribution of labeling theory to cultural studies is noted by Tony Bennett (1982a, 296):

> Although this does not deny the cogency of inquiring why it is that the members of some social groups are more likely to engage in such forms of behaviour than are the members of other groups, it does entail a shift of interest away from the behaviour of the so-called deviant towards an examination of the social and cultural processes whereby the attribution of the label of deviance is made to some acts and not to others and of the functions which the nomination of such acts as deviant fulfils in relation to the wider social order.

British cultural studies found in deviance theory the formulation of certain questions about the mechanisms of the social reality of crime, consensus, and deviance, often with significant attention paid to youth. From Richard Hoggart's

(1958, 247) description of the milk bar, with its teddy boys and juke boxes, through to Iain Chambers's (1986) "profane" style-conscious semioticians, youth has reappeared frequently as a favorite object of British cultural investigation. Cultural studies has tended to fetishize youth as a social location where the contradictions of how we live our "imaginary relations" to real conditions of existence are laid bare. But, importantly, the significatory power of youth-as-problem is always at the fore. Here the lived contradictions of youth involve an understanding of the troubling and troubled qualities discussed previously.

It is not surprising, then, that *Resistance Through Rituals: Youth Subcultures in Post-War Britain* (Hall and Jefferson 1976) begins with an acknowledgment of Becker's work as a significant contribution to the study of deviance and criminology and as a source of inspiration. The difference from that earlier American approach is that public reaction is not seen to exhaust the explanations of deviance. *Resistance Through Rituals* concerns both the structural determinants of social action and labeling theory's interest in social reaction. Importantly, in the place of acts of individual deviance, the central focus becomes the determining features of the structural differences between social groups. This constitutes a significant move to subculture theory as conceived in the British context. Youth is demonstrative, by which the authors are specifically referring to conspicuous consumption and the display of affluence. They suggest that a dialectic exists between the social category of youth and the industrial production of a youth market.

Comprising a fundamental ingredient of contemporary youth culture, this dialectic was constituted as the object of analysis, to be deconstructed and, through subculture theory, recuperated as a structurally defined social space with certain possibilities for social action. The three aspects of subculture were seen to be structure, culture, and biography (Hall and Jefferson 1976, 57); or, alternately, determinations, expressions, and agency (as they were understood respectively). To map the articulations of these three social conditions and their consequences, the project required a text that could be read openly, such that a wedge could be placed among the production of culture, consumption, and experience. Increasingly, "style" became that text.

As a privileged site of cultural analysis, style constitutes an "expressive form," a communicative medium that speaks the experience of social position. Young people in particular are seen to employ the strategy of style as a way to negotiate and advance "their own" distinctive symbolic response to their social position of disenfranchisement. Style is the display that marks youth's difference from the broader, parent culture and from other subcultures. It constructs a unity and opens a cultural space for certain expressions and activities to take place. Frequently, this is taken in its most romantic sense: Not only does subcultural style speak a collective voice, but, as an expression of malaise, it is also a resistant one.

Hebdige's *Subculture: The Meaning of Style* (1979) is a sophisticated semiotic version of this perspective. Taking the communicative aspect of subcultural style—that we can read style as an expression of identity—he explores the construction of this "language." In his conception, rastas, punks, and teddy boys are Claude Levi-Strauss's "everyday engineers" constructing their subcultural voice through the appropriation of banal artifacts. This activity of bricolage is not random; instead, it occurs and is arranged through some form of logic. Hebdige sees his task as the identification of homologies between the elements of subcultural style that will allow him to read and comprehend that expression of identity and the experience of social position. Subcultures arise in the appropriation of elements from the dominant culture; commodities and their recontextualization provide a site for the expression of "forbidden identities." Popular culture provides an endless inventory of "everyday" artifacts to work within the process of constructing and expressing cultural identity. The act of bricolage disrupts the "natural" connection between signifiers and signifieds by making their association provisional. Thus, subcultural style is a semiotic challenge.

Because of the "unnaturalness" of the appropriation and use of cultural artifacts, style begs to be noticed and interpreted. The display value, the visibility, is a precondition of the availability of style as a text. Moreover, it is also the very location of cultural identity—where it can be discerned, where it resides. It is always the *demonstrated* difference from the dominant culture and other subcultural groupings that establishes the significatory weight of style. The codes are on the surface, on display, and are therefore easily appropriated once again—by those whose social position is not authentically associated with the stylistic expression or by the dominant culture.

This is the confounding problem of incorporation for subculture theory. A number of responses have been offered. First, the more traditional subculture theory response is to argue that there is authenticity of expression. Once musical style, argot, and fashion are incorporated back into the dominant, there is no longer the oppositional potential that was once available. However, it is ambiguous how and when this occurs, for the markers of the dominant and the subculture are not always easy to pin down with precision. To deal with this, a second response argues that there may be a dominant culture and subcultures but that the question of authenticity, of what is authentically rooted in which culture, does not matter. If cultural expressions and cultural identities are on the surface, then anyone cannot only express but also live that subcultural relation (see Chambers 1986). A final position argues that all members of the contemporary world are people involved in the construction of their own identity. Here popular culture acts as a resource of elements for people to use as they wish, with equal access. Thus, the difference between a dominant culture and a subculture cannot be discerned with any precision and possibly does not matter anyway (see Fiske 1987). Social position cannot be read directly from style in the manner that subculture theory suggests. This position in effect says that the notion of subculture no longer designates a unique relation.

Although I am sympathetic to this conclusion, it often leads to the further conclusion that there is no specificity to social position either, a dangerous mis-theorization to say the least. This problem was brought to the fore in Angela McRobbie's (1980, 45) early critique of subculture theory's insensitivity to issues of gender, insisting on a consideration of the fact that "walking on the wild side— it's different for girls."

Subculture theory is important as one attempt to deal with the question of youth's uncertain position in the social, its "deviant" or threatening nature. The theory's emphasis upon the expressive forms of youth culture has been significant, but subculture theory has been less successful in dealing with the complex determinations of what youth comes to signify. In other words, subculture theory reads homologies of style as expressions of social position and identity often at the expense of the discursive indication and construction of articulated identities as they are made meaningful. To evince the qualities of social position as undertaken by subculture theory, assumptions are made concerning the correspondences between expression (style) and experience (felt contradiction). But subculture theory cannot deal with the circulation of the imagined unity of youth against the diverse populations of punk women, rasta men, or glitter androgyny.

Crime, Crisis, and Hegemony

As suggested by labeling theory, crimes are taken to be expressive by the specularizing practices of "dramatization." One of the central assumptions about deviant activity in general is that it tells us something about those involved, about the context in which the activity occurred, and about those who are threatened or disturbed. Crimes come to indicate social problems, psychological disorders, and emotional incapacities, and, conversely, they suggest the bounds of acceptability in so many varied respects. They speak, or rather they are made to speak; and various forms of representational practice not only presume that the actions of the deviant speak but also that it is possible to gain access to that voice. The visibility and spectacular qualities of youth—youth-as-problem, youth as both troubled and troubling—figure strongly in crime and deviance. In one respect, youth is always deviant, always a problem, always in need of managing, guiding, and surveillance.

One of the most sophisticated analyses of criminal youth and social order is *Policing the Crisis*. In attempting to comprehend the British "mugging crisis" of the early 1970s, the authors examine "why and how the themes of race, crime, and youth—condensed into the image of 'mugging'—come to serve as the articulator of the crisis, as its ideological conductor" (Hall et al. 1978, viii). Hall and his colleagues employ a complex variant of labeling theory informed by semiotics to discuss how certain social concerns and connotative effects are mobilized. Starting with the very precise and contained events of mugging, they work outward to describe a general crisis in the postwar hegemony. This focus upon the historical moment contextualizes what they describe as the "politics of mugging"—that is, how this particular type of crime comes to act as a site at which certain political projects are enacted. "How has the 'law-and-order' ideology been constructed? What social forces are constrained and contained by its construction? What forces stand to benefit from it? What role has the state played in its construction? What real fears and anxieties is it mobilising? These are some of the things we mean by 'mugging' as a social phenomenon" (p. viii). This approach represents a significant alteration of the usual object of study in criminology. The crime itself is not the locus of investigation; rather, the authors are concerned with "the relation between the deviant act and the reaction of the public and the control agencies to the act" (p. 17; from Cohen 1972, 28). In taking the term *deviant act* as a cultural construct, *Policing the Crisis* exposes exactly who benefits from such definitions, to what ends they are used, and with what broader social effects, particularly with respect to the construction of a hegemonic position. Theoretically speaking, *Policing the Crisis* considers deviance not just as a marker of consensus but also as a site of hegemonic struggle.

One way to understand this process of a seemingly consensual concern about a particular issue or event, suggested by Stanley Cohen (1972) in *Folk Devils and Moral Panics: The Creation of Mods and Rockers* is through the notion of a moral panic. According to Cohen (p. 9), this panic occurs when

> a condition, episode, person or group of persons emerges to become defined as a threat to societal values and interests; its nature is presented in a stylized and stereotypical fashion by the mass media; the moral barricades are manned by editors, bishops, politicians and other right-thinking people; socially accredited experts pronounce their diagnoses and solutions; ways of coping are evolved or (more often) resorted to; the condition then disappears, submerges or deteriorates and becomes more visible.

The condition of a moral panic suggests that there is an active attempt across social institutions to make sense of a point of interest, an event, or a series of occurrences. The complexity of this social activity of constituting and securing the significance of a common concern is described in Hall et al. (1978, 52):

> These agencies [media, judiciary, police] must be understood as actively and continuously part of the whole process to which, also, they are "reacting." They are active in defining situations, in selecting targets, in initiating "campaigns," in structuring these campaigns, in selectively signifying their actions to the public at large, in legitimating their actions through the accounts of situations which they produce. They do not simply respond to "moral panics." They form part of the circle out of which "moral panics" develop. It is part of the paradox that they also, advertently and inadvertently, amplify the deviancy they seem so absolutely committed to controlling. This tends to suggest that, though they are crucial actors in the drama of the "moral panic," they, too, are acting out a script which they do not write.

In other words, to explicate the political charge of the mugging crisis and the specificity of its development, the authors are obliged to consider a broader field of focus. How does there come to be a certain compliance across agencies to recognize a "panic"? How are such campaigns initiated and with what consequences? The contemporary scene, the popular and cultural environment of Britain in the late 1960s and early 1970s, provides the context for the conjunctural analysis of *Policing the Crisis*. In fact, the latter half of the book, in the interest of historical specificity, presents a history of the social and political formations of postwar Britain to ground the precise significance of the appearance of mugging.

Although *Policing the Crisis* emerged from a very different context to speak to a specific situation, it has certain theoretical similarities to the work of Michel Foucault. Foucault studies the complexly structured forms of social knowledge and power. In his work, power is multifaceted and cannot be said to be singularly located. It operates in and through epistemology; the very mechanisms that order our relations to the world in an intelligible fashion and that make something comprehensible to us are equally relations of power. For instance, in *Discipline and Punish: The Birth of the Prison* (1979), Foucault writes the history of the discourses of knowledge and ethics that facilitated the application of particular tactics of dealing with criminals. The tendential repercussions have little to do with the efficiency or effectiveness of the "prison." For instance, these consequences include the establishment of a "criminal class," the contingent development of a number of "scientific" discourses that explain and reinforce the procedures of incarceration, and, most generally, the installment of a "society of surveillance," which Foucault describes as the diffused manner in which "soft" tactics of discipline are evidenced in many aspects of contemporary social existence. When *Policing the Crisis* is read with this in mind, a Foucauldian sense of the discursive construction of knowledge, necessarily a relation of power as well, encounters a Gramscian notion of cultural leadership and class alliance to provide a comprehensive analysis of the articulations of deviance and social power as mediated through and motivated by the mass media of news reporting.

Panics, as the concentration of popular concern, trigger the structured responses of social institutions and do not occur in an isolated manner on an irregular basis. Certainly, crises differ from one another in the scope and intensity to which they shake up the social apparatus and are experienced at a popular level. Yet crisis, or at least the threat thereof, is equally a normal and everyday aspect in many arenas; otherwise there would be no need for such regulatory bodies as the police, the military, the judiciary, and religious orders. After all, there is always the possibility of a "crime wave." Crime is at some level a "coming apart" of "order" without necessarily contradicting its everydayness, its banality. Crime is the dual play of normal/deviant, inside/outside, legal/criminal, that indicates the particularities of hegemony through crisis. Crisis is thus a term reserved to describe the movement between the bifurcated realms of prosocial/antisocial. When Hall et al. describe a general crisis, they are describing a historical moment. On the contrary, I am suggesting that crisis as discourse, which is experienced and determined historically, is omnipresent in the formation of hegemonic alliances. Crisis operates as a *mobile signifier* that migrates from debate to debate and carries with it a field of connotations and referen⁺ial indices. It implies a common set of standards, values, and ethical questions that set the debate in motion and guide the institutional responses. The discourse of crisis is a potential point of conjuncture or a series of such points; it is the logic of a form of hegemony.

Instead of a crisis of hegemony, I want to install the notion of hegemony through crisis. For instance, in Britain World War II has become increasingly codified and mythologized as the last heroic moment in which England was for the English. This rhetoric continues to inform the racism inherent in British public policy concerning immigrants. Furthermore, this rhetoric was particularly evident in the Falklands War, where the discourses of empire were given a momentary shot of life through an appeal to the narratives of a still-recent history of colonialism (see Hall 1984). In the United States, this axiom has impelled foreign and domestic policy from the cold war, to the attacks upon Libya, Grenada, Panama, and Iraq, to the proclamation of an "enemy within and without" with the War on Drugs. The frenzied responses of patriotism associated with these state initiatives are strong arguments for their effectiveness as consenus-forming events.

The project of hegemony through crisis is not always a question of massive rallying around single battles; it equally consists of numerous debates that infuse the predilections of popular imagination and particular political agendas. Various Others may always be present, but at times some are more prominently displayed, with more specifically material and strategically destructive consequences, than at others. This is precisely what is taking place with contemporary youth in the United States. Youth—and this is doubly true for African-American and Hispanic-American youth—is increasingly symbolically central as that internal Other defined as a threat to the stability of the social order but central in the composition of that order. As such, the connotative purchase of youth has a profound political stake.

Crime, violent or otherwise, is about deviance, sexuality, morality, justice, class, race, social crisis, and so forth. These discourses cross and shift, giving shape to the meaning and effectivity of crime. The event (item, thing, artifact, practice) emerges as material, as evidence, and can thus be designated as socially productive. In this way, crime figures prominently in the structures of hegemony. Duncan Webster (1988, 207) writes, "On both sides of the Atlantic crime has played an important part in populist politics. 'Law and order' campaigns by the right have worked to criminalize protest and have often acted as a disguised appeal to racism as well as drawing on more general moral themes of declining national values with promises of a restoration of past virtues and certainties." The threat crime poses to a particular order of things is a key place to elucidate the values and specificities of that "order." It mobilizes concern and energies. This is the political import of "folk devils" as "visible reminders of what we should not be" (Cohen 1972, 10). They are neatly sown as the agents of the moral panics and become the recipients of discipline and surveillance. They come to be identified as particular brands of deviants and "outsiders." And as Cohen notes, "One of the most recurrent types of moral panic in Britain since the war has been associated with the emergence of various forms of youth culture ... whose behaviour is deviant or delinquent" (p. 9). This statement is equally true of the Unitied States.

There was no actual rise in adolescent crime during the 1950s to precipitate the vociferous public response witnessed in the form of debates concerning censorship, television effects, comic books, and rock 'n' roll (see Gilbert 1986). Even during the hysteria of the period, Daniel Bell (1960) described "the myth of the crime wave." It is evident that juvenile delinquency, and youth in general, had become the focus of fears of changing class, gender, and racial boundaries; youth violence was a site invested with energy, concern, and paranoia. In other words, discourses of crisis intersected in the category of juvenile deviance. Similarly, it appears that in the contemporary scene, varying forms of social concern are being secured at that particular site as well. In each instance, the construction of a location where certain discourses of crisis converge is the process of initiating and augmenting a moral panic.

The trajectory from "murder as entertainment" through to hegemonic articulations of the social imaginary is extensive and tangled. Along the way we encounter an endless host of accidents colliding, confounding, *and* determining the relative fixity of articulations. Gramsci (1971, 324) writes that "the starting-point of critical elaboration is the consciousness of what one really is, and is 'knowing thyself' as a product of the historical process to date which has deposited in you an infinity of traces, without leaving an inventory." The next line, a crucial one omitted from the standard translation, states, "Such an inventory must therefore be made at the outset" (Forgacs 1988, 326). Though Gramsci is referring to the study of philosophy, arguing for a historically grounded approach, this remark is equally appropriate as a description of the complexity of historical relations that designate an "event" and its consequences, ideological and otherwise, in the popular.

In the endless host of accidents that make up the complex determinations of history, something emerges: points that announce the particularities of the social formation. Therefore, how, at the intersection of youth and violent forms of deviance, is a site constructed in which our fears and desires are housed, exemplified, and substantiated? How does this operation act to add yet another building block to the continued (conservative) project of patching the cracks in the discursive boundaries of sex, class, ethnicity—that is, those vectors along which the measures of crisis and social order are struggled over?

Considering the white-on-white violent crime committed by a young man against a young woman—the notorious "preppy murder"—the vectors of determination elucidate how this event figures in the process of hegemony. The following chapters map some of these "accidents," these "traces, without an inventory," through an analysis of the discourses of popular crime and their relation to a broader spectacular crisis of American youth.

PART TWO

Murder

3
News and Sensations: On Images of Crime

These few remarks sketch a kind of differential table of photographic conno-
tations, showing, if nothing else, that connotation extends a long way. Is
this to say that a pure denotation, a this-side of language, is impossible? If
such denotation exists, it is perhaps not at the level of what ordinary lan-
guage calls the insignificant, the neutral, the objective, but on the contrary,
at the level of absolutely traumatic images. The trauma is a suspension of
language, a blocking of meaning.

—Roland Barthes, *Image, Music, Text*

Robert Chambers, nineteen, strangled Jennifer Levin, eighteen, in Central Park on August 26, 1986, an incident that was soon to be popularly known as the preppy murder. Levin and Chambers had dated a few times that summer, and on that evening they had met at Dorrian's Red Hand Restaurant. The events that took place between the time they left the club together at approximately 3 A.M. and the discovery of Levin's body three hours later are uncertain; with no witnesses, only Chambers's version, an elaborately conceived tale of his own molestation at the hands of Levin, is available. Coupled with Chambers's fortuitous talent for the sensational, the murder rapidly became a full-blown media extravaganza, complete with lurid tabloid headlines ("Sex Play 'Got Rough'" and "Wild Sex Killed Jenny") and a front-page article in the *New York Times* that screamed concern for the "darkness beneath the glitter" of the life of upper-class youth (Freedman 1986a, 1).

The media covered Jennifer Levin's murder extensively for over a year and a half. It was front-page news for a number of weeks in the fall of 1986 and in the spring and summer of 1988. Even its naming as the preppy murder indicated a high degree of familiarity with the case; few occurrences of this kind receive the dubious honor of a nomenclature. Although the precise details of the crime may never be known for certain, an issue I address in the next chapter, there was something particularly significant about the considerable energy expended in the process of organizing the meaning of the crime. This sort of extensive coverage and speculation is an index of *cultural investment.*

Crime Stories

News produces meaning by associating one event with other familiar narratives, stories, or events that already make sense to us. This is true regardless of the "quality" of the coverage or the pretenses to "objectivity." In turn, given the currency of events like the preppy murder, the way in which the telling is "resolved" will affect the telling of other events. As news reporting produces a form of knowledge about a specific event, it also links events and circulates certain perspectives, thus creating a form of knowledge about the world in general. Keith Soothill and Sylvia Walby (1991) show that the demands upon the practice of popular news reporting—the desire to inform the public and the need to sell papers—are often conflicting. Consequently, certain characters, images, and knowledges appear that can satisfy such contradictory demands. In their study, Soothill and Walby trace the development of the category "sex crime" in the press and demonstrate how it has informed popular knowledge about rape, sexual assault, and murder.

Importantly, the social significance of crime is never inherent in the event itself. There is a whole fabric of forces that act upon crime, designating the nature of its deviance, the understanding of those victims and perpetrators involved, the appropriate social response, and the associated punishment. News reporting is an important initial moment of this definitional process. Events do not speak their newsworthiness; rather, this culturally defined category stands as an informal set of criteria informing what is to enter a position of public and popular scrutiny. Furthermore, the "story" transforms the raw data of "what occurred" (itself a problematic category) into what is suitable for broadcast or publication through various codes and conventions, all of which necessarily inflect the report in a number of different ways, drawing references to other events, constructing a narrative, and indexing certain values and beliefs. In this way, the complex social function of news reporting operates as a *technology of power;* as we begin to "know" an event, we enter under the weight of the power to organize, to moralize, to valorize—a power that is enacted upon events and our understanding of events. Hence, that power is enacted upon us. The question is not whether the news coverage is accurate; rather, it is what powers circulate in the explanation, accentuation, and mobilization of these events.

But the process does not stop there. The news is only one mechanism of discourse, with its own particularities. Part of what is intriguing about sensational crimes is the way in which they are taken up in a variety of different contexts: as television movies, as the topic of talk shows, as references in fictional films and television programs, and so on. Spectacular crimes circulate and capture public imagination, becoming examples of how we understand crime, criminals, race relations, sexuality, contemporary life, and the like. At times they are evidence of social change, the need for social change, or triggers of nostalgia.

Sensational crimes are distinguished by the way in which they rework the presumed "informational" function of the news. Coinciding with the move from event to sensational crime—to murder as entertainment—is an entire industry of cultural production. Like Amy Fisher's attempted murder, Tawana Brawley's charges of rape, the assault on Rodney King, and the murder of Yusuf Hawkins, the more celebrated crimes appear in a variety of different contexts: as the topic of talk shows, biographical features, editorials, movies, and so on. For example, the preppy murder has been the subject of at least six magazine feature articles; two magazine covers; three talk shows; two book-length journalistic accounts—*The Preppy Murder Trial* by Bryna Taubman (1988) and *Wasted: The Preppy Murder* by Linda Wolfe (1989)—with a third in preparation for Doubleday by Jennifer's mother, Ellen Levin; a made-for-television movie; and another film based on Wolfe's account in preproduction.[1] The two "star" lawyers who tried the case were not only familiar with this kind of attention; they also attracted it in their own right. Prosecuting attorney Linda Fairstein was chief of the New York Sex Crimes Unit. Her career had already been the subject of a made-for-television movie, with Valerie Harper in the lead role. Defense attorney Jack Litman was no stranger to high-profile cases, perhaps the most notorious of which was the Bonnie Garland murder, in which he argued successfully that her murderer, an ex-boyfriend, could not bear the emotional stress of Garland's wanting to see other people and therefore was not responsible for his own actions.

Crime stories of this nature are always fascinated with their own status as sensation. The story of the crime is inflected with an interest in the telling of the story itself; as such, there are often ample references to the coverage itself. Only a few days after the preppy murder, the *New York Times* reported that "the crime, with its elements of wealth and sex, has dominated the news all week" (Gross 1986, 29). Even over a year later, the *Times* reiterated the point under the subtitle of "sensational press attention": "The case, with its combination of sex and violence set amid the privileged prep-school world in which Mr. Chambers and Miss Levin moved, has attracted sensational media attention and inspired a yearlong police crackdown against underage drinking" (Johnson 1987, 33). These two examples demonstrate that reporting employs self-reflexivity as a way to suggest a consensual concern and that this is indeed a media event. The fact of coverage explains and legitimizes additional coverage, not in terms of competition but as an indicator of a consensus in the media and, by implication, the public, given the traditional ideological role of the press in the United States.

A *Newsweek* article of January 18, 1988, is illustrative. In its first line it references other reports of the same crime: "It was the kind of crime story the media play big" (Hackett 1988, 31). The article reiterates this later in the same paragraph: "The tabloids quickly dubbed the case the 'preppy murder'" (p. 31). On the one hand, the article uses the telling of the story of this event in the past as part of its own telling. On the other hand, it employs this moment of self-reflexivity to distance itself from those reports. The tabloid interpretation is the "sensational" one. This marks a difference against which the present article, embedded in the more "respectable" *Newsweek,* becomes the more accurate interpretation. Attention shifts away from the act of telling in the present article and focuses on the telling elsewhere. References to the inadequacies of the "dark tales" of the tabloids and suggestions that the event is "more than a sensational story" allow the present telling to be disguised behind the narratives it exposes as misinterpretations.

The media response to the preppy murder is far from unusual. Though only selected crimes become the object of such intensive investigation, there always exist similar sites of cultural investment. In this respect, the agenda-setting function of the media operates by increasing the salience of certain problems posed by crime. The consequence is always to marginalize other stories and other possible perspectives. For instance, at approximately the same time as the Levin murder, an East Harlem nun was raped (Stokes 1986). In upstate New York, a "brutal rape and murder" occurred that was actually witnessed by police officers, who did nothing to prevent the crime (May 1986). Both of these sex-specific crimes, given the conventions of newspaper coverage, could have easily lent themselves to a sensational response. And yet they were buried in favor of the Levin murder. What was it about this murder, the preppy murder, that led to its acceptance as a site of cultural investment?

Roughly, two principal elements gave the preppy murder its sensational qualities. First, Chambers and Levin were both white, young, attractive, and affluent. According to the conventions of news reporting, this is not the usual profile of individuals involved in this type of crime; this difference indicated the event's status as a unique, and therefore sensational, occurrence. By contrast, African-American violence generally becomes sensational in terms of its scale (numbers of people involved) and randomness (the extent to which any [white] person is a potential victim). Individual acts of violence are deemphasized in favor of the scope and prevalence of black crime. Unlike individualistic crimes such as the preppy murder, the "mass" black crime leaves little room to romanticize the perpetrator. In this respect, the news of African-American violence involves the construction of a chronology, which forms a general racially defined category spiraling out of control. There is no better example than the depiction of gangs, the reference points of which include turf, loyalty and ritual, membership, arms, drugs, and violence. These terms frame "gang-related" activity through oblique references to an *alien* presence. The suggestion is that this presence involves the development of a separate, dangerous counterorder. Semantically, "gang-related," and the coterminous "drug-related," activities describe nothing in particular, on the one hand, but connotatively signal a societal breakdown, on the other.

Gang-related violence predominantly involves blacks victimizing blacks. When this violence becomes volatile black-on-white violence, there is significant news and media attention. Here, suddenly, it is presumed that race speaks. The Central

Park "wilding" incident in which approximately two dozen black youths "spontaneously" went on a rampage of mugging, assault, and rape is a striking example. Culminating in a white investment banker being left for dead after being gang-raped and severely beaten, the wilding was disturbing because of the young age of the perpetrators (between fourteen and sixteen) and its senselessness. This was not "organized" gang activity; it was for "fun," as the young criminals were quoted as saying. This image of inarticulate but dangerous black youths led the associated discussion to characterize the perpetrators as "uncivilized and irrational." With Donald Trump's public plea for the execution of these "savages," there was no doubt that discourses of race composed the lens through which the wilding was popularly understood.[2] In other words, this crime, it was believed, revealed something of the "nature" of the urban African-American, something different from, and ultimately feared by, white society: a crazed, violent, and sexually aggressive black mass.

The randomness of this crime is a crucial determinant of the threat posed. Even organized gang violence at least has a perfectly logical economic motive; it is easily understood as a reasonable response to an impossible situation. Random violence provides no such mark of intelligibility and moves with a heightened ambiguity. As explanations contest one another, the status of the random crime increases to the level of general societal threat. Furthermore, it is these instances that become international news most frequently, next to organized student political protest as witnessed in South Korea over the last few years, China in 1989, and Greece in 1991. In 1990 and 1991, France and Britain saw riots developing from what were seen to be "apolitical" circumstances. In Vaulx-en-Velin, teenagers vandalized and then burned an entire shopping complex to the ground. The violence was generally conceived as frustrated responses to "urban apartheid," a term used to describe the social isolation experienced by youth living in suburban environments (Fraser 1990, B1).

These are partly the terrors of the *mass* mind; without reason and predictability, random youth violence is understood to be a terrible aberrant growth of the social. The image is that of a virus, where parts of society begin to attack others. The natural order of the social has been thrown askew with rogue elements upsetting the balance, so the image suggests. The body of the social has come under siege from a malignant force spun out from contemporary youth. But there are targets that, when attacked, draw the most attention, including investment bankers, shopping malls, and public parks. This suggests that perhaps these actions are not so random. In France, this particular youth riot was explained as having to do with social isolation and immigration. In the case of the Central Park wilding, this terrifying viral crime was linked to a question of race because it was black-on-white violence. The underlying supposition, then, was that the banker was attacked in Central Park, not because she was female, but *because she was white.*[3]

Whereas discourses of race molded the Central Park wilding, the preppy murder was filtered through discourses of sexuality, the second element that announced the preppy murder's qualities as a sensational crime. With the preppy

murder's white-on-white violence, racial concerns were absented, thus supporting the attention given to sex, youth and class. Centrally, there was Jennifer Levin's reported complicity in the sexual activity of that evening; she was described as
having "pursued" Robert Chambers, having initiated sexual advances, and having
suggested a bondage game. The source of this information was Chambers's videotape confession, in which he acted out the murder and Levin's sexual advances. It
is in this statement that Chambers made the initial tie between Levin's sexuality
and her own death, an association that was to govern the popular and judicial interpretations of the crime and its implications. Chambers's attorney, Jack Litman,
capitalized on this aspect when he demanded to see Levin's diary, which he said
chronicled "kinky and aggressive sexual activity" (Glynn 1988, 46). Though Judge
Howard Bell examined the diary and concluded that it included nothing pertinent to the case, the connotative power of Jennifer Levin's "deviant" sexuality remained and guided the understanding of her murder. No report failed to mention
the alleged kinkiness, despite the fact that there was no evidence to support
Litman's claim concerning the diary's content. In many respects, Levin's sexuality
came to be the enigma of the case; if it could be deciphered, then the crime would
be solved.

Images and the Obviousness of Crime

How does an incident like the preppy murder come to be situated in this manner?
Why was this association so successful, so evocative, so compelling? Published
and broadcast images of the crime are an ideal place to begin. News photographs
are crucial players in the formation of the agreed-upon meanings of crime and
social order.

Photographs are part of the cycle of evidence. They attest to the existence of key
elements in the story. Their status involves a process of marking and demonstrating claims, organizing what comes to be the narrative. They are a different form
of forensics, publishable and harboring a truth value that appears beyond dispute.
Like Walter Benjamin's ([1935] 1968) art in the age of mechanical reproduction,
this is evidence that is being reproduced, disseminated, and, in the context of
American ideologies of the free press, democratized. Where Benjamin refers to
the disappearance of the aura of art, the news photo carries a sort of reproducible
existential aura that attests to the veracity of the written claims. The ontology of
the photographic image is always confounding; this is taking place, this has taken
place, here is something, here is a representation of something. The photographic
image is a ghostly presence, never really what happened, never really accurate, but
impossible to dismiss.

This ontological relation becomes more evident with the circulation of particular sets of images. Reading news photographs requires paying attention to the
breadth and frequency of their reproduction as a composite historical record.
With sensational crimes like the preppy murder, no image stands alone. Instead,

Jennifer Levin (right) poses with friends Larissa Thomson (left) and Laura Robertson the night before her death.

camera setup will show the victim, played by Lara Flynn Boyle, lying under a plastic sheet.

Baldwin is one of four acting brothers (the best known is Alec, whose films include "Married to the Mob"). William faced unexpected animosity from his friends after the casting was announced. "I heard some groans when I told them. They didn't feel the whole thing deserved a TV-movie, that it would be exploitative."

Baldwin, however, saw it as "a great showcase for an actor—especially an unknown actor. For a case that got so much publicity, nobody knows much about Robert Chambers. No matter how I play it, the audience will have

diary" that Levin supposedly kept were vividly played up in the media. When the jury became hopelessly deadlocked, Chambers was allowed to plead guilty

Figure 3.1 *This snapshot of Jennifer Levin (right) and friends was widely circulated in* People *magazine and other publications.*

composites of various images are assembled and become the photographs of the crime. Soon they are not seen individually but in relation to other photographs. A photo of Levin does not make sense without a photo of Chambers or at least the memory of such a photo. There is a narrative link, however loose. The relationship between images reveals the story, its tensions and resolutions.

There she is: her face, her clothes, her hair (Figure 3.1). This innocuous snapshot of Levin, with all its codes of amateurishness, can never appear without a connection to what was then about to take place. Taken usually as haphazard souvenirs—as though one decides "I want to remember this"—snapshots are about places and friends, about relationships and sentiments. In other words, they are most often about things that cannot be photographed—memory and emotion. And this connotative impulse is not surely set; instead, it bounces between the material presence of the photograph as evidence of the past, of what memory is organized around, and the process of remembering, of setting the story straight, as it were.

This image circulates as the terrible evidence of the everyday whose significance has changed. This snapshot will never have the luxury of being lost amid the mess of similar images collected over the years. This was probably the last snapshot taken of Levin; we cannot look at this image without thinking that this

Park Mu
Ends

NEW YORK, March 26
Friday, after eight and a
jury deliberations in the
of Robert E. Chambers
rate dramas were near
acts.

In the jury room, tl
panel was falling apa
notes came out from in
seeking to be removed
One man burst into tea
judge and said his e
had been destroyed b
noon, two notes came
time — one from the
saying the panel was
the other from an ind
ing there was no im
verdict was still poss!

In the judge's ch:
hall, the plea-bargai
end the case a few
coming together, dr
clear signs of chaos
and the threat — in
jury or a mistria
would have to be
thing neither the
defense wanted.

Finally, sometir
general terms wel
bers would plead
manslaughter fr
Levin on Aug 26
ceive a sentence
mum 8⅓ to 25 ye

Few De

The New York Times/John Sotomayor

Robert E. Chambers Jr., being led to a car yesterday for the trip from
his parents' apartment to the jail on Rikers Island in New York.

But according
court transcrip
day, few other
those final hour
hearing. Indee
rangement, ur
bers admitted
cause serious
Levin and the
were not fully
ties until mir
the courtroon

Meanwhile
ating. Jurors
were swingi
ing and acqu

Cries of 'Murderer' Amid the Rain

By LISA W. FODERARO

As protesters, neighbors, reporters
and the curious looked on in a soft,
steady rain, Robert E. Chambers Jr.
left his home yesterday, stepped into a
black Cadillac and headed off to jail.
At exactly 10 A.M., Mr. Chambers,
... his pants and an

Mr. Chambers, who pleaded guilty on
Friday to first-degree manslaughter in
the death of Jennifer Levin, faces a
prison term of 5 to 15 years. Several of
the friends on the roof were in the
courtroom late Friday afternoon, some
distraught and others tearful, as Mr.
Chambers told Justice Howard E. Bell
... intended to cause Miss
thus ...

Figure 3.2 *The face of a killer? Robert Chambers's handsome visage was often showcased in
the daily newspapers.*

young woman is about to die. Roland Barthes (1981, 95) describes a similar reaction in examining the photograph of a man about to be executed: "He is dead and he is going to die." The frozen instant captures our imagination. Searching it for clues, for understandings, we come up empty-handed, except with a sense of what an utter waste Jennifer Levin's death was.

Analogously, is it possible to look at an image of Robert Chambers and not think that this man killed Jennifer Levin? This boyish visage is the face of a killer. And what does the killer look like? Pleasant, wealthy, athletic, sexy, charming, indifferent, smug, vile, cold? (See Figure 3.2.)

Faces pose a particular interpretive problem. The human face is always a myriad of expressions and meanings that are ambiguously communicated. Faces, images of faces and their expressions, are in many ways indecipherable, always escaping precision of description and understanding. Yet they draw us and insist upon our critical attentions. Generally, part of the process of coming to know someone is being able to draw correspondences between bodily expression and internal states. And part of our coming to know Levin and Chambers, as distant and mediated as that process may be, is founded upon assumptions that are made with respect to our own abilities to read their faces. The anchoring capacity of photo captions is central. But the materiality of the expressions, and of our understanding of those expressions, can undercut other interpretations.

Here are the seeds of the criminal identity. Compare this to the most widely circulated photos of the Central Park wilding (Figure 3.3). Clearly, the grouping of six photographs of the suspects is a marked contrast to the common portraits of Chambers. The wilding suspects' faces are turned, almost hiding, seemingly shameful, not permitting identification or even recognition. The Chambers photograph, with his defiant gaze and almost arrogant demeanor, informs the text concerning his criminality by suggesting a certain complexity to his character. His identity emerges as complicated, contradictory, and, most important, worthy of consideration. He is romantic, tragic, sexy, and cruel. Furthermore, he is a star, a public and popular persona. The wilding suspects, by comparison, are denied this form of exposure and individuality; instead, they are criminality. They are the young, black, and wild. Their names are public record, but this is overshadowed by their numbers. The Chambers photo testifies to his individual existence and identity. The wilding suspects' photos testify to their existence as criminals and to the charges of a general social disintegration. Although the racism of the judicial system and of the media in the wilding case was met with a terrific public response, both in the press itself and through the scrutiny of the trial by black activists, nothing could undo the discursive pull of the suspects as the mass suspect.

The respective framing of each crime on the cover of *People Weekly* is particularly indicative of these differences. Whereas the preppy murder is a "case," the wilding is an "outrage." A consensual public response to the wilding, in other words, is a given and is woven into the story. The preppy murder issue employs a formula composition, one that appeared on at least two magazine covers and one

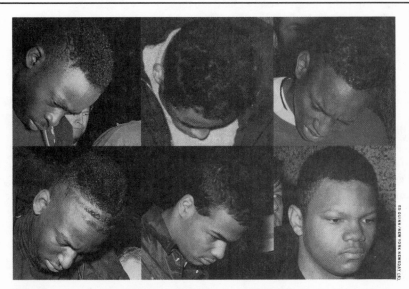

ED QUINN/NEW YORK NEWSDAY (6)

ir consent, but and broad meadows in the heart of Man- lasted 30 minutes. They pummeled
ad chronicled the hattan. Some areas seem as unspoiled as her with fists, smashed her face and head
y of the young the Forest of Arden, offering peace, seclu- ̄ with stones and a metal, threw rocks at car
rom the hazy hell trees on her left she could see the illumi- and bicyclists, robbed a 52-year-old His
her progress, she was nated blue spire of the Empire State Build- panic man and assaulted at least four oti
ion, and it remained ing, the red neon joggers before p<
she would ever re- RCA logo atop lice captured th<
and physical capaci- Rockefeller Cen- **It remained highly doubtful** first five of the b<
We're taking it one ter, the glittering at about 11 P.M. I
silver Art Deco **that the victim would ever fully** the cops didn't
crown of the **recover. "We're taking it one** know about the
), had begun un- Chrysler Building. **miracle at a time," her** rape, and the wo
year-old investment The only sound an had lain brok
she settled in at her was the gentle **father said.** and bleeding for
finance department whoosh of the city's more than three
, the Wall Street in- traffic, like surf on hours before pa:
>use where she a far-off shore. ersby discovere<
nultimillion-dollar Then, at about 10 P.M., police say, as her and summoned help. She had by th
is industry. After a many as a dozen youths fell upon her. Ac- lost two-thirds of her blood, and her bo
day, she headed cording to the official account, which is temperature had fallen to 80 degrees.
fth-floor apartment largely based on the often conflicting

Figure 3.3   *The Central Park wilding suspects, as presented to the public.*

book cover: a full-page portrait of Chambers, taken in a formal photo session, with an inset photo of Levin (see Figure 3.4). Chambers's more recent and larger photo connotes his present, his life, whereas the older, smaller, and generally more amateurish photo of Levin (snapped at parties, in clubs, on vacation) suggests her past, her deadness. Their images are discrete with borders to separate them. But their names and their respective roles are clear.

The Central Park wilding issue does not present the names or the faces of those involved. Like the other circulated images of that crime, its very "facelessness" sets

Figure 3.4   *The preppy murder cover of* People, *1988.*

it apart. Instead, "the ultimate urban nightmare" was perpetrated by "dozens of teenagers [who] came out of the darkness," attacking in "packs," "savagely." The full-page photograph of deserted Central Park at night (Figure 3.5) is analogous to the Chambers portrait on the cover of *People;* it is the park, the night, the "darkness," that we must be fearful of, so the magazine suggests. The inset photo of the victim is tinted and obscured. The only fact it announces, the only fact discernible in the image that is not mentioned elsewhere on the cover, is her whiteness.

There are other genres of news photographs—for instance, those that, unlike the shots of Jennifer Levin, connote present repercussions. The most frequent are those of the crime scene, with and without Levin's sheet-covered body, and those of Chambers entering and exiting court. These images capture the story as it is unfolding, but always along fixed paths. Certain sites are privileged and transformed into pieces of evidence. The crime scene is a prime example. A shaded spot behind the Metropolitan Museum of Art in Central Park, the elm tree, and the distance from the road all become significant, reread as holding part of the story of the crime and as being available for popular scrutiny. Similarly, the images of individuals become victim, suspect, lawyer, judge, and jury—all the necessary actors to complete the structural arrangement of this narrative of crime and justice and injustice.

The video stills, probably among the most reproduced images of this crime, are arguably *the* images of the crime. The representation of Chambers confessing, his calm yet eager reenactment of what he said happened, is made all the more powerful by the fact that this confession takes place on the same day that he killed her. And the grainy quality of these stills, the cinema verité of the informally performed drama, and the drab surroundings summon a voyeuristic delight. The image reproduces a usually hidden and secret encounter: the application of state power through police interrogation.

The videotape of the Rodney King beating operated in a similar manner; it captured a cruel encounter between police officers and a civilian, one that is not supposed to occur and certainly is not supposed to be seen. Immediately, the video was forceful evidence of ideas that many already accepted: that police brutality is not uncommon, that this treatment is unfairly directed at African-Americans, and that there are criminal police officers and practices. The riots in Los Angeles and elsewhere following the not-guilty verdict at the officers' first trial were an expression of class conflict and frustration with the unbelievable security of systemic racism. Additionally, the riots were an acknowledgment of a faith in this videotape image as a sign of social disparity in the United States.

Another videotape in the preppy murder case, the "party video" showing a candid Chambers at a slumber party, was sold to and broadcast by *A Current Affair* just after his conviction in 1988. It attracted significant audience numbers and pushed the case back into the news, in some cases to the front page. The following is one report on that video:

Figure 3.5 *The wilding cover of* People, *1989.*

It was a grim epitaph for Jennifer Levin, whose strangling during rough sex in Central Park inspired accounts of privileged youth gone awry. Last week, FOX TV network aired a home video showing Robert Chambers, 21, who pleaded guilty to manslaughter, in another escapade. In the tape, made after Levin's death and before the trial, Chambers frolics with scantily clad women. Grinning, he plays with a doll, twisting its head: "I think I've killed it." Showing the tape stirred controversy, but the program's staff said it provided important insights. ("Playing with Dolls" 1988, 9)

The documentary *Video, Vigilantes and Voyeurism* (Fenton Bailey and Randy Barbato, 1993) marked the preppy murder case as the key turning point for tabloid television. In particular, the party video demonstrated the potential interest to television audiences of this brand of sensational news story and encouraged a wave of other tabloid format shows. And for the coverage of the preppy murder, the video provided a final image, one that seemed to give a sense of closure to the case: the image of Chambers twisting the head of a doll, with three blurred women in the background looking on at his performance.

Finally, the absent police photographs of Levin's body also come into play. Though they are never seen by the public, we know their forensic status. We know the reactions of the jury, described in detail in the press, and the strength they lent to the prosecution's case; the photographs said that this death could have been no accident. Even in the video confession, the cool Chambers is flustered only when he is shown these images.

With this discussion, the photographs of a crime are once again appearing as evidence. They are being examined and prodded for clues and insights into the mechanisms of meaning formation. They exist in this context for the purposes of my own scrutiny and hence for the encouraged—perhaps forced—look of the reader. It is impossible for me not to be involved in the whole process of representation, of retelling the story, albeit through a set of critical discourses. But rather than wave the flag of metacritical distance and shout claims of sensitivity or even privilege, I want to acknowledge my own immersion in a project of representation and to understand the political import of such an enterprise. In this way, I hope to take advantage of this immersion and make the story one about the social meaning of order and crisis, about violence against women, and about the insidiousness of racism and sexism. But it is still a story, one among many.

And in this story both of these violent attacks against women are seen through the social boundaries they are understood to transgress. These boundaries themselves are largely invisible under ideal instances of settlement and order. But they are announced in instances of disruption, such as these crimes. Whereas the preppy murder involved a class-specific breach of gender relations, an argument to be developed in the next chapter, the wilding was seen as a more profound violation of both class and racial divisions. To say that the media coverage of each event was racist or sexist does not really explain very much because, in the final analysis, all popular renderings are filtered through the discourses of race, sex, gender, class, and so on. This is the case regardless of how absent or explicit these qualities may be in the discussion. Instead, these sensational crimes act as social telescopes, isolating and drawing nearer aspects of racism and sexism that are always present. Hence, they are ideal moments in which to observe the fabric of the distribution of social meanings, concerns, and powers.

4

"Tall, Dark, and Lethal": The Discourses of Sexual Transgression in the Preppy Murder

"Public opinion" about crime does not simply form up at random. It exhibits a shape and structure. It follows a sequence. It is a social process, not a mystery. Even at the lowest threshold of visibility—in talk, in rumour, in the exchange of quick views and common-sense judgements—crime talk is not socially innocent; already it is informed and penetrated by the lay opinions and ideologies about crime as a public topic.

—Stuart Hall et al., **Policing the Crisis**

A *Newsweek* article on the preppy murder introduced Jennifer Levin as follows: "On a late-summer morning in New York's Central Park, a bicyclist came upon the nearly nude body of a pretty 18-year-old girl" (Hackett 1988, 31). The rest of the article reinforced the titillation of sexual fantasy invited here. The description of the "nearly nude body" and reference to the "prettiness" of the murdered corpse seemed a rather obvious attempt to construct Levin as an object of desire. The narrative codes of romantic fiction ("on a late-summer morning") were employed to set up a situation in which a potentially erotic encounter could take place—be it

---

"Tall, dark, and lethal" is a description of Robert Chambers appropriated from the cover of Bryna Taubman's *The Preppy Murder Trial* (1988). A version of this chapter appeared in the *Journal of Communication Inquiry* 15.2 (Summer 1991):140–158.

between Levin and Chambers, the bicyclist and the "pretty" corpse, or the reader and a fantasized Levin, described later in the report as a "sexual tigress."

In contrast, the introduction to Robert Chambers described him as "a handsome prep-school graduate and former altar boy" (p. 31). While the article reduced Levin to a body without a history—a generic icon of sexual fantasy—it afforded Chambers a past as an altar boy and a future as a graduate. These were signifiers of his innocence and youth. His involvement was then a fall from grace, a story that could not be told of Levin given her narrative construction.

A fundamental aspect to the intelligibility of a crime is an understanding of the key actors. Who were they, and what were they like? In the narrative construction of these individuals, certain recognizable personalities emerged, as supported by what came to be understood as particularly salient demonstrations of these traits. This construction involved the identification of evidence deemed to be specifically indicative of their character. And these identities played a significant role in the legal proceeding where the discernment of a motive and its inextricable ties to the intentions of an individual were central.

Even immediately following the crime, a certain tacit agreement concerning the representation of Levin and Chambers was in place. The first *New York* feature article on the preppy murder was representative of this agreement. The article began with the stated intention of probing the question, "How, people asked, could an apparently innocent teenage tryst end in death?" (Stone 1986, 42). As captured here, an imagined group of inquiring people, assumed to be the magazine's readership, was the catalyst for the investigation. This naturalized the story as a response to a demand for information and simultaneously as a demand for the commodity of the magazine itself. The subtitle definitively stated that the preppy murder was "a death that shocked a city." But what elements made it shocking? And what role did the news media play in constructing its shocking nature? The representational consistencies of the preppy murder invite such an analysis.

Certain aspects of Jennifer Levin's and Robert Chambers's lives were given significant credence over others and were seen to be particularly consequential to the case. Without fail, there was an emphasis upon the physical attractiveness of Levin and Chambers. For example, "Chambers's tall good looks—he's six four and about 220 pounds—and secretive manner made him something of a legend among the younger private-school girls" (p. 47), and "another pretty student, Jennifer Levin ... was high-spirited and popular" (p. 42). Though they were from different social contexts, Chambers from an old Manhattan Irish-Catholic family and Levin from a Long Island suburban Jewish family, continuities were stressed. The similarities in their backgrounds rested largely on the social "scene" in which they both took part. The depiction of the scene was such that it included many young people, often with the intimation that these youths were also potential victims. As such, the fears of social permissiveness, particularly as it affected upper-class youth, was a recurring concern.

The world of Levin and Chambers had its shadows. Both came from broken homes, and both had embraced a troubling scene—a particular community of private-school students in which drug use, alcohol, casual sex, and chronic under-achievement sometimes start when the students are as young as thirteen.

Of course, not all young people are part of the scene, and not all want to be. But it draws from the city's best-known private schools, luring students with its aura of glitter and elitism. Both Levin and Chambers probably understood the shortcomings of their young social world—Chambers, in fact, had told friends he hated its superficiality. Other students no doubt feel the same way. But they also say the scene provides them with a sense of belonging that they don't get elsewhere. (p. 44)

The social environment, described as "the world of Levin and Chambers," is seen here as a living beast "luring students" from their "elite" positions and true vocations. Similarly, the lack of traditional familial relations is implicated, another similarity between Levin and Chambers that came to be understood as a determining feature in the crime. Absent parents (a term that easily slides to connote "working mothers") force youth to find a "sense of belonging that they don't get elsewhere."

Typically, Chambers's personal history received much attention. The representation was one of a clean-cut boy, a preppy, with significant potential. "He was an altar boy at his parish church, a member of the Children of the American Revolution, and an officer in the Knickerbocker Greys" (p. 42). Additionally, "Chambers graduated from York in June and was accepted by the College of Basic Studies at Boston University, in part ... because of his high test scores" (p. 48). And most tragically, "Chambers's admirers say he was turning his life around in the weeks before the killing" (p. 44). In contrast, the depiction of Levin's past consisted not so much of what she had done or accomplished, but how, "coming from a Long Island suburb, she adapted quickly to the hipper styles and sensibilities of her Baldwin classmates" (p. 48). Some effort was made to suggest that she was not terribly bright: "Friends say that Levin had a reading disability," and "Levin described herself as 'street-smart, not book-smart' and was proud of her ability to handle people" (p. 48).

But in reference to their relationships with members of the opposite sex, their differences were dramatically stated, constructing very distinct personalities and sexualities. Chambers becomes, "'always very gentle, very sensitive. He used to write me poetry.' Still Chambers's girlfriend broke up with him in the spring after hearing he had 'fooled around' with another girl" (p. 45). And "his on-again, off-again girlfriend of two years ... had broke up with him, and friends say he was crushed when she began seeing ... a veteran of the scene" (p. 49). Note how it was "Chambers's girlfriend who broke up with him" and that it was he who "was crushed" when an ex-girlfriend began dating someone else, despite the suggestion of his infidelity. Compare this with the following depictions of Jennifer Levin: "Despite her romance with Pernice, she had casual affairs with other boys" (p. 48), and [according to a friend, at a job interview,] "'she just grabbed him by the shoulders and told him that she was great with people and about all the jobs she'd had selling, and she made him fall in love with her'" (p. 49). Another "friend" is quoted as saying, "'She was very flirtatious, definitely outgoing. You could tell by the way she flashed her eyes. She kissed me when we were introduced, and she didn't even know me'" (p. 51). With reference to her "casual affairs," Levin's aggressivity and promiscuity were seen as a direct contrast to Chambers's sensitivity and passivity. She was exactly the type who posed a threat to Chambers's emotional well-being: "A friend recalls that girls from surrounding schools used to camp out on the steps of the brownstone where he lived. He hated to be pursued that way" (p. 47).

The article depicted Chambers as a victim hounded by some women and dumped by others. In fact, a calculating and seemingly predatory female sexuality was a recurring reference point in the biographies of Chambers, rendering him an emotional victim of the desires and actions of the women in his life. The depiction of Levin suggested that she was not one to shy away from something she wanted sexually; in fact, she was represented as being pushy and domineering. So when a close friend of Chambers's described him as "a 'wimp, not capable of violence,'" it seemed entirely plausible (p. 47). Similarly, when Levin was said to be "direct and feisty," someone who "would rarely back down," this, too, contributed to a wholly consistent profile (p. 48). Someone was quoted stating that "'two nights before she died, she nearly got in a fistfight in Danceteria ... with some guy she thought had pinched her'" (p. 48). And, of course, this view was not terribly far removed from the image of Jennifer Levin constructed by Robert Chambers in his videotape confession. According to Chambers, she "pursued" him for sex so forcefully that he had to resort to violence to protect himself. This report established a fit between Chambers's self-representations and these reconstructions offered in the popular press.

The similarities between Levin and Chambers—young, white, attractive, part of the same social circle, and with similar class backgrounds and aspirations— gave license to the presumption that the crime indicated something about the social context, specifically about youth and class. In other words, these similarities became evidence of certain cultural developments, certain trends, and general social anxieties about those trends. Furthermore, the distinct sexualities of Levin and Chambers signaled the qualities of masculinity and femininity, which, once transgressed, were a prime explanation for the crime and figured prominently in the assignment of legal responsibility. Briefly put, we are left with very distinct and stereotypical personalities: the pushy Jewish-American princess who cannot take "no" for an answer tormenting the poor Catholic altar boy. This was accentuated after the bail hearing when it became apparent that certain members of the Catholic clergy had written letters attesting to Chambers's good character.

This *New York* feature article was by no means an exception. In fact, immediately following the homicide, an informal consensus seemed to be established concerning their biographies and personality profiles. This should not be mistaken for accuracy. Given the evidence provided in the same reports, there is no reason the roles could not have been reversed. However, the roles were assigned in this way because of certain practices of representation that overdetermine the construction of the image. This means that the raw material of the narrative or discourse is structurally secure. The details need only be filled in to arrive at the composite image.

The later coverage demonstrated a shift, not in Levin's favor, but in the tendency to portray Chambers as a "pseudo-preppy" and, at times, as a sociopath. These later reports presented Chambers as upwardly mobile rather than a "true" member of the upper class, with his mother being depicted as a key figure who pushed him in this direction. As an example of this representational shift, *New York Times* reports originally described Chambers as "a 19-year-old graduate of an Eastside preparatory school" (Farber 1986, B10) and later began referring to him as a "college drop-out" (Johnson 1987, 33). This was equally true of Levin and the other members of the scene, who were represented as spoiled and unable to deal with their privileged position. In other words, throwing doubt upon their class standing meant that the case could less obviously be understood through a critique of class. Instead, issues of sexuality remained at the center.

The "Rough Sex" Explanation

As central to this crime as the murder itself was the ambiguous notion of Jennifer Levin's "kinky and aggressive sexual activity." No article failed to mention either the diary or Levin's sexual behavior, and yet the kinky and aggressive characterization was never defined with any more precision. It stood as a signifier for virtually all sexual practice. It collapsed any form of sexual variation into a single semantic location and evaluated it as deviant or at least as not quite in the realm of the normal. Gayle Rubin (1984, 279) observes that "modern Western societies appraise sex acts according to a hierarchical system of sexual value." She points to the "need to draw and maintain an imaginary line between good and bad sex," making sex "a vector of oppression" (pp. 282, 293). A good example of how these boundaries operate is demonstrated by the easy slippage between descriptions of Levin as "sexually active" and "sexually aggressive." This slippage finds its source in general assumptions about female sexuality where there appears to be no distinction between the two descriptions. In this way, the condemning connotations of the less acceptable aggressive sexuality transfer to the more innocent label.

One of the reasons for the popular currency and circulation of the preppy murder was that "normal" gender identities were breached. As Chris Weedon (1987, 118) asserts, "Sexuality is seen as a primary locus of power in contemporary society, constituting subjects and governing them by exercising control through their bodies." Part of the consequence of the popular scrutiny was to police and restore the temporarily transgressed boundaries. As Foucault (1978, 103) writes, "Sexuality is not the most intractable element in power relations, but rather one of those endowed with the greatest instrumentality: useful for the greatest number of maneuvers and capable of serving as a point of support, as a linchpin, for the most varied strategies." Sexuality, and its links to gendered behavior, is a site at which the technologies of the social are enacted, forming what Teresa de Lauretis (1987) calls "the sex/gender system." In brief, the reference to sexuality in the preppy murder was never just reported; it was evaluated, made sense of, moralized. Consequently, this case exemplifies the ongoing process of arresting the shifts of boundaries between acceptable and unacceptable sexual practice.

Though the value-laden description of aggressive sexuality was often brought into doubt by the various reports, it was also the case that "rough sex" or some similar phrase usually appeared prominently as either a title or a caption to a photo of Levin. This validated, if not the claim's accuracy, at least its currency and weight as the summation of the entire event of her death. Rough sex was thus an imprecise signifier for the murder that effectively told a variety of stories. First, there was the suggestion of Jennifer Levin's complicity in that evening's sexual activity. Though the charge of attempted rape would have been equally supported given the evidence, it would have contradicted Levin's agency, which the majority of the narrative explanations evoked. Defense attorney Litman was quoted as saying that Chambers "didn't go to the park to rape her. She had sex with him before" (Raab 1986, 29). This strange comment assumes that it is not possible for a woman to be raped by someone with whom she has previously had sex. Though the legality of the statement varies (some states, surprisingly, still agree with this argument), it maintains the status of a "commonsense" reasoning, echoed by Chambers's attorney.

Second, the taboo nature of the entire situation further implicated Levin. As one report put it, "Chambers's supporters insist he didn't lure her there for sex. After all, his mother was working that night, so they could have made love at his home, a short distance away" (Stone 1986, 51). The possibility that either of them *wanted* to have sex in the park was ruled out, forcing the acceptance of other explanations (e.g., Levin was a crazed nymphomaniac, raping boys). In terms of the conventions of sexual behavior, a number of "crimes" were committed: sex in a public place, sex with an acquaintance, sex without love or commitment, bondage, and rough sex. This list is only to suggest that, the law notwithstanding, a number of *cultural crimes* were also committed. In the popular press and the legal system, these deviancies were weighed against one another, the effect of which was to accuse Levin just as her killer has been accused. The crime of murder was shared, and thus seen to be a less severe criminal act, with an ambiguously defined set of sexual crimes. Interestingly, since the trial of the preppy murder, the rough sex defense has become an increasingly popular way in which husbands and boyfriends explain the death of their lovers (Lacayo 1988).

The more striking examples of the centrality of sexuality in this case were those articles that openly capitalized on the image of Jennifer Levin raping Robert

Chambers. *Mademoiselle* opened its report with, "They were pretty kids, rich—and reckless. There was something spoiled about Robert. Something wild about Jennifer. Something very, very sad about the way they lived and the way she died" (Heller 1987, 145). Here both were victims, but the potential for being out of control was once again associated with Levin. The reference to the then-popular film *Something Wild* (Jonathon Demme, 1987) was a metaphoric descriptive device that was not infrequently employed to describe the preppy murder. This was presumably an allusion to the "wild" female lead in the film (and, more distantly, to the bondage game she initiates with the male lead).

The *Mademoiselle* article described Chambers as "exceptionally handsome: six foot three with wide blue eyes, a chiseled jawline and a discus thrower's beautifully proportioned body" (p. 145). It argued that "the boy Levin pursued so persistently—the boy now accused of murdering her—seemed, ironically, neither particularly bold nor particularly bad. Childhood friends and teachers describe Robert Chambers as helpful, docile, not too bright—a somewhat passive kid whom no one ever saw angry, let alone violent" (p. 146). As referenced in the preceding quotation, Levin was endowed with a near monomaniacal potential for violence, having "pursued so persistently" that "passive kid." This was further evidenced in the following passage: "Jennifer Levin, for one, seems to have had a wilder side. At Baldwin, the $8000-a-year West Side prep school she attended for four years, she was known as entirely 'outgoing,' 'bubbly,' 'popular with everyone.' ... But in other places, including Dorrian's, where even friends say she got 'falling-down drunk,' she was viewed as troubled and more than usually aggressive" (p. 175). In fact, her seductive intentions to "conquer" Chambers the evening of her murder were made completely unambiguous; for "on August 25, Levin, dressed casually and provocatively in a pink miniskirt and blue-jean jacket, went looking for Chambers" (p. 175). Dressed to kill or dressed to be killed—either way, the author described Levin's "provocative" attire, if not as a causal agent, at least as an indicator of intention.

The article developed the image of Jennifer Levin the rapist fully, an image suggested explicitly in the tabloids and more implicitly in "respectable" sources:

> Jennifer Levin was a girl of her time and place. She pursued men, and she pursued them assertively—even, in the case of Chambers, aggressively. Some of the things she said and did in Dorrian's are almost a caricature of what bold, bad boys traditionally do. But bold, bad boys don't get blamed for asserting themselves sexually—and they don't get killed. For Jennifer Levin, the gender difference could have made the difference between life and death. (p. 146)

"Normal" sexual practice and gender behavior had been transgressed by Levin, and not only on the evening of her murder. As "a girl of her time and place," Levin is understood to have embodied many of the attributes of other contemporary women—aggressive, demanding, and desirous. The subtle suggestion was that the modern woman, the product of years of feminism, presented a danger to herself and others. Her death became a punishment of sorts, one that demonstrated the importance of the maintenance of the "natural" order of gendered sexual behavior. The article in *Mademoiselle* concluded by moralizing about the dangers of playing with traditional gender roles.

> Whether or not Levin and Chambers were playing sadomasochistic games with each other, they were acting out roles. The remarkable thing is that each was playing a part we would expect the other one to play.
>   Levin seems to have been impersonating a guy who knows who and what he wants—and can be aggressive about getting it. Chambers seems to have been in the same position as many good-looking, "not too bright," insecure girls 15 years ago: sought after for his sex appeal but never acknowledged as a person. It wouldn't be surprising if he felt that he was being "used." (p. 176)

Another May 1987 *Mademoiselle* article provides a good example of how the seemingly consensual kinky sex understanding of the murder was indexed as evidence to support a moral position. At that point in time, the "correctness" of that interpretation of the preppy murder was presumed; rough sex was the taken-for-granted explanation of Levin's death. And the assured reference to that version further stabilized it as the "true" one. "Rough Sex Gets Real" opened with an antipornography crusader's worst fears: "She first got turned on to the idea by something she saw" (Coburn 1987, 238). The article, in typical form, described three fictionalized "confessions" of two women and a man's individual experiences with rough sex. The author continued by suggesting that "something wild is going on—something wild and potentially perilous. Increasingly, what was once forbidden, even considered a sickness, appears to be moving into the mainstream" (p. 239). As evidence, the author alluded to films (*9 1/2 Weeks* [Adrian Lyne, 1986], *Blue Velvet* [David Lynch, 1986], *After Hours* [Martin Scorsese, 1985], and four references to *Something Wild*), "pop culture and commercials" in general, and the preppy murder specifically.

While acknowledging the potential for "an arousing excursion" (p. 239), the article took a quick turn to construct, in a highly nonspecific manner, the boundaries of acceptable sexual practice. The subtitle explicitly referenced this, reading, "When erotic fantasies cross the line, anything can happen." In and of itself, the subtitle seems appealing enough, but given the obvious agenda of the author, it was not far removed from the tabloid headlines concerning the preppy murder. An array of experts, M.D.s and Ph.D.s, responded to questions about what rough sex is, whether it is healthy, and at what point it can be said to be dangerous. The ubiquitous feminist Barbara Ehrenreich was quoted as pointing out that "one possible redeeming factor" (Coburn's comment) was an inversion of the traditional male-dominant/female-submissive roles, citing *Something Wild* as one positive piece of evidence (p. 266). But this was contradicted by the overall tenor of the article, which warned of the dangers involved in such sexual practices as exemplified by the "out-of-control sex" of Jennifer Levin and Robert Chambers (p. 266).

Thus, a number of points become clear concerning the discourses of sexuality that circulated in the representations of the preppy murder. Levin's sexual behavior was seen to be deviant, and her assumed sexual taste (sadomasochism, aggressivity, promiscuity) acted to validate her fate. In this light, the frequent reminders of Chambers's problems, his domineering mother, and his betrayal by other women were significant. In short, *he was depicted as a victim of a new social environment as embodied in one of the most powerful indices of contemporary social change, the "modern woman."* Moreover, their age was seen to be particularly telling. Their youth was often employed as a site at which all of these other concerns and transgressions got condensed. In many respects, even though youth is a time in which the bounds of the acceptable can be experimented with, the preppy murder was taken to demonstrate the dangers of *playing* with sexuality, with gender roles, with being an adult. The youth of the murdered and the murderer made this tragedy that much more significant and was thus taken to say something about contemporary youth in general.

The Influence of the Social

"'This scene is very sick. It all came together and it's all f—d up. I can't get it out of my mind. You're going back to school. You're so lucky you're getting out of here'—one girl to another in the ladies' room at Dorrian's Red Hand, New York City" (Van Biema 1986, 56). Acquired by an eavesdropping reporter in a public washroom (and, if the quote is authentic, by a man in a women's restroom), this passage provides proof of the reporter's infiltration into the "scene"; it says that the gap between writing and actuality has been closed, implying that here the real, the environment, speaks. Accordingly, the location of the truth of the crime, the truth spoken, is "out there."

The shift from the initial coverage of an event to editorials and features is an important ideological move. As well as being an indication of the significance of a story, editorials tend to allow the authors to take a specific position, which is forbidden to "good, objective reporting." Features provide more extensive coverage of various explanations or histories (of people involved, similar events, etc.). As the authors of *Policing the Crisis* (Hall et al. 1978, 88) note, "If primary-news stories are presented in 'the form of a question,' editorials and features provide two, different kinds of 'answers.'" We must therefore ask, Where editorials can, given the codes of news production, openly advocate a position, what positions do they adopt? Similarly, Hall et al. write that features "are *inherently* ideological, for what they seek to do is to 'contextualize' the event, place it in the social world" (p. 96).

The restroom conversation could have been pulled from any of the contemporary novels or films about sex, drugs, and kids with too much money, such as Jay McInerney's *Bright Lights, Big City* (1985) and Ellis's *Less Than Zero*. It is the romantic urban myth of the evils and thrills of big city living and life on the edge. Levin's murder was framed to fit this narrative; the "scene" was full of "children of privilege" for whom "'the circuit' provided an underage singles' scene that often led to casual sex in nearby Central Park" (Van Biema 1986, 56). One patron was quoted as saying that Dorrian's was "the meat market ... and the park [was] the grill" (p. 56).

This featured article in *People Weekly*, typical of the many editorials, constructed the Levin murder as an awakening for the scene as a whole: "youngsters getting their first taste of the harshest of realities" (p. 57). Since the crime, sexual activity was being curbed; for "leather jackets have replaced polo shirts here tonight, cunning long sweaters supplanting last week's tank tops. The 'grill' will be closed tonight" (p. 58). The suggestion is that perhaps Levin's death was an inevitable consequence of the scene and that it provided a shock to the young patrons, who now realized the dangers with which they were playing.

This was one of the central narratives employed to frame the crime: The murder was the result of transgressions in the social environment, such as peer pressure, negligent parents, underage drinking, and social permissiveness in general. One result was to alleviate some of the direct implications of Chambers's guilt. He was only a member of the scene, a victim of his cold environment. And, not surprisingly, Levin became increasingly more central as the agent of her own death, for she willingly participated in the scene. The only photo of her that accompanied the article, aside from the long shot of her sheet-covered corpse in Central Park, was a photo of her "at a party." The *People Weekly* article described the impact of the crime as one of increased awareness about the problems of contemporary youth and the obligations of "good parenting": "For days career-obsessed parents looked up from their work and feared for their own children" (p. 57).

The initial local coverage of the murder was quick to associate the crime with that of underage drinking, largely based on the evidence of two pieces of fake identification found on Levin's body. The *New York Times* framed this with the headline "Underage Drinking Sparks a Tragedy and Debates" (Freedman 1986c), to be followed the next day with a story that a local group had previously reported minors drinking at Dorrian's Red Hand (Freedman 1986d). On September 3, 1986, the *New York Times* reported a "citywide crackdown to begin against under-age drinking" (Lambert 1986, 1). On September 11, police charged three individuals with forging identification to be sold to underage college students ("Three Store Employees" 1986); four employees of Dorrian's Red Hand were charged with serving liquor to minors on November 16, 1986 ("Four at Dorrian's" 1986); and a year later, the New York State Liquor Authority suspended Dorrian's license to sell alcohol for the same offense ("License Is Suspended" 1987).

What is significant is that the reports tied each of these events directly to the preppy murder. For instance, on the first anniversary of the murder, the *New York Times* ran a feature editorial that discussed the failure of the crackdown on underage drinking ("Crackdown" 1987). Simply put, the murder in some way indicated the necessity for increased state surveillance of minors or at least provided the alibi for that particular activity. The fact that only marginal traces of alcohol and no drugs were found in either Chambers and Levin (in other words, both were legally sober at the time of the crime) did little to hamper this association. These reports and city policy drew a trajectory between the murder and alcohol abuse by minors. The murder became enveloped in a larger current debate that served to explain the crime and to empower an agenda of increased surveillance of minors.

A typical instance of the linkages between discourse and the diverse aspects of the crime was the *New York Times* front-page editorial "Death in Park: Difficult Questions for Parents:" "Is it harder to rear children amid the glitter and vice of the big city? Is it inevitable to lose control of a 19-year-old? Or have some parents in demanding, high-paying professions substituted money for affection and freedom for supervision? Have they abdicated their role as parents to surrogates?" (Freedman 1986b, B1). The rhetorical tactic of asking these questions as though they are common sense obscures the process of framing and narrativization. And as promised, the article suggests an adequate resolution: "The young people most likely to fall into the aimless nocturnal life, educators and psychologists say, are those without strong ties to their parents. The increasing divorce rate, the entry of many women into the full-time work force, and the declining importance of socializing forces such as religion, ethnicity, and extended family all contribute to the atrophy of authority, specialists say" (p. B10).

Here a number of popular discourses come into play: the changing configuration of the family unit, the waning of respect for authority, and the severing of ties with tradition. These are popular indices of contemporary social change. And equally they are understood as products of feminists, social progressives, liberals, anarchists, and atheists. The tenor of the editorial—and let me stress that it is by no means anomalous—situates the Levin murder in the context of a social upheaval in which, it argues, young people are understandably confused about their place in the world and are easily led astray. This is a popular rendition of Durkheim's ([1897] 1951) anomie theory, nicely revealing its conservative heart. In this instance, it works to magically lift the blame from Chambers and at least partially transfer it to those perpetrators of social change. This is one definition of "backlash."

Discourses of Transgression

Levin's murder is made to be meaningful as it is organized in the context of other cultural developments. And, of course, the legal system is involved here as well. Before the proceedings of a trial can begin, the legal system engages in the process of determining what evidence is to be admitted in court and what is not. The result is a restriction on disparate elements that could have an influence on the direction of the trial; some are given a central position, while others are ruled out of the realm of judicial consideration. The consequence is that a closure is set such that only some stories are possible. This process designates other stories as immaterial, even oppositional, to the workings of justice.

In the case of the preppy murder, three of Chambers's versions of the events of August 26, 1986, were initially admitted in court: that Chambers and Levin parted company at Dorrian's, that they had left Dorrian's together but had quarreled and then parted, and that Chambers had acted in self-defense, which was the story captured in the videotape confession. The contradicting stories could have been used as evidence of guilt but not of murder, which requires proof of intent to kill. The trial thus revolved around an attempt by prosecuting attorney Linda Fairstein to assign intentionality to Chambers's killing of Levin given the manner in which she was killed. Fairstein's argument was that if Levin was strangled for roughly fifteen seconds before she died, Chambers must have realized what he was doing and therefore was guilty of murder. If, however, the strangulation was shorter than that, then the incident would have been an accident, with manslaughter being the maximum charge. Defense attorney Jack Litman only had to present conflicting medical testimonies concerning the length of time Chambers strangled Levin to cast sufficient doubt on Chambers's motives.

In turn, the defense was permitted to introduce testimony concerning Levin's sexual and personal history. This was to give credence to Chambers's argument that Levin "pursued" and molested him. Conversely, the court decided that much of Chambers's own past was immaterial. Fairstein could not mention Chambers's drug history, his cocaine addiction—which was amply documented—or his involvement in burglaries and check forging. Consequently, in what seemed a surprising decision, the fact the Levin had been robbed that evening could not be introduced as evidence. Approximately $70 in cash, her fake diamond earrings, and her jeans jacket, all of which she had had when she left Dorrian's with Chambers, were missing from her body the next morning. And though this fact would appear to have been a central consideration in the events surrounding Levin's murder, the court suppressed it, declaring it inadmissible as evidence. So a photograph of Levin at Dorrian's on the evening of her murder presented to the jury had a piece of white tape covering Levin's ear so that the earring and its absence from other photos would not enter the legal debate or prejudice the jury.

In the end, with the threat of a hung jury, a plea bargain was struck. Chambers agreed to admit guilt, and to read a public statement to that effect, in return for a reduced sentence of voluntary manslaughter and three counts of second-degree burglary and the guarantee that he could not be tried for other crimes should additional evidence turn up. The actual sentence was relatively short; Chambers was given five to fifteen years, which was more in line with a second-degree manslaughter charge.[1] As a point of comparision, David Fillyaw, an African-American, pleaded guilty to burglaries he had committed with Chambers as well as to attempted murder of a Columbia University student and attempted assault. He received ten to twenty years for the attempted murder, five to ten for the burglaries, and two to four for the attempted assault.

In many respects, the plea bargain was a conclusion without a resolution. The jury could not decide; the parties reached an agreement acting outside the public arm of the judicial system. This is the not-uncommon spectacle of the justice system stalled. While giving credence to the defense, it announces the supposedly ad hoc nature of the legal system; each crime is taken on its own. The possibility that the judicial system will not come to a resolution defines an internalized limit to its powers; in effect, its fallibility implies that it is working, that it is just. This is central to its brilliant invisibility, where the process of the definition and evaluation of "the criminal" is made to appear natural. The machinations of how certain elements are constructed as salient evidence of particular actions, while others are not, are supplanted by a system that appears to be reconstituted in each new instance it must consider.

Certain popular discourses ground what we know of the preppy murder—discourses about trials, murders, lawyers, sexuality, youth, affluence, and so on. Who the individuals involved become is who and what we recognize in them—the flirtatious young woman, the sullen young man, the "darkly handsome" hunk (Glynn 1988, 46), the sexually adventurous, the sexually dangerous, the victim of male aggression, the victims of inadequate parenting, schooling, state control, or the "live fast, die young" social scene of the young, white, and rich.

Through a series of spurious connections, the Levin murder was explained with respect to class (the abuse of their affluence), age (youths trying to grow up too fast), sexuality (bondage and rough sex), and gender behavior (the sexually aggressive Jennifer Levin versus the sexually passive Robert Chambers). This last point facilitated the popular and legal interpretation of the murder in which Levin was playing the more "appropriately" male role of rapist, while Chambers played the transgressive role of "not-too-bright bimbo."

The event becomes enveloped in numerous discourses, all of which attempt to make sense of it. As metaphors, labels, and descriptions become attached to the event—"rough sex," "preppy murder," "underage drinking," "negligent parents"—a site of concern is constituted around which energies can be mobilized. Though this does not indicate a seamless consensus, these discourses mark the sites at which the qualities of the social are discerned. There is a circulation of social power in this process; the realms of deviance and normalcy, their inhabitants and their qualities, assure the visibility of their boundaries. The frontiers of normalcy, then, involve the discursive link between the expressive and the disciplined. In other words, the way the evidence of crime is made meaningful, this being largely a process of description and narrative, is bound up in a question of judgment, evaluation, and moralization. Our understandings of sexuality, gender specificity, affluence, race, and age are never value free. Our "common sense" frames the significance of things. As such, the ideologies of common sense inhabit the assumptions attributed to social consensus.

Murder is always "precipitated by," "having repercussions on," "causing," or "motivated following"; and the way that each of the fill-in-the-blanks is completed frame the act, making it meaningful in a particular context. The discursive solutions to the crime are articulated within certain institutions with demonstrable, if localized, effects: the attack on negligent parents, feminists, and underage drinking; the renewed concern about increasing social permissiveness; Levin as a victim of her own actions; and, not to be left out, the sparking of an ad hoc victim's rights group. What occurred is not only obscured but rewritten. The accuracy of Chambers's confession does not enter the question. As soon as Levin's sexual aggressivity, for instance, is referenced, other elements, discourses, and images enter, in effect, to construct the story. In a sense, after the crime Jennifer Dawn Levin's fate was written for her.

5

The Subject in Crime: Confessions as a Site of "Self-Evidence"

Let everything be produced, be read, become real, visible, and marked with the sign of effectiveness; let everything be transcribed into force relations, into conceptual systems or into calculable energy; let everything be said, gathered, indexed and registered. ... Ours is a culture of "monstration" and demonstration, of "productive" monstruosity (the "confession" so well analyzed by Foucault is one of its forms).

—Jean Baudrillard, *Forget Foucault*

A report in the *New York Times* on August 9, 1989, almost three years after Jennifer Levin's murder, begins: "There was a body sprawled beneath a tree. There were clusters of detectives and an ambulance parked behind the Metropolitan Museum of Art. And there was the suspect, graciously giving interviews. Beneath a bright blue sky yesterday, Central Park again became the scene of an ugly crime" (Hays 1989, B4). The article, "A Film on the Levin Case Is 'Really Creepy,'" concerns the filming of the television movie *The Preppy Murder* (John Herzfeld, 1989). Written to elicit a sense of déjà vu, with an accompanying photo of the crime scene that only on closer examination proves to be a film set, the report questions the desirability of this additional exploitation of the case. Although the New Yorkers quoted seem to think "it's pretty disgusting," the article assures the reader that this is to be a "docudrama," with particular sensitivity paid to detail, realism, and tasteful presentation. The week of its broadcast, *TV Guide* printed a similar article (Brown 1989). "Accuracy" and "sensitivity" are again the two central justifications given for why this particular rendering of the Levin murder is credible and, importantly, not like all those other sensational versions.

Common sense dictates that a sensational crime is one that exhibits an increasing distance between the representation and the actual event, usually through the registers of "entertainment" value. The more sensational the representation is, the less it has to do with the materiality of the crime, instead relying upon the codes and conventions of various genres for its reconstruction. In this respect, the event becomes increasingly wrapped up in popular forms that translate and interpret the significance of the crime. Importantly, this process also designates the associated emotionality, portraying the tragic or retributive reactions of participants and the broader public outrage or abhorrence. The differences between the "meaning" of the crime and the (presumed or supposed) public reaction are blurred and rendered indistinguishable. The sensational has to do primarily with emotion and only secondarily with information.

There are twists in this definition, however. What counts as the original event, the identification of the salient elements, is not straightforward and unambiguous. There is a materiality to crime; violent acts occur, there are victims, and there are perpetrators. And yet the meaning of criminal activity, the sense it makes, is not so simply determined; it is bound up in the representation of the "appropriate" public response. There is a certain discursive reach that stretches into all aspects of the knowable. Even the most material of moments, such as murder, are not immune. There are a number of different categories of "killing," each with a specific referential order and associated moral and legal connotations. For instance, the distinction among first-degree murder, second-degree murder, manslaughter, and criminal negligence, not to mention executions and killings that occur during times of martial conflict, differ in terms of their *culturally defined and sanctioned significance,* not in terms of the loss of life involved.

Therefore, what comes to be the "obvious" materiality of a crime, the "ground zero" measure of the sensational, has as much to do with the context in which it takes place, and in which it comes to be situated, as it does with the act itself. In short, even though a greater frequency and variety of representation can be indicated, a representation's *distance* from the originary moment is not always conspicuously manifested. The operations of popular and legal explanation work equally on the appearance of and agreement upon the initial event of the crime as on its subsequent formulations and connotative weight. The movement from crime to sensational crime is not direct and without intricate senses of materiality. In the end, discerning the less "mediated," or the more "authentic," rendering of the event is an untenable task. To refer to the increasing distance from the actual event as a way to talk about a sensational response makes intuitive sense, though in actuality it is next to impossible to measure with any degree of accuracy or predictability. Instead, access to the event of the crime is always gained through an entangled set of representational practices—images, narratives, and language. The actuality of the crime is left obscured and in the dark.

A striking example of this problematic is evidenced in the ABC made-for-TV movie *The Preppy Murder.* Detective Mike Sheehan, the NYPD officer in charge of the investigation into the death of Jennifer Levin, sold the movie rights to his version of the story to ABC. The film tells the story primarily from the detective's point of view. *The Preppy Murder* makes a concerted effort to be a docudrama; the first half, in particular, has a gritty, pseudodocumentary feel. Low-key naturalistic lighting replaces the typical television "cafeteria" lighting; there is ample hand-held camera work and a significant amount of attention to diegetic background noise. Many of the actors are not professionals. For instance, the squad room scenes are shot on location with actual police officers as extras. And perhaps the most interesting move is the casting of Mike Sheehan himself as his own superior, Lieutenant Doyle.[1]

The narrative turning point in the film is Chambers's (William Baldwin) first admission of guilt. A lengthy interrogation scene, in which Detective Sheehan (Danny Aiello) and Assistant District Attorney Steve Saracco repeatedly question their suspect about his activities on the night of the murder, precedes the confession scene. Chambers begins to contradict himself but still does not confess. The two detectives take a break, leaving the room to get some food, and Doyle tries the "good cop" routine. In an intimate two-shot close-up, Doyle, almost whispering, tells Chambers that he likes him and sympathizes with his position. Chambers begins to open up and nod to Doyle's questions concerning his involvement. The scene ends with Doyle ordering his detectives to get the statement in writing and to get Chambers's confession on videotape.

Although the movie rewrites the sequence of events (the confession was not elicited in precisely this manner, and at least one other detective, Mike Sheehan himself, was present when Chambers first broke), it still pays attention to the minutest of details (when Doyle asks Chambers how he strangled Levin, Chambers responds silently and cryptically by raising his left arm, indicating his watch). The scene is partly a reenactment with one of the original participants and partly a fictional dramatic interpretation. In the sensational form of the made-for-TV movie, we find moments that retrieve the incident as a tangible source of facts. The confession scene fixes the "actuality" of the crime; at least for the moment, the possible shifting interpretations and representations have been arrested. And, paradoxically, this certainty is engendered in the context of a "fictionalized" narrative.

Even though sensational crimes are particularly interesting for their conspicuous representation of the complicated relations between the real and its depiction, they are by no means unique in this respect. The obfuscated distinctions among materiality, reenactment, and fictionalization are precisely the problematic of all representational forms. The question of "accuracy" is consigned to conjecture. Rather, the movement of selection, organization, and interpretation of texts and facts is the focus. This allows a tracing of the logic of conventions of representation in popular forms. How is the highly codified nature of popular representational forms to be read? And with respect to the present concerns, what are the links among the realms of the material event of the crime, its retelling and re-

presentation, and its fictionalization? One site where this discursive effectivity in-
tersects is the confession.

The confession scene in *The Preppy Murder* shifts the direction of the narrative
from the crime and the investigation to the trial. Similarly, the tone and intensity
of the response to the crime were in many ways a consequence of the bizarre and
fantastic nature of the events as narrated by Chambers himself. His videotape
confession and the later party video were central to his rise to infamy and media
"stardom." The preppy murder was sensational not solely because the public was
intrigued by the strange events, but also because it kept being replayed and performed in so many different forms. The implausible and elaborate testimony of
Chambers, who seemed so willing to perform the incident in such a blasé manner,
provided a text that governed the legal and popular response.

Directly across the street from the scene of the murder stands the Metropolitan
Museum of Art. There a surveillance video camera mounted on a wall would have
captured the crime as it was taking place had the camera not been out of service
that night. Thus, Chambers missed his first chance to perform in a "snuff" video,
something he would not hesitate to approximate later. On so many different occasions, there have been additional reworkings and re-presentations of Levin's murder; her death is enacted over and over again.

Stories of Murder

After being apprehended by the police, Chambers began telling stories about the
night before: stories about being attacked by his cat to explain the scratches on his
face and chest, about Jennifer bumming a cigarette from him as she left Dorrian's
alone for a Korean deli, about heading home alone to watch a movie and stopping
at a donut shop on the way, about quarreling with Jennifer on Lexington Avenue
and getting scratched by her as a result, about quarreling with Jennifer on Park
Avenue and being introduced to a friend of hers there. The events of the evening
were reworked repeatedly during the police interrogation until a satisfactory version, a conventional and coherent narrative, was agreed upon, one that was not
wholly plausible but that chronicled Chambers's involvement in Levin's death.
Chambers's statement of confession, written and signed on the same day of the
murder, August 26, 1986, reads as follows:

> I, Robert Chambers was present at Dorrian's Restaurant on 84th and Second Avenue.
> I met Jennifer Levin there about twelve midnight. I had known her about two
> months. During that time, I had sex with Jennifer three times, twice at a friend's
> house and once on the roof on the West Side.
> I didn't plan to meet her that night. We just ran into each other. A girl I didn't
> know but recognized was a friend of Jennifer's said she said I was better in bed than
> her boyfriend Brock.

Alex Kapp was angry at me, and Jennifer laughed as I was being yelled at. I was pissed off. Jennifer stated that she wanted to speak to me in the vestibule while I finished a shot of tequila.

We walked down 86th Street. Jennifer suggested Central Park where we could talk. At Fifth Avenue, Jennifer suggested a particular path, and inside Jennifer suggested we go behind the museum, so we crossed the road and went under a tree. It was darker than near the museum, and no one could see us.

We started talking about why I wasn't interested in her. She freaked out and began screeching and scratched my face with her hands. I stood up and started to leave. She apologized and still wanted to talk. I agreed if she didn't sit next to me. I was sitting on the ground, facing the museum.

Jennifer excused herself and then came up behind me. She massaged my shoulder and said I looked cute, but I would look cuter tied up. Jennifer began cackling and tied me with her panties.

She pushed me down and took off my pants. She grabbed my dick and jerked me off. I said it hurt. She picked up a stick and hit my dick with it. I yelled out, and a jogger passed and asked if everything was alright. She sat on my face and dug her nails into my chest. I screamed, and she squeezed my balls.

I couldn't take any more. I got a hand free and around her neck. She flipped over and landed on her side, twisted next to a tree. I stood up, pulled on my pants, and said, "Let's go."

I shook the body, but it didn't move. I knew then something was wrong. I walked to the museum and sat on the wall. I saw the woman with a bike, saw a police car come and an ambulance. I went home and went to sleep.

All this time, all this jerking off, and I didn't come.

P.S. I told Jennifer after she scratched my face I would talk to her, and she began kissing my hands. I tried to pull away, and then she bit my hands. It didn't hurt then, but it does now. I also hurt my right pinky knuckle when I leaned on it as she flipped over.

The bare minimum of a narrative is captured here, but it certainly portrays a horrific sequence of events, which the coldness of the tone only amplifies. Embedded in this initial statement are the grains of the subsequent direction of the investigation and the case's popular engagement. Most notably, though this is Chambers's version, Levin is the central agent. She is the one who acts; Chambers is acted upon. She laughed at Chambers, she suggested what they were to do, she scratched him, she tied him up, she "cackled" at his pain, and so on. Even in her own death, Levin is the principal actor: "She flipped over," as though of her own volition. The connotative weight of this image of a cackling, emotionally unpredictable woman significantly tainted the accepted versions of the crime. And importantly, this initial statement makes the tie between Levin's sexuality and her own death. Conversely, we learn almost nothing about Chambers's sexuality directly—"better in bed than her boyfriend"—except that it is hard to imagine a six foot four inch, 220-pound man being subdued, bound, and molested for an extended period of time by a five foot eight inch, 120-pound woman without a degree of complicity on his part.[2]

Supposedly, confessions are spontaneously suggested, without undue pressure from the interrogators. But, of course, though they may appear to be an unmediated rendering of the sequence of events from the point of view of one of the participants, confessions take place in structured settings, with particular practices of extracting and making sense of such statements. The process is one of constructing a coherent story from the suspect's perspective. This activity involves sifting through a variety of information, in effect coding statements and suggestions as either pertinent or irrelevant. Simply put, what may be important to the suspect may not be of any interest to the procedures of legal investigation and prosecution. For instance, the postscript of the Chambers confession was added upon the insistence of Chambers, who felt the point was a significant omission from the statement. And yet it played virtually no role in the subsequent proceedings.

Confessions belie the problematizing of the original moment of the event; under the guise of an autobiographical discourse, they operate to mask the complicated relationship between the "author" of the confession and the institutional obligation to "speak." The preceding statement, endorsed by Chambers as *his* own version, was not written by him. First, it was the product of a highly codified process of sense-making, the police interrogation, whose objective was to elicit legally comprehensible evidence. This institutional "will to knowledge" provided the structured and regulated space in which the suspect was to speak as well as a certain imperative to do so. Second, the statement was actually written by Detective Mike Sheehan, as is quite routine in the process of police investigation. He constructed the narrative from notes taken during the interrogation, then handed it back to Chambers for editing and endorsement. Verbal prompting and the efforts of the police officers to make his story make sense could not be revealed. And when they were, they played a significant role in the trial. For instance, it was disclosed that the final line, "All this time, all this jerking off, and I didn't come," had not been volunteered by Chambers, but rather had been a response to a question. This led to some questioning concerning the validity of the Chambers confession. Nonetheless, the ideological necessity of the "spontaneous" confession was not contradicted in this instance; for the force of "individual" speech, of the autobiographical and its discursive import as unmediated and "true," pushes aside the visible interventions of police and legal proceedings. The enunciative voice of the self obscures even the most conspicuous manifestations of power.

Immediately following the signing of the written statement, Chambers's version was recorded on videotape. The sixty-five-minute video consists of Chambers responding to questions from Saracco and Sheehan. The questions were sometimes clearly leading the suspect to answer in particular ways, which again raised problems during the trial about the nature of Chambers's treatment by the arresting officers. Some of the more sarcastic comments by Saracco had to be deleted when the tape was played for the jury. Chambers did not testify at his own trial; the videotape statement was Chambers's proxy for the jury.

Certainly, the video of Chambers's statement is one of the main reasons for the notoriety and public fascination with the case. It records a handsome, clean-cut young man elaborately recounting and reenacting the events leading to and including Levin's death. He acts out his own "molestation": Levin "jerking him off," freeing his hands, and "flipping" Levin over. And all of this is done with a certain clinical distance and stone-faced indifference. The only instance in which Chambers reacts, becoming momentarily flustered, is when he is shown pictures of Levin's body. The transcript of the videotape statement is much too lengthy to reproduce here in its entirety. The following are some of the more frequently quoted excerpts.

Saracco: She had laughed at you in the bar that night?

Chambers: Yeah. And—she'd also spit on me—after scratching me. Didn't really say anything. Didn't call me any names. She just had this look on her that she—I don't know. She was insane. I don't know what was wrong with her. ... And she seemed calmed down and she came over and she seemed really nice, giving me the massage. ... She said I looked really cute and that I'd look cuter tied up. And I thought, you know, that she was just horsing around. ... I started to say that this is crazy, whatever. I mean, she scooped my hands with both her arms and like held them together. ... And she wrapped her underwear around my wrists so they were locked and they were behind my back ... because I was leaning on my hands. And she just pushed me back. Like this. And then got on top of my chest and she was facing my feet. ... And, she started to take off my pants, and she started to play with me. She started jerking me off. ... And she was doing it really hard ... and it really hurt me and I, you know, I started to say, "Stop it. Stop it. It hurts." And she kind of laughed in a weird way—like more like a cackle or something. ... And she then sat up ... and she like sat on my face and then she dug her nails into my chest. ... And then she squeezed my—she squeezed my balls. And this really hurt. And I just—I couldn't take it anymore and I was screaming in pain. ... And I managed to get my left hand free. So I sat up a little and just grabbed her. ...

Chambers: She ... she molested me in the park. She hit me with ...

Saracco: How did she molest you? You're—we're talking about ... ?

Chambers: What, girls ... girls cannot—girls cannot do it to a guy?

Saracco: But you can't—tell me, she's ... she's raping you in the park? Robert, come on.

Chambers: She's having her way with me without my consent. With my hands behind my back. Hurting me. The jogger heard me scream.

Saracco: Are we from Iowa or someplace? What ... ?

The fantastic nature of Chambers's confession provided ample fodder for the tabloid press. "Wild Sex Killed Jenny" and "She Raped Me" were two of the most infamous headlines. And although the tabloid press stated the lurid facts of the case in an extreme fashion, this tack was nonetheless a definite undercurrent, and often not a covert one, during the course of the trial. Sex and death are a perfect combination for popular interest; with the additional element of "kinky" sex, white photogenic youths, and gender-role reversal, the preppy murder engages public imagination and supposition. And it is apparent that though Chambers is confessing, his own narrative and the subsequent press coverage exonerate him to a certain degree. Thus, attention focuses upon the powerfully resonant discourse of the grave consequences of transgressing sexual normalcy.

What begins to take shape is an elaborate tale of male hysteria and sexual panic, which are partly what make this "crime of passion" distinct. At a number of moments, Chambers recounts the pain of humiliation caused by women laughing at him. Early that evening, according to many witnesses, Alex Kapp, Chambers's girlfriend, argued very loudly with Chambers in Dorrion's. The quarrel ended with Kapp throwing a package of condoms at Chambers and saying, "Use these with someone else, because you won't get a chance to use them with me." Chambers refers to the incident in the videotape as follows:

> Chambers: And—while this is going on Jennifer was laughing at me and talking to another guy at the same time.
>
> Saracco: Did this get you annoyed?
>
> Chambers: Yeah, because she came—she asked me to come over and talk to her and—then I's getting in trouble and she's laughing at me and also the fact that the girl I was supposed to meet, Alex, the girl I like, was yelling at me in front of everybody, so it was embarrassing.

Later Chambers slips and confuses the two women; his anger is directed toward both, each of whom is seen to have injured him. Chambers clouds the individual identities of his victim and his girlfriend.

> Chambers: That I had hurt Alex ... not Alex, Jennifer. Sorry.
>
> Saracco: Alex was the other girl?
>
> Chambers: Yeah.

As the confession provides a detailed account of the (sexual) body in crime, the precise activity, position, and movement of the bodies of Levin and Chambers become points of evidence. The crime and the appropriate judicial conclusions are read from the sketch of these bodies in motion. The text—that is, Chambers's text, which, given the operations of criminal justice, becomes the text of the crime to be debated in court—involves the articulation of female adolescent sexuality and *Levin's* criminal intentions (molestation). Equally, Chambers's account rests on the very absence of his own sexuality except as something acted upon by others. There is no male desire in this text, only a kind of paralysis; this is part of his hysteria.

The confession is expected to speak the truth of the crime, which in this case means the truth of female adolescent sexuality. To comprehend fully the Chambers confession and its centrality in the entire case, we must address the ideology of confession as a particular discourse of authority.

Murder Confessions and Misogyny

Foucault (1975, xi) writes in the forward to *I, Pierre Rivière, Having Slaughtered My Mother, My Sister, and My Brother* ... , "The reason we decided to publish these documents was to draw a map, so to speak, of those combats, to reconstruct these confrontations and battles, to rediscover the interaction of those discourses as weapons of attack and defense in the relations of power and knowledge." The book contains the documents that were produced as a consequence of a case of parricide committed in 1835: medical testimony, newspaper articles, accounts from witnesses, judges' opinion, legal testimony, and, most notable, the elaborately detailed written confession of the murderer himself. The case is intriguing because it so comprehensibly captures a conflict of two discourses of knowledge: those that read the evidence presented to construct Rivière as a madman and those that find Rivière a criminal, with clear intentions and a carefully calculated scheme.

Much of the confrontation originates from the confession itself. Central to Rivière's trial is a debate concerning the relationship among the written document, the murder, and Rivière himself. On the one hand, how could an insane man produce such an eloquent and intricate text? Did he not *intend* to produce this statement explaining the reasons for the murders prior to their enactment? Does he not refer to *playing* the madman? On the other hand, Rivière employs a skewed and peculiar logic to explain his murders. He kills his mother because of the wrongs she has done his father; he kills his sister for being in league with his mother; but he kills his brother because his father loved him so much. In this way, his father will hate Rivière most for this act, thus assuring that his father will not grieve for Rivière after his inevitable execution. Is this the logic of a sane man? Additionally, much of the evidence presented, from the confession and witnesses, testifies to Rivière's history of "bizarre behavior."

The short essays following the collection of documents on the case describe the context and discourses that operated to "make sense" of Rivière's actions, his madness or criminality. And the confession as a source of evidence and insight into the soul and person of Rivière is at the center of these discursive struggles to elicit the "truth" of the murders. As Alexandre Fontana (1975, 284) writes in his note, "A charitable 'trap' was laid for the criminal to enable him to tell the truth about his act by speaking or writing. The criminal's or 'madman's' speech therefore served as final proof when all others had failed." The confession is ineluctable; it documents the mind and motives of the suspect. While it is to speak its own truth, *what truth it is to speak* is the struggle of competing discourses of knowledge. In other words, the confession is a form of irrefutable evidence, though the proof it serves as is not guaranteed and is instead the product of discursive and interpretive intervention. The act of murder recedes; the materiality of the confession, the murderer's speech, moves to become the focal point of legal, medical, and moral investigation. Foucault writes that the confession "did not so much throw light on, or account for, the crime as form part of it" (p. 200). There is an inescapable coupling of murder and narrative, of weapon and discourse. This interplay between murder and its discursive constitution is where Foucault understands the popular panic and fascination with such crimes.

> [Murder] posits the relation between power and the people, stripped down to essentials: the command to kill, the prohibition against killing; to be killed, to be executed; voluntary sacrifice, punishment inflicted; memory, oblivion. Murder prowls the confines of the law, on one side or the other, above or below it; it frequents power, sometimes against and sometimes with it. The narrative of murder settles into this dangerous area; it provides the communication between interdict and subjection, anonymity and heroism; through it infamy attains immortality. (p. 206)

The *mis-en-discours,* the enunciation, activates this "dangerous area" of murder. Discursive powers guide the possible renditions of murder toward the social formation of deviancy and normalcy. The "communication between interdict and subjection" is precisely the threat of epistemological uncertainty. "To know" is to govern that communication. It is for this reason that murder and speech, the crime and its significatory design, are inextricably entwined. And the confession, having "priority over any other kind of evidence" (p. 38), is a convergence of the two.

Interestingly, Rivière appears to be not unaware of this relation. Not only does he speak of the idea of his memoirs in direct association with the plan to murder his mother and siblings; he also describes the malleability of this narrative. For instance, "I conceived the design of playing the role which I played at the beginning of my imprisonment. ... I thought therefore that I must not say that I represented myself, I must say that I was inspired by God, I was his instrument and was obeying his orders; that I had seen him and his angels too. I embraced this method of defence with great regret, but I thought it would serve my purpose" (pp. 116–117).

This interrelationship of crime and discourse makes the case of Pierre Rivière and that of Robert Chambers analogous; both involve the centrality of the confession, serving as the terrain and evidence for the ensuing legal and public debate. Rather than being framed by the discourses of madness and criminality, the preppy murder is purely one of legal responsibility engulfed in conflicting *moral* agendas. An investigation into female adolescent sexuality designates the terms of the debate. In the preppy murder case, the criminal confession is also a sexual confession, providing dual evidence of the body in crime and the sexual body. Chambers's double roleplaying is far more dangerous than that of Rivière. First, there is the narrativizing of the night of Levin's death and his performance of her sexual advances. Second, there is the volatile, and ultimately fatal, gender-role exchange, where the potential "female rapist" signals a true panic concerning the state of the social and moral consensus. After all, following the popular interpretation, Chambers is playing a woman who is playing a man.

Rivière's misogyny is especially exaggerated to the point where it becomes further evidence of his madness. And yet the origins of his rationale are unquestionably from the central institution of the moral code of his day, the Catholic church. In exhibiting a certain religious fanaticism, Rivière believes that women, as the embodiment of original sin, emit a contaminating fluid that infects men, resulting in temptation and the possibility of incest. When he acts to protect his father from the schemes and insults of his mother and sister, he is acting out the extremes of an extended history of male fear of women. The crime of Robert Chambers is similarly situated. His own recounting of the public and private embarrassment caused by his female acquaintances and his tale of being attacked demonstrate this. The striking thing is that there is nothing particularly unusual about this logic; the construction of masculinity facilitates what could be called a forbearance of the violent excesses of a misogynistic culture. It remains to be explained why what is intuitively and rationally horrific remains, in the final analysis, so predictable.

Subjectivity and the "Self-Evidence" of Confession

As a particular mode of self-narrativization in which a private thought or action is made public, confessions are very much part of the everyday; we engage in that form of discourse willingly and routinely to create intimacy, to share a piece of ourselves, to solicit emotional responses and compassion. Similarly, the confession is an integral part of so many practices of investigation, including medicine, law, and the social sciences. Carole Spitzack (1990) has discussed the intricate relation between the secular confession and medical power in the production of discourses about women's health, in particular body reduction. Andrew Tolson (1990) points out how the historical emergence of the sociological interview in the mid-nineteenth century was a key tactic of surveillance, as significant as photography. As practiced and popularized by nineteenth-century British sociologist Henry Mayhew, through the interview "a new kind of 'social visibility' was constructed" (p. 116). The imperative was to speak and to be questioned about oneself. And this social visibility was central in two areas, in the British context, one having to do with "the moral condition of the working class," and the other concerning "the development of a new kind of 'criminological' interest in the reform of 'delinquents'" (p. 116).

Besides the conjuncture of the interview and the historical appearance of the delinquent, the confession has so imbued such a wide variety of institutional procedures that Foucault (1978, 59) writes, "The most defenseless tenderness and the bloodiest of powers have a similar need of confession. Western man has become a confessing animal." And yet when this activity is also a tactic of discipline, as opposed to an aspect of interpersonal communication, it is sometimes difficult to imagine why one would engage in a self-incriminating discourse. Why surrender? Tantamount to understanding the self-incrimination of confession is an assumed *impulse* to do so. In Fydodor Dostoyevsky's *Crime and Punishment,* Raskolnikov, afflicted with guilt for having committed a multiple murder, is compelled to reveal his heinous actions. In effect, Raskolnikov seeks to be punished for what he recognizes to be wrong.

The notion of a desire to be punished, to tell of one's guilt, has come to be ideologically entwined with the practice of confession. Such works as Erik Berggren's *The Psychology of Confession* (1975) and Theodor Reik's *Compulsion to Confess: On the Psychoanalysis of Crime and Punishment* (1966) explore the existence of an innate need to confess one's misconducts. In this perspective, the act of confession alleviates the associated anxiety and guilt and provides a sense of catharsis and liberation. This position has greatly influenced the extraction of confessions, techniques of interrogation, and the selection of what can count as legal evidence in confessional testimony.

The commonsensical notion of the motivation to confession and its psychological origins is decisive in the ideology of confession. Although some sort of impulse to confess may exist, what it means to confess, the consequences, and the appropriate instances and responses are not universal. By examining the specificities of confession, how it has come to indicate certain things, and how it has been incorporated into particular institutional frameworks, we can reveal its ideological undergirding.

Mike Hepworth's and Bryan Turner's invaluable work, *Confession: Studies in Deviance and Religion* (1982), takes the essentialist position to task, demonstrating the historically specific determinations of confession and the way in which confession legitimizes hierarchies of authority. "Confession lies at the sensitive intersection between the interior freedom of individual conscience and the exterior requirements of public order. Confession is a social activity shot through by contradictions between spontaneity and compulsion, between disinterested confessions and confessions as part of 'bargain justice,' between moral consensus and political force" (p. 15). Confessions occur in the context of certain structured relations of power, whether formally instituted, as in the case of the Catholic confessional, or informally conceived, as when an intimate confession between two acquaintances of equal social stature still operates as a mutual recognition of a taken-for-granted "transgression." In this way, the confession is a point of convergence where the social organizes and impinges upon individual conscience, always with public results or the alibi of public necessity.

In brief, the act of confession can be seen as the multiply composed practice of (1) relating one's own story (autobiography), (2) in a discursively assembled location at which one is given license and encouraged to speak, (3) where the admission of guilt (intention and motive) becomes evidence of agency, and (4) where there exist structured practices of identifying salient elements and reconstituting the confession as legal, medical, scientific, evidence.

Hepworth and Turner argue that labeling theory (as discussed in Chapter 2) has been interested in "rituals of social exclusion"; that is, those activities and procedures that operate to label and define what is exterior to the social consensus. Labeling theory thus assumes a certain uniformity of social response, which is primarily negative, in the constitution of the realm of the deviant. But the nature of social consensus is not so clearly marked in terms of inside/outside; there are many disputes and contradictions that problematize the homogeneity of social normativity. Hepworth and Turner suggest that one must deal with the movement between deviance and normalcy, or what they refer to as "rituals of social closure" that monitor and regulate the boundaries of these two fields. There exist "moral gateways" through which one can pass from deviance to normalcy, such as the legal pardon, "paying one's debt to society," mercy, and the confession. These are "rituals of social inclusion" because they permit the reorientation of the deviant within the domain of the moral structure of the social, thus reinscribing the deviant in the prevailing consensual arrangement and acknowledging the existence of a negatively valued "outside." In this respect, "confession also has important ideological consequences in legitimating the moral order and legal force" (p. 37).

Controlling the movement between the inside and the outside is an important application of social power. It is an example of how both ideology and power can be found in the most precise and seemingly isolated locations. Gilles Deleuze (1988, 26) clarifies Foucault's use of the "local," which "has two very different meanings: power is local because it is never global, but it is not local or localized because it is diffuse." Foucault argues that there is a gap between the potentiality and effectivity of power. He writes of the discursive constitution of sites of social and critical gaze, which, while repressive, equally open up a certain space for potential empowerment. This is the important contribution of *The History of Sexuality: An Introduction* (1978), which argues that the Victorian era and its agenda of moral censure, far from initiating sexual prohibitions, actually invented and gave voice to a range of practices. This is not a simplistic, and politically dangerous, version of "the power of the oppressed"; rather, Foucault explores the conditions and practices of epistemological investigation in the formation of the realms of the inside and the outside and their institutional incorporation (e.g., ways of understanding madness and the asylum, methods of dealing with crime and the prison).

For Foucault, the confession is not a unidirectional "moral gateway." There are other powers, of enablement and confinement, at work, with both calculated and residual effects. Hubert Dreyfus and Paul Rabinow (1982, 169) succinctly characterize Foucault's position as follows: "It was through the technology of confession that several factors ... of bio-power—the body, knowledge, discourse, and power—were brought into a common localization." The confession is a site at which the "truth" is to speak; in so doing, in the course of presenting the "evidence" of oneself, the "truth" of the self speaks. The confessing subject is a moment in which the self becomes visible. It is evident, then, that there is a particular articulation between the individual and the social involved in the space of the confession; and it is an articulation that is dependent upon a notion of individual agency and the assignment of the moral consensus, particularly as formally enforced by the legal system. Hepworth and Turner (1982, 11) argue that "the morality of the conscience was associated with a new emphasis on intention, subjectivity, the person and grace." Historically, with particular shifts in the constitution of the realms of public and private, and in the relations of production, the Catholic church turned to confession as a way to gain access to a newly burgeoning social sphere—the domestic family. The Lateran Canon in 1216 instituted formal procedures of confessing and hearing confession as well as allocating certain powers of judgment to priests. In a good example of the gap between power and its effectivity, whether the tactic of the confession caused a decrease in activities of iniquity is quite ambiguous.[3] If the confession is to stifle "sinful" behavior, then it is certainly a failure. Clearly, other considerations are behind its institution and perpetuation.

Instead, its incorporation rested on the power of enunciation and on an ability, and obligation, to speak the truth about oneself. In turn, the inevitable bestowal of forgiveness exhibited the unlimited powers of the church. This not only transpired as an attempt to solidify the authority of the church over practices of the individual—in effect, to dictate boundaries of the moral structure. But it also equally coincided with the appearance of the self, the individual conscience. The operation of the confession, then, needs to be seen as both a consequence of the emerging qualities of the individual and a site of its discursive constitution.

Thus, confessions are enunciations of the intersection of the individual with social powers.[4] This is the case for two reasons: First, what counts as suitable for confession has to do with the socially constituted category of the transgressive; and second, it is a practice that corresponds to a recognition of the authority of the one who hears the confession. This exchange of information, whether in the context of interpersonal conversation or in the structured realm of police interrogation, is always a question of authority—not the authority to speak, but the *authority to hear,* to be made a confidant, to then assimilate and interpret the information without the additional consent or consideration of the original speaker. The confessor is but a voice; the true "authors" are those who hear. For they construct the space to be inhabited by the speaker, they police who enters, they enforce the confessor's obligation to speak, and they pry into the confession to give it an "authorized" meaning.

To make all of those relations of power invisible, and therefore to be entirely acceptable, the confession must be spontaneous. Confessional testimony must seem to come from the individual voluntarily and not be provoked. This seizes the individual not only as the "author" of the crime but also as one who has the moral fiber to identify the transgressive nature of the crime and the legitimacy of the moral consensus. If a confession is coerced, there is the possibility of its falsity, which would elide the agency of the individual's own will to confess. Thus, it becomes conceivable to imagine that there is nothing particularly intrinsic or natural about the authority structure of the confession. The need or impulse to confess becomes a way to downplay attention to the context in which confessions take place. But, of course, there is clearly little that is spontaneous and natural about police interrogation.

The confessing subject as the agent of the narrative and of the crime appears to act freely and to possess an individual consciousness with intentions and social autonomy. Concurrently, the confession needs an institutional framework to make it meaningful to particular cultural agencies with respect to an expressed moral structure. The encounters between the registers of individual consciousness and representatives of public authority are starting points for the discursive and ideological constitution of the self and the realization of one's relation to the social. One is recognized and one is self-recognized in the light of the social. So, paradoxically, even though confession is a moment of self-incrimination, the absence of guilt and remorse (the presumed motivating emotions for confession) is considered to be equally pathological. To confess is to admit to a form of deviance, and not to demonstrate remorse is to risk being labeled a sociopath. In this respect, the confessor must *want* to confess and must *display* remorse to fully "return to the social."

One of the most significant contributions of contemporary critical theory has been the ideological analysis of intentionality. As Deleuze (1988, 104) writes, "This is Foucault's major achievement: the conversion of phenomenology into epistemology." The critique rewrites the idealism of phenomenology as a system of knowledge, an arrangement of relations of force that allow us "to know." Intention and motivation are ways of understanding within which the pretense of universality operates to mask their historical conditioning.

Criminal subjectivity is the result of a whole apparatus of discourses designed to designate and explain the deviant and related practices. The subject-in-crime becomes wrapped up in the ideology of individuality and individual agency. Joel Black (1991) shows how this notion of intentionality constructs certain affinities between the murderer and the artist. In fact, his argument rests almost entirely upon reports concerning the desire, motivation, and objectives of the murderer, which, he claims, demonstrate an artistic temperament and what could be called an awareness of aesthetic. For Black, murder at one level is a form of communication, expressing otherwise incomprehensible demands and emotions. Hence, murder demands a witness or an audience. The practice of confession is one way to guarantee this. According to Black, the requisite witness assures the social function of criminal intentionality—that is, criminal subjectivity. Becoming a *subject* refers to being rendered a topic or site of inquiry *and* a participant in that process and to being *subjected to* certain powers. In confessions, one's own story becomes evidence. The self and a moment of self-definition work as evidence of agency, deviance, and the power of the moral consensus and its representative institutions. One is situated within the reach of certain operations of consensus, order, normalcy. And, importantly, the public nature of these operations means that the subject-in-crime is evidence for other diverse forms of knowledge, such as those pertaining to sexuality.

The Disciplinary Power of the Sexual Confession

Confession and sexuality have a particular historical association. This is one of the propositions of Foucault's *The History of Sexuality.* Not only has sexual activity been a dominant theme of confession; it also came to be presumed that the act of speaking about sex enunciated the "truth" about it. Sexuality was to speak its own truth through its articulation in the confession. "For us, it is in the confession that truth and sex are joined, through the obligatory and exhaustive expression of an individual secret. But this time it is truth that serves as a medium for sex and its manifestations" (Foucault 1978, 61). In this way, there is an articulation of the truth value of the sexual confession and the impulse to confess. Here, with the ideological *truth in sex,* "we demand that it tells us our truth, or rather, the deeply buried truth of that truth about ourselves which we think we possess in our immediate consciousness" (p. 69). The discourses of the self, sex, and truth intersect in the confession, for "causality in the subject, the unconscious of the subject, the truth of the subject in the other who knows, the knowledge he holds unbeknown to him, all this found an opportunity to deploy itself in the discourse of sex. Not, however, by reason of some natural property inherent in sex itself, but by virtue of the tactics of power immanent in this discourse" (p. 70). There is a twist on the sexual confession as a tactic of power; though sex speaks its own truth as well as our truth, it requires interpretation, a formal structure of expertise in which the truth, once enunciated, can be discerned and heard. This intervention is the dual location of knowledge and the realization of power. It is the investment of the faculties of speech and listening with the socially guided exercise of diagnosis, judgment, consolation, reprimand, and discipline.

The significance of this discussion in the present context is that it is evident that Robert Chambers's confession to Jennifer Levin's death is intricately composed as a confession to murder and a sexual confession. The truth it speaks of the crime of murder is intertwined with the truth it speaks of adolescent sexuality, in particular that of young women, but also that of the hysterical adolescent male. Furthermore, the confession speaks of the criminality of both activities; Levin's death is doubly composed as a crime of violence (legally designated as manslaughter) and a crime of transgressive sex. Robert Chambers acts as a witness, and victim, to the second "crime." Levin, utterly speechless in this process, has been "confessed for," and hence her example operates as proof of certain aspects of contemporary youth. Her case reveals previously hidden or unsubstantiated knowledges concerning youth sexuality and its links to a certain social crisis. The evidential procedures of the confession are such that Jennifer Levin becomes the terrible metonym for adolescent sexuality, its licentiousness, its permissiveness, its possible perversity, and hence its threat to the order of the acceptable.

Chambers is the confessing subject, and all of the aforementioned forces act upon him, bringing him into the sights of the social formation. Yet he avoids taking up the position by placing the agency of the crime on Levin, which, of course, is the tactic of any self-defense plea. The power of the speaking (confessing) subject accounts for the "truth" that Chambers describes of the crime. Nonetheless, he effectively shifts the blame or at least casts sufficient doubt upon his own participation that at the end of the trial, the jury cannot make up its mind about Chambers's guilt. The decision goes to a plea bargain for a reduced sentence instead. Chambers rejects the confession as a "gateway" back into the accepted ranks of the social order: He does not show any remorse for having caused Levin's death, nor does he entirely accept his own position as murderer. In fact, much is made of his emotional vacancy. The plea bargain requires Chambers to read publicly a statement admitting his guilt. He does so, but woodenly, shaking his head as though he disagrees with the words he is saying. This and earlier demonstrations of remorselessness, more than any other single factor, encourage a reconsideration of the authenticity of his story.

So, then, are his statements to the police really confessions? Insomuch as they are personally contrived and endorsed narratives of his own part in Levin's death, yes, they are confessions. Though his version is perplexing, it is clearly an admission of guilt; in the final version Chambers does not deny having killed Levin. The disciplinary power of confession renders Chambers a subject of the judicial system; he is caught in the gaze of legal and police procedures, of judgment and discipline. But thrown on the tracks of this process is the evidence of Levin's sexual performance. This "self-evidence" of Levin's sexuality, as depicted by Chambers, is to be evaluated with respect to Chambers's guilt; it is to accept a degree of the charge of "authorship" of the crime. This process of evaluation, then, is the role of the trial. The confession makes Levin's (sexual) body reappear as evidence and as a potential suspect.

The appearance of Levin's "sex diary" augments this direction. The strategic demand to see the small appointment book effectively draws public attention to Levin's sexuality, lending increasing support to Chambers's claims of molestation. The absent and legally immaterial appointment book is transformed into a written document of self-incriminating evidence, an unintended confession of sexual transgression. As such, it is thought to speak the truth not of the crime of murder directly but of Levin's sexuality. Even without the actual document, Levin is "hailed" by Chambers's attorney and the scrutiny of the public into a position as a confessing subject. She does not speak; her words are made to speak as a confession after the fact. The sex diary, a monstrous creation of Jack Litman's blame-the-victim defense, even in its absence, legitimizes Chambers's testimony. It is another point of investigation into the truth of the sexual body in crime—or rather, into the criminal sexual body of the female adolescent.

On the Spectacle of Confession

The individual details of the death of Levin alone cannot account for the popular interest in the crime. Certainly, there are many aspects that make this case distinct and unusual, not the least of which are the two videotape "performances" of Robert Chambers and the alleged existence of Jennifer Levin's sex diary. Equally, Chambers and Levin's photogenic qualities also contribute to the spectacular nature of the crime, as much as any of the lurid specifics. Briefly put, the crime and the confession must be seen in the context of their own exhibition in popular culture. The confession in particular cannot be comprehended unless we sketch its position with respect to a variety of modes of popular confession—that is, confessions that take place in popular culture for a popular audience.

The space of the confession assumes the a priori existence of a moral order, however heterogeneous, from which a rendition of the consensual can be formed. The hearer of the confession is the representative of that order, interpellated as a subject of and on the "inside." In effect, the listener is the witness to this "ritual of social inclusion." The confessing subject is confined and enabled by the space of the confession. The listening subject is an accomplice in the link between the "self-evidence" of the confession/confessor and its public import. This is the deeply significant nature of the performance of confession.

To perform is to be caught in the gaze of an audience. In the case of the spectacular confession, the performance occurs for a number of witnesses, most notably the representatives of the institutional structures of authority (police officers, lawyers, priests, doctors, etc.) and popular audiences—that is, those with a different sort of *authority to hear,* one having to do with membership inside a moral community. Popular audiences are without direct and sanctioned authority to judge and interpret; yet the hearer as a socially interpellated subject has a certain authority. The popular audience engages in the "authorization" of the confession and the confessional space through its scrutinizing or distracted gaze. The presentation, enactment, and reconstruction of confessions in popular culture transpire with astonishing frequency. There is a popular fascination with the drama of self-incrimination and the supposedly cathartic release in the admission of guilt, a sensation of attraction and repulsion. It would be banal to read this as though it is only a drama of the outside that is being replayed continually, one that delineates the consensus and makes us feel safe on the inside. Although surely this is partly at work, it cannot explain the sustained intensity of our popular passions for the "entertainment" of the confessing subject. Our fascination has residual effects.

As already indicated, Foucault took the confession as a site of the "self," where there is an engagement of disciplinary power to form the individual subject and to compose a source of knowledge of that social being. But the confession is equally a power managed and conducted through its public performance. The ideological force is not limited to that of the enunciating subject, at least not any more. Today we witness far more (mediated) confessions than we ever engage in. The theater of public confession consists partly of a reenactment of familiar, though often twisted and perverse, narratives. In brief, at this level of analysis the performance of confession as a tactic of disciplinary power must be examined.

In their heyday, public executions did not operate purely in the intended fashion of political ritual and admonition; they were also occasions for celebration and festival. The decline of the spectacle of execution in the nineteenth century brought on other forms of spectacularizing deviance and retribution. In tandem, the confession, as popularly conceived, sustained an

> increasing preoccupation with criminal psychology (particularly the notion of mental pathology), a corresponding shift in the kinds of explanations acceptable to the general public, the growth of modern forensic criminology geared to scientific detection, and much later the development of scientific interrogation drawing upon the insights of experimental psychology, behaviouristic psychiatry, and technological innovation. (Hepworth and Turner 1982, 137–138)

The secularization of confession meant that it suffused into so many varied areas and institutional practices. Concerning the increasing deployment of the confession in diverse public locations, Hepworth and Turner write that "the process of secularisation ... was accompanied by the emergence of murder as mass entertainment" (p. 137). Confession as represented in the broadsheet press brought the concealed activities of the criminal and criminal investigation out for public consumption.

Such mediated reports are seen as unambiguous acknowledgments of the act and its status as deviant; they are self-evident, incontrovertibly offering the self-narrative—the "truth" of the confessing subject—and the self as evidence. However, as previously discussed, confessions are not as self-evident as they are presumed to be. They are tactics of power; they are put into play, enunciated, and located in discourses of authoritative explanation, of the production of knowledge. Their status as evidence works only as a consequence of discourse. What is worthy of confession is bound up in social definitions of the deviant, itself a product of its public nature.

The drama of the self-incriminating and remorseful deviant becomes a spectacle attracting public attention, but with a twist, for the spectacle of confession implies a double stake in its status as evidence. Not only is it a realization of the self in relation to particular narratives and discourses—the microphysics of power; it is also an instance in which the private is drawn into the realm of public and popular scrutiny and observation. Consequently, while we investigate the problematic of how to read such instances of self-evidence, we must also consider the recuperative *and* enabling moments of the popularity of particular crimes and criminal confessions. Western people may be, as Foucault has said, confessing animals. But even more forcefully, *we are slaves to the drama of confession.* It is not our own confessions, but those of others, that we find so beguiling. And what is being confessed seems to matter little; it is the act, the performance, itself that appeals.

PART THREE

Spectacle

6

Crisis and Display:
The Nature of Evidence
on the Daytime Television
Talk Show

*The "news" thus becomes no more than another category through which
any available televised event is capable of migrating. Simple depiction su-
percedes any issue of depictability. The newsperson's talking head registers
authority, represents judgement. The succession of images of this apparatus
of preference constitutes TV's minimum, the repetition of the declaration "It
is, it is, it is, it is." It's the raw form of TV ontology.*

—**Michael Sorkin, "Simulations: Faking It"**

In a tawdry and abhorrent display, Morton Downey, Jr. acted out Robert
Chambers's version of the killing of Jennifer Levin. On his late night television talk
show, known for its tastelessness and the aggressiveness of its host, Downey's
hands were bound with a pair of panties, and a female guest sat on top of him on
the studio floor. Downey then struggled to free his hands and to strangle the guest.

The success of this brand of journalism, or "trash TV," as it has been disparag-
ingly labeled, is phenomenal. Trash TV has been used to describe the magazine
format of *A Current Affair*, the reconstructed dramas of *America's Most Wanted*,
and the daytime talk shows like *Geraldo*. Often seen as a shift in news coverage toward the excesses of the tabloid press, these shows are never too far from dominant currents and trends. Geraldo Rivera himself (1988, 45) provides a clear analysis of his own fit with respect to the news media in general: "Oh, about trash TV.
Do I think it's a fair label? I think it's an appallingly unfair label. I think that
Newsweek magazine, which coined the phrase, was guilty of the grossest kind of

hypocrisy. During the week of the presidential election, the most important domestic news that happens only once every four years, they put me on the cover."

The popularity of trash TV is indisputable. For instance, Rivera's prime-time report on satanism in the United States aired on NBC in October 1988—the week of Halloween—and was the highest rated two-hour documentary ever to be broadcast on network television (Waters 1988, 73). This occurred despite the fact that the network lost $2 million of advertising revenue at the last minute when advertisers became apprehensive about the topic (Rivera 1988, 44). Kevin Glynn (1990) explains trash TV in terms of its carnivalesque appeal, its subversion of bourgeois taste and the assumptions of liberal journalism. Certainly, there is a heady delight taken in the exhibition of various perversities and aberrations.

Daytime talk shows differ from the nighttime versions in that the former wish to maintain the pretense of their informational and news functions. The nighttime versions, including *Tonight with Jay Leno, Late Show with David Letterman,* and *The Arsenio Hall Show,* tend to be entirely wrapped up in the environment of commercial entertainment, acting as variety shows and promotional opportunities for other television shows, movies, and so forth. Daytime talk shows such as *Geraldo, The Oprah Winfrey Show,* and *Donahue* center on special topics and popular concerns. These distinctions are difficult to ascribe with certainty, particularly with *Oprah,* where movie stars or authors often appear to promote their latest projects. However, the daytime talk shows have in common the devotion of an entire hour, sometimes an entire week, to a single focus of interest. For example, in the fall of 1989 *Geraldo* ran what it referred to as "Bad Girls Week," which included such remarkably different topics as mothers in prison, nymphomaniacs, and women who have affairs with married men.[1]

These programs are the prized products of syndication. Most syndicators have found it difficult to sell original programming to the networks, relying instead on reruns. But the daytime talk show is an important element in opening the door to increased market share for syndicators. Interestingly, the affiliates targeted by the "syndies" are those already carrying one of the other talk shows (Dempsey 1987). The consequence is the creation of "strips" of afternoon talk shows where, for instance, *Geraldo* and *Oprah* are back to back. Syndicators also sell them as good lead-ins to the local evening news or as lead-outs from morning programs such as *Today* and *Good Morning America.* A typical 1989 weekday schedule, as exemplified here by that of WPTZ (NBC) Plattsburgh, New York, is as follows:

7:00 A.M.	*Today*
9:00 A.M.	*Donahue*
10:00 A.M.	*Joan Rivers*
4:00 P.M.	*Oprah*
5:00 P.M.	*Geraldo*
6:00 P.M.	*News* (local)
6:30 P.M.	*News* (national)

These two strips of four and three hours, respectively, make up the daytime informational scheduling for this particular affiliate. This lineup represents a total of four hours of daytime talk shows, strategically positioned in pairs (*Donahue-Rivers* and *Oprah-Geraldo*) to form a ministrip within the longer news-information programming strip.

Critical responses to the popularity of talk shows have been relentlessly harsh. For instance, an outraged editorial in the *Wall Street Journal,* published shortly after the Aryan Nation fight with black activists on *Geraldo,* comments, "*Geraldo* is like a Who's Who of deviant behavior—the weird, the depraved and the twisted. Aren't there any normal segments of society? Aren't there any big, important issues worth talking about?" (Goldberg 1988, A14). Television talk shows do seem to pillage the darkest corners of human behavior, ever vigilant for extreme items of deviancy. Nothing loathsome and grisly is outside the purview of the talk show. What Robert Goldberg misses in his editorial, and what popular critics often overlook as well, is that the "normal" is written into these programs throughout. As references to "the weird, the depraved and the twisted" abound, these shows also strike subtle reminders of the order that is outside and supposedly disappearing. In the final analysis, they are in fact always about "big, important issues," though their individual topics may seem inconsequential. This is because in the talk show, the aberrant is laced with the seeds of social disturbance and the paranoia of a shaken order. This is the industry of the representation of the socially subversive. What operations act to constitute the appearance of certain concerns and their association with larger issues and crises? More specifically, what mechanisms and forms of evidence function to affirm the nature of a contemporary crisis of youth? Or, put differently, in a demonstration such as the one in which Morton Downey, Jr. reenacts the preppy murder, what is being ascertained, and how does this figure with respect to a general understanding of the crime?

Aspects of the Daytime Talk Show's Evidential Procedures

One quality that is consistent and fundamental to the evidential particularities of daytime talk shows is a broad notion of television stardom. Apart from being defined around the star persona of their host, these shows are premised on the rapid replacement of guests. They move through a diverse population of individuals who are invited to take center stage, to speak and be attended to by the audience. It is highly unlikely that there will be a repeat visitor on a given show, unlike the nighttime talk shows, which schedule habitual guests and which have rather predictable reappearances. Though it is not unusual for certain people to appear on different daytime talk shows, to do the circuit, so to speak, their reappearance is most rare over a number of years. Additionally, the guest is as likely to be Michael Hersch ("heavy metal music fan") as Tipper Gore ("author" and "wife of the vice president"), Sia ("teenage runaway") as Jello Biafra ("former lead singer, The Dead

Kennedys"), John C. McQuinn ("principal, Bryuan High") as Sylvester Stallone ("actor/writer/producer"). An odd sense of celebrity status is exhibited; a guest, famous or not, gets the same spotlight for a moment. And the representative guests, who act as the metonymic figures of vast realms of social activity, are never heard from again. Their names (Michael Hersch, Sia) are much less meaningful than their illustrative caste as archetypes of social crisis (heavy metal music fan, teenage runaway). In this way, the associations made by their metonymic function augment their status as "ordinary" guests; they are taken as representative of a sample, as voices that speak of and for broad social concerns and activity.

A breakdown of the audience-performer distinction amplifies this transitory sense of stardom. With the host situated within the audience, the program devotes a significant portion of its time to the comments of audience members, who often relate their own associated stories. In fact, there are usually planted guests in the audience who are called upon to comment and respond to the principal guests on the stage. Often, there are few characteristics that distinguish the guests in the audience from the ones on the stage (e.g., "This audience is filled with kids in crisis" in reference to teenage runaways present in an episode of *Oprah*). Establishing shots before and after commercial breaks present the geography of the studio, including the position of the audience with respect to the guests on stage and the standing, moving figure of the host. The establishing shots tend to track around the perimeter, circling and encompassing the space in which the debate is to take place, often with the host as an imprecise axis around which the trajectory of the camera moves. The majority of the show consists of alternating shots between speaking subject and silent reaction shot, either of audience or guest. This creates a sense of dialogue as the two groups converse back and forth. The alternating shots establish the space of that dialogue between audience and guest and also the rhythm of the exchange. The following is an example of how a talk show debate progresses.

"Teens in Crisis" was the focus of the September 16, 1987, *Oprah*. It was followed the next day by the less panicky topic "Fathers and Sons." The following week, *Geraldo* broadcast "How to Spot a Child Molester," which reiterated many of the suggestions and positions of *Oprah*'s "Teens in Crisis" show. This particular episode begins with Oprah Winfrey setting up the questions and situation to be addressed: "This audience is filled with kids in crisis. Some are runaways, unwanted and feeling unloved, living on the streets, often trading sex for a hot meal. Others are victims of family neglect and have been thrown out of their homes with nowhere to go. And others have gotten involved with drugs, turning to a career of crime." This introduction, with its rapid and rough association of youth, prostitution, drugs, crime, and family neglect, is the extent of the investigation of the "crisis" mentioned in the title. The majority of the show consists of testimonies of youths, all of which further substantiate the initial concerns.

From the introduction, the show moves to a short prerecorded video segment, shot "on the streets," of two "real" runaway/drug user/abuse victim/prostitutes.

Each interview provides a brief narrative of the teenager's situation. The first female teenager states, "I mean, when I got caught from being a runaway I was up at the lake, and they took me to my house and my mother said, 'Take her to the police station.' And I see, you know, prostitution, drug dealing, and I was helping sell reefer and everything, you know. I'm afraid of my future. I'm afraid what I might turn into." These "confessions from the street" provide the staple evidence from which, upon returning to the live studio, the other stories build. Winfrey introduces the guests, which include three "teens in crisis," an "expert" who runs a program called Children of the Night to help runaways, and a former child runaway. Winfrey then asks one of the guests to relate her story of family neglect, attempted suicide, drug abuse, and life on the streets. Next Winfrey introduces another guest by reading a letter she had sent to Winfrey's office: "Ever since I've been 13 I have been running away. I've been a drug addict, an alcoholic. I've tried committing suicide, I was raped as a virgin, I've gone to a girls' home, juvenile hall and spent time in the women's county jail. I was 15 then. I've had a very hard life." As the stories are told and retold, there are frequent reaction shots of the audience listening intently.

Winfrey, standing in the audience, orchestrates the movement among the guests' testimonies, questions and comments from the audience, and those who telephone. The first caller is a mother of two runaways, and the remaining two calls are runaways themselves. Eleven audience members make comments. Two question the guests directly, and another shares the experience of being in a play about runaways. The other eight are all teens in crisis who relate similar stories of abuse, drug use, and prostitution. Though the formal structure of the studio separates audience and invited guests, the movement between the groups as they are chosen to speak begins to break this distinction. There is the creation of a closed environment of teens in crisis in which at every turn there is a substantiation of Winfrey's opening thesis. The show glides from street interview, to guest confession, to audience member confession, to the anonymous phone confession. The cursory authoritative comments of the social worker add little to the dense arrangement of the often repetitive testimonies of the teenagers.

Different points in the "Teens in Crisis" episode suggest probable causes and solutions. For instance, Dr. Lois Lee, the director of Children of the Night, coments, "Kids are not going to follow rules because rules are right or because there's pay-offs. It's because they do it to please people who care about them, because they think that that's what they're supposed to do. Without that kind of connectedness, no home is going to work, whether it's a foster home, whether it's a natural home, whether it's a program, regardless of what it is." Providing little insight, this commentary reiterates the positions of previous testimonies of teens in crisis. It is general enough to be easily pertinent to a number of situations. Clearly, the focus of interest lies in the personal narratives. The statements of experts legitimate the stories of firsthand experience of the topic. There is frequent negotiation between the two types of testimony, as guided by Winfrey.

Dr. Lee: Most commonly what you hear from women is, the new husband is not going to put up with it. And the kid literally experiences the fact that the mother has chosen another man over their own child.

Winfrey: Anybody here experience that?

Tomi: Right here.

Winfrey: Yeah. You too, Sia?

Sia: Yeah.

This is not to say that these shows are about consensus on an issue. In fact, quite the opposite is the case; each episode thrives on animated discussion, ideally to the point of vexed dissension. The shows move along by alternatingly challenging and supporting each enunciated statement. The nature of a response, the direction of defense or attack, is less certain than the fact that there will be a response, any response. Without exception, the debate hinges upon the testimonial assertions of individuals who have been exposed to the situation in question. Their statements are incontrovertible and act to corroborate varying perspectives. The shows are about crisis as told and substantiated by those affected.

The qualities of the daytime talk show—the immediate obsolescence of guests; the broad, if fleeting, sense of television stardom; the reworking of the audience-performer distinction; and the privileged position of personal testimony–all operate to effect the construction of the issue and the manner of its treatment. Elspeth Probyn (1989, 30) comments, "Oprah Winfrey is also of prime interest to feminist criticism because of the ways in which the program stitches together autobiographical descriptions of the experiences of both the host and her audiences." This, Probyn argues, is complexly arranged in the formal and extratextual considerations—for instance, Winfrey's unique status as a black woman star—all of which create a particular mode of feminine address.

Talk shows target and frame the alluring qualities of psychological terror and the inescapable horrors of the guilty mind. Grounded in the compelling and often revolting nature of the description of such states and experiences, the myth of the "talking cure" lurks never too far behind the proceedings. This self-narrativization (what I later discuss as an act of confession) is seen to be good for the speaker, as this activity shares the ordeal with the audience. The authority of the host has little to do with the topic at hand; hosts are not experts. They are concerned citizens, interlocutors, operators who bring audience and guest together in the roles of confessors and hearers of confession. The experts who appear as guests verify the authenticity of the experiences related by the other guests, placing the stories into comprehensible orders that speak particular problems, solutions, and situations. In an inadvertent metacommentary on the centrality of confessional testimony in the television talk show, Geraldo Rivera ends a show on incest with the cryptic epitaph "And remember, you are only as sick as your secrets."

Television and Talk

Talk and television: The relation has been suggested and explored extensively. For such diverse theorists of the medium as John Ellis (1982), John Fiske (1987), and Marshall McLuhan (1964), television is primarily an aural technology, relying upon sound to carry the image lacking detail and complexity. More than a few seconds of silence is highly unusual. In fact, the norm is continuous talk from on-screen talking heads or from disembodied voices. Not surprisingly, then, programs that feature talk abound: daytime talk shows, nighttime talk shows, news, and interviews. Anyone who caught a glimpse of Oliver North's appearance at the Iran-Contra hearing or the Clarence Thomas–Anita Hill hearing knows how televisually apt that mode of drama is. The live, real-time, and interrogatory nature of the hearings perfectly melded to their extended daytime coverage.

Margaret Morse (1985) refers to the particularities of television as "discourse space." This involves "the inclusion of the act of narration in the representation of a story; it spreads itself like another plane over the story space of television and encompasses our living room as well" (p. 4–5). Unlike the "objective story space" of cinema, premised upon the invisibility of the narrator, television makes the process of telling the story explicit. Thus, "the subject-narrator of television is 'confessional,' holding a one-way conversation" (p. 5). Whereas cinematic narrative *unfolds for,* television *talks to,* engendering a self-referential moment of enunciation to the television audience. From this, Morse reads "the impression of discourse" created by television and the "quasi-subjectivity" that it initiates. This "impression" is bound up in television's "reality effect," with the prevalence of direct address, its star machine of ordinary people, and the connotative assertion of its own immediacy and "live"ness.[2]

Television's confidential mode, and our position as silent partners in the process of hearing and validating the enunciations, needs to be emphasized. I agree, but it is misleading to presume only an *impression* of discourse; for this belies the actuality of the community of address—what Ellis (1982) refers to as the audience's "citizenship"—and erases the particular activities of the television audience as it participates in the validation of the said. As Ellis notes concerning television, the *glance* replaces the cinematic gaze, "hence the crucial role of sound in ensuring continuity of attention and producing the utterances of direct address ('I' to 'you')" (p. 137). Different from the cinema's substitution of the camera for the spectator—the ideal viewing position leading the spectator through the "winding corridor" of the narrative (Bordwell et al. 1985, 37)—television inures an inclusive mode of address. And this mode of address harbors the pretenses of community and complicity. "Broadcast TV recruits the interest of its viewers by creating a complicity of viewing: the TV look at the world becomes a surrogate look for the viewers" (Ellis 1982, 163).

Moreover, the mode of direct address creates a space that designates a particular community of viewers. Viewing entails an entry into a position approximating

citizenship and in this respect entails participation in proceedings, even if participation only means acceptance of the "delegation of the look" of television (p.
169). In this context, the daytime talk show is a mode of popular confessional
practice, as Morse suggests of television as a whole. What are the content and context of a genre of confession, prized for its emotionality, sincerity, and demonstration of anguish? And how do the qualities of the confession figure in the presentation and authorization of particular concerns?

There is a 900 telephone service in which the caller can anonymously listen in
on women's "secret confessions." The television advertisement for the service
(just what is being served anyway?) consists of images of women crying into telephone receivers, repeating such repentant phrases as "I can't believe what I've
done," "I'm sorry," and "Please forgive me." Speaking to an absent structure of
authority, exactly whose forgiveness is being sought? After all, the invitation is *not*
to confess but to listen in on others (women) recite their transgressions, crimes,
and sins. As with the talk show, the audience—again, a presumed female, or femi-
nized, audience—is always an absent presence of authority to whom the testimonies are addressed. To understand this mode of confession, we cannot presume a
direct social effectivity of self-incrimination. Instead, with the telephone confession line and the daytime talk show, it is the exhibition value, the performance,
that is proffered.

As seen in the previous chapter, confession refers to a personal narrative, an individually formed and related story in which the narrator figures centrally.
Hepworth and Turner (1982, 151) perceptively note that "confessions were not of
great interest ... because they illuminated the dark corners of an alien criminal
mind but precisely because they were acts of communication which confirmed
the existence of a shared ethical view and a common human nature." The truth of
confession is taken for granted; in fact, confessions are so naturalized as the legitimate story of personal experience that their truth value is not questioned and furthermore *does not matter.* Confessions are communicative acts that capture, artic-
ulate, and confirm something that is "shared" in a culture—about deviance,
transgression, and the emotion of guilt.

With respect to the talk show as a mode of popular confessional practice, it is
the *act,* not its subsequent deployment as evidence or the associate penalties, that
is of importance. This is what is meant by the performance of confession: a drama
of social inclusion, always with the implication of the stability of the social order.
The performance of confession involves the intersection of the individual, the
popular, and the social order. The self-incriminating subject in popular discourse
always introduces the double suggestion of how the speakers are just like us, with
a similar moral structure and responses to right and wrong, and how they are so
utterly different. In fact, on talk shows there is a frequent alternation between extreme horrors and mundane problems as topics; with the horrors, the limits of the
social are not contested, and with the trivial concerns, our position inside the social is clear. In both instances, this constitutes a community of address.

On television there is a prominence not just of sound and speech but also of personal enunciation. What is said, the actual content of the testimony, melts into a cacophony of voices, of confessing subjects. "The grain of the voice" punctures the surface of the utterance. Barthes (1977, 181) writes that the grain refers to "the very precise space (genre) of *the encounter between a language and a voice*." There the expressed consists of an emotional weave from which its force arises. The pathos of the enunciative voice unsettle the dimension of meaning. The consistency of passionate displays subsumes the variety of narratives in the environment of talk show television. The stress shifts to the performance, to the act of telling, its grain. The significance of this form of self-narrativization, and of the placement of that narrative into the context of particular social concerns and interests, is lodged in the display value of the telling, the performance of the confession. What is confessed—the manner of the confessor's own implication in particular transgressions—dissolves in the face of the spectacle of its enactment.

With these aspects of the talk shows' evidential procedures, and particularly with the important place of the performance of confession, the specificities of the talk show debate can be grasped. Significantly, we can begin to describe how the diverse and varied topics coalesce into a commonsense logic of crisis-in-process.

Mobile Evidence

Oprah broadcast a show on the Hedda Nussbaum–Joel Steinberg case, in which a battered woman, Nussbaum, was accused of having "done nothing" to stop the abuse and subsequent death of their child. The guests included Susan Brownmiller, who had just published a novel based on the case, *Waverly Place* (1989), and who felt that Nussbaum was guilty; Naomi Wise, a friend of Nussbaum who believed Steinberg was entirely to blame; and Susan Schecter, who worked with battered women and understood that "failure to act" is a typical response to a dangerous situation. Later in the show two former battered women joined the guests. The course of the show dealt with what counts as a "reasonable" attempt to get a child out of such a situation, what being a battered woman is like and its effects on self-esteem and motivation, the role of drug use in the crime, and what it means to be "without power" in a relationship and in society. The audience's comments were split between "save the mother" and "save the child" as priorities. Battered women in the audience read the case according to their experience, with differing conclusions. Quite evocative statements, such as "If you are not white, middle class, and male, it's to hell with you in this society," from one former battered woman in the audience, were met with normative statements concerning a mother's responsibilities to her child. Steinberg's responsibilities as a father, or as an adult, were not addressed once.

The show was a quite overt struggle to understand the case with respect to the exigencies of motherhood or the consequences of women's social disempowerment. Though the proceedings seemed to favor a demonization of Nussbaum as a failed mother/wife, there was no resolution. Furthermore, the counterposition, the radically charged claim that a woman cannot be held responsible in a situation in which at every other instance she is being told she is powerless, was stated incontrovertibly. But it was made perfectly clear that there was a considerable amount at stake in which position was to be supported. The debate was passionate and relentless, and it exposed the operations of sense-making—that is, the operations of articulation.

Talk shows and "infotainment" programs, such as *A Current Affair* and *America's Most Wanted*, are important moments of articulation similar to newspaper editorials and features. They are all instances that downplay *reportage* and that afford a certain amount of freedom to construct relations between events and issues. Here "critical" investigation and interpretation take off. Daytime talk shows tend to focus on an issue or concern. Within the individual show, representative events are discussed. For instance, in the Nussbaum episode of *Oprah,* the experiences of battered women present in the audience, as invited guests, and on the telephone are employed to provide insight into the case and into Nussbaum's psychological makeup. The frame already exists; the auspice of the topic situates the investigation.

On May 24, 1988, Jennifer Levin's mother, Ellen, made an appearance on *Donahue,* framed by the topic of victims' rights. The course of the program reiterated the by-then-familiar story, though with twists that passed unchallenged. For example, Donahue described Robert Chambers as having been under the influence of alcohol and "chemicals" during Jennifer Levin's death and commented on his unreasonably "pushy mother," who, in Donahue's opinion, was partly responsible for Chambers's behavior in general and the murder more specifically. The questions from Donahue and from the audience repeatedly wanted to pin the crime on particular elements, to understand it in an uncomplicated fashion. And to her credit, Ellen Levin resisted, saying that the cause of the crime "wasn't the hour and it wasn't Central Park." Nonetheless, the episode made a series of assertions to understand the crime, most of which were not novel in any way; Chambers as drug user, Chambers as social climber, Chambers as spoiled rich kid, Chambers as mugger, Chambers as impotent man, Chambers as rapist, Levin as dupe, Levin as victim of media sensationalism, Levin as victim of a "travesty of justice." Rendered intelligible in one context, for instance, as a case in which the victim was put on trial, the crime can be equally situated with respect to another understanding, namely, the nature of contemporary pressures on today's youth. There is not necessarily a contradiction here; definitive "solutions" do not have to exist.

This is a continuation of the process discussed earlier with respect to sensational crimes: After a crime comes into focus, into popular recognition, and can be precisely related as a narrative, it then serves as evidence in other locations. Sensational crimes by definition are complex and have multiple "solutions" or manners in which they can be understood. In this respect, they are excellent rhetorical devices and exceptionally convincing ones. George Bush's use of the Willy Horton case during the 1988 presidential campaign is perhaps one of the best recent examples of the startling effectiveness of mobilizing crime and people's fears of lawlessness to a specific political end. Briefly put, the location—that is, the rhetorical, enunciative, and discursive context—renders the *evidential* aspects of the crime intelligible. This, of course, is the opposite of the presupposition of investigation: that evidence leads to the "solution," to intelligibility.

Given the popularity and high-profile status of daytime television talk shows, they are significant players in the arena of popular political activity. But predominantly, the erratic nature of the subject matter makes generalizations about political tendencies and ideology difficult. *Oprah* is likely to feature black feminists or spoiled brats. *Geraldo* is likely to discuss racism or sexual addiction. The abundance of social concerns as depicted on these programs suggests that no single crisis seems to carry much weight. There are some staples, in particular the family, sexuality, and contemporary youth, but their representation is not guaranteed and is far from consistent. Thus, it would be misleading to draw ideological conclusions from a *single* episode or even from a *single* talk show for the simple reason that any statement or position is as likely as not to be contradicted the next day.

Dealing with the intractable nature of the talk show suggests that the pinpointing of ideology as a readable text is provisional at best. It cannot be discerned only from what is said. Ideological critique needs to consider other dimensions, most notably the very flow and passage of concerns. This is an instance in which the faculties of context are fleetingly exercised, where the focus of ideology is vague. Most significantly, then, the politics of these programs needs to be figured with respect to the rapid exhaustion of concerns and crises and with the observation that the only assured and recurring element is the talk show's *affective constitution.*

Evidence, Bodily Display, and Crisis in the Making

The chair was real because it hit Geraldo Rivera on the shoulder. The wildly swung punch was real because it broke Rivera's nose. Hence, the anger, the passion, the racism, and the out-of-control youth were all real. On an episode of *Geraldo* in which the invited guests included black activist Roy Innis and white supremacist youths, a fight broke out that spread to include studio audience members and the host. One of the principal participants of the fight, Innis, had already been involved in a minor altercation on *The Morton Downey, Jr. Show,* in which he pushed another guest, Reverend Al Sharpton, backward in his chair to the ground. The fight on *Geraldo* was much more spectacular: more participants, blood, and the chaotic destruction of a television studio. In short, it was ideal news and an occurrence rarely seen outside of professional sports: the brawl.

Of all the possible aspects of the incident, it was the movement of that chair through the air as well as the swift, frenzied motion of the fist and its contact with Rivera's face that made this event spectacular. A demonstration of the issue in question, of young hatemongers, that agitated and violent contact brought together previously dispersed elements: youth gone wild and the reporter as defender of a "free" United States. Rivera later commented, "These racist thugs are like roaches who scurry in the light of exposure" ("Geraldo Rivera's Nose Broken" 1988, B3). Fascistic youth becomes unavoidably apparent; Rivera as a moderator/ animator, whose role is to confront and challenge as well as mediate, is the casualty of this particular struggle. The evidence of Geraldo's broken nose condenses the activities of reporter/participant and a conflict of passions, of generations, of political agendas, of races, in a single location.

Interestingly, this now-famous episode broke few codes of the genre. We might initially assume that such actual violence, unforeseeable and uncontrollable, would shatter the propriety of this cool medium. Instead, the fight fit perfectly. It was spontaneous and immediate, a form of "eyewitness news." The fight slid neatly into those powerful connotative aspects of the omnipresence of television—unscheduled, impromptu, *live.* Talk shows are always in part a controlled breakdown of the audience/guest distinction; the riot is but a step further. The host is precisely to act as instigator, drawing out stories and, most important, emotions that would otherwise remain unspoken. And the blood on Rivera's face and on his shirt marks his incursion as an undaunted investigative journalist. It announces the dangers of getting too close to a social crisis (fascistic youth is of central concern here and, contrary to the billing, not racism) and the necessity, the civic duty, of doing so. The blood marks that encounter; the blood is news and provides evidence of the issues addressed. The crisis is there because Rivera is there; see him bleed.

Given that the codes were not broken, Rivera had little alternative but to proceed with the show ... and then the taping of two more! The blood and his broken nose conspicuously display his mettle and the social significance of his intrepid enterprise. This is not to trivialize the incident. In many respects, it was a watershed moment for trash television. Various forms of news media now reported concern about the sensationalized forms of television reportage. Not surprisingly, even *Geraldo* reinscribed the incident in the episode "Has TV Gone Too Far?" In this incident lies the ontology of the television talk show, as Michael Sorkin puts it, "the declaration 'It is, it is, it is, it is'": speech and bodily display. The whole apparatus of these shows consists of enunciations explaining the emotive demonstrations. Geraldo Rivera's standard demand on his guests, particularly after a trying or powerfully personal experience, is "Describe what you are feeling." The host is our guide to the revelation and presentation of emotions. In the environment of talk show television, no single topic stands over any other. Instead, the display value of emotions is the most significant evidential aspect, and this in turn points to the central importance of the confession, the essence of the ideology of the performance of confession.

No single concern or issue seems to matter differently; everything matters, everything, that is, that elicits a passionate response. What is central is not the particular issue but the emotional intensity; a response, either positive or negative, needs to be elicited. Or at least there is the drama of emotionality, which discloses the importance of the signifiers of tears and hysteria, disgust and intense interest. And the discursive space of the talk show allows the audience to witness this; furthermore, with generic pretensions toward the disruption of the differentiation of the guest and the audience, the appeal furnishes a space of participation, one based largely on empathy. The topics themselves recede, particularly if the programs are viewed in their strips or across shows. The constant, the continuum, is the emotive response.

The framing of the show within a topic, the background information provided, and the interpretive activity of the host all work to provide a structure in which the emotive responses can be comprehended. The emotional demonstrations are remarkably similar; yet they are taken to indicate various conclusions and preoccupations. Emotional displays are politicized as they are linked to concerns and interests. Thus, a central aspect of the ideology of the performance of confession is a politics of empathy. Such a politics has to do with the irrefutable testimonial power—the power of the confession—of an individual's experience, of guilt, errors of judgment, errors of conscience, lapses of morality, and so forth. Because empathy does not operate on a rational level, such a politics cannot be refuted on the level of logic. A politics of empathy mobilizes issues such that they can be articulated with positions and agendas. It always provides an incontestable site of evidence, bound and assured by the mark of the experiential.

The emotional displays of the talk show possess a noticeable mobility. Relocated easily in various contexts and in relation to vastly divergent concerns, the indisputable fact of passion and compassion seems to be a basic thread of extension. Issues and concerns enter and depart rapidly, though not thoroughly, mined for their affective import—strip-mined, so to speak. The energy of emotive investment conversely matches the exhaustion of this substitution, of this topographical investigation. The fetishization of the topic itself over the investigation collapses the possibilities of critical examination into the exhibition of those who have been there. Topics begin to be indistinguishable, for they garner identical responses; the residual effect is precisely the affective. What remains, episode after episode, day after day, is that this (issue, cause, concern, problem) is worth caring about. It states that people, these people, care about the difference between moral and amoral, guilty and innocent, victim and perpetrator, normal and deviant. Talk shows are bound to the spectacle of the investment in those differences, in the display value of things that matter to people.

Confessions must be guaranteed as authentic. As noted in the previous chapter, signs of emotional involvement must be visible to certify the testimony. This is no different on the talk show, where the accounts enunciated must be demonstrably legitimate to carry any weight. There is a certain authoritative quality that accompanies personal experience and encounters with a topic of interest. Nonetheless, this prerogative is assured through the display of the presumed marks of that encounter. Hence, we witness a certain preoccupation with the *bodily displays* that accompany the spoken testimonies and narratives. They attest to the authenticity of the emotional trespasses of the talk show host and to the actual passion of the response. Bodily displays provide a certain evidential text, one that the talk show fetishizes and prizes. Most effective are tears, which appear with startling frequency, yet are still languished. The response typically involves a reverential pause—usually of mock respect—silence, and a slow zoom. It is not uncommon for the host's hand to appear in shot to provide an encouraging squeeze on the shoulder, implying, "I know, we all know, we understand and empathize. This is hard, but please continue. Your tears let us share your experience with you. And we need that, we need to know ... to know that this matters to you." Tears verify the emotional display, and in turn this evidential quality of the authentic bodily exhibition is the confirmation of the topic at hand, its warrant for consideration.

The least mediated moments—crying and, rarer, bleeding—attest to a certain invisibility of television. The tearful, confessing guest makes the cameras vanish. There is always a certain inappropriateness to such displays, to "make a spectacle of oneself." Mary Russo (1986) writes that this is particularly true of women in patriarchy, where the "excess" of the female body is a carnivalesque spectacle. The daytime television talk show uses the "femaleness" of its confession-performance to capitalize on the entertainment value of this form of carnival, presenting women in trauma or extreme hilarity, women with "out-of-control" sexualities or criminalities. An elusive and indecorous spectacle of masculinity is also fetishized: male tears. Simultaneously inappropriate and always applauded as a cathartic shattering of the yoke of masculinity, male tears seem to attest profoundly to the experience and the significance of their enunciation. In the demonstration of the new male sensitivity, once again is the fulfillment of the talk show's confessional promise.

Morton Downey's reenactment of the story of the preppy murder feeds on the audience's morbid curiosity. Could Robert Chambers's story be true? Is what he described physically possible? Though these questions provide a vague impetus for the reenactment, it would be mistaken to assume that Downey's performance has anything to do with shedding light on a perplexing crime. Instead, his own bodily display, hands bound by panties and a woman squatting on his chest, assembles a text that runs parallel to that of the actual murder. Certifying the Chambers confession, making the story of the crime inseparable from the crime, and further complicating the difference between display and evidence—between the telling and the tale—Downey's performance lifts the murder to the realm of entertainment. There Chambers's performance-confession and Downey's bodily display are equally incontrovertible. Their evidential nature is mutually assured, one authorizing the other.

Rivera pisses into a jar for a live, and discreetly on-camera, drug test. His urine is "clean." He passes the test. In tandem, he authorizes a naturalization of the procedures and objectives of such policing tactics. Geraldo Rivera's urine: It is as real as it gets.

The Domestic and Crisis-in-Process

Ellis (1982) describes television's normative confirmation of the domestic as one of "citizenship." He sees the "citizen" of television's direct address as being roped into a position of conformity. It is a sort of group pressure of and in domestic isolation that accomplishes this. On this, Lynn Spigel (1988) describes the "installation" of the television into the home and reveals the way it constructed certain ideas about American domesticity, and the role of women therein, through advertisements and formal aspects of the programs themselves. But contrary to Ellis's ideas, the contradictions of the daytime television talk show hardly suggest conformity. Although the material and structurally enforced condition of domestic isolation, most pronounced for women during the day, remains intact, the talk show's involvement is more than simple reinforcement of that condition. For though its mode of address is clearly domestic, presuming an audience of primarily women in the home, it most frequently involves a process of estrangement from that environment. Whether it is the discussion of such frivolities as "When Your Daughter's a Lousy Mother" on *Oprah* or more sensationalized topics such as "The Murderer Next Door" on *Geraldo*, domestic space is the location of trouble and disruption. Strangely, domestic isolation becomes a promise; instead, there is a perpetual invasion of that space of supposed sanctuary. The domestic is far from being equated with the necessarily normal and secure; rather, the premise of the talk show rests upon a pathology of the everyday and an exposition of the "ordinary" threats of domesticity. The community addressed consists of a seemingly complicated and unsettled formation of domestic activity. And, of course, one of the most unsettling elements is youth in crisis.

An episode of *Geraldo* entitled "Children Who Kill Other Children" aired in September 1989 and began with the following introduction by the show's indomitable host located in a studio control room:

> You don't need me to tell you we live in an increasingly violent society; one in which it's become almost commonplace to talk about the latest, most dreadful crime committed in the neighborhood. But as horrified as we are, nothing, no crime is as sickening as one committed against a child. But what happens when the perpetrator, when the *murderer,* is also a child. That's what today's program is about. You'll soon

be hearing some pretty tough stuff. So before we begin, I want to suggest strongly parental guidance. This one may be about kids but it is strictly for adults only. Okay.

(Credit sequence, then Rivera in the studio)

It is a tragic reality of modern life that most of us have heard about, or maybe even know, a youngster who has been killed, either by accident, parental abuse, *even by random murder*. But increasingly we are hearing of children who are murdered *by other children* in gang fights, drug wars, or just for the fun of it. Just for the fun of it.

This opening is typical of the scope of talk shows, whose worldview is firmly entrenched in the sensibility that "we live in an increasingly violent society." In fact, a brief local advertisement, "Teens and Satan, on the next *PM Magazine*," precedes this introduction—a report that, one and a half hours after the conclusion of this particular episode of *Geraldo*, referred to some of the same incidents and reiterated identical concerns. As affirmed by Rivera's introduction, without exception talk shows suggest the possibility of the viewer's own encounters with the concerns, violent or otherwise, in question. Troubled and troubling youth are everywhere. The crimes are "committed in the neighborhood," where we "may even know" of someone affected. The issues' proximity to the domestic, or the possibility of direct encounter with the threats under consideration, importantly implicates the viewer and intends to interest in this manner. The talk show addresses a particular community, one composed of people who recognize the probability that certain hypothetical dangers may be directed toward themselves or their neighbors. This particular quality of social disorder is a distinctive aspect of the citizenship of the talk show. The suggestion that an epidemic of youth in crisis is evident, that the incidents referred to are not isolated, and that their increasingly frequent occurrence cannot be ignored all sanction the program's prurient interest and investigations. Imbued with this form of authorization, the talk show engages in an intractable activity of sounding alarms concerning contemporary youth.

Both the official and "unofficial" witnesses and participants present ample evidence of the crisis. The signs of crisis are but mentioned and are drawn from diverse situations such as drug use and statutory rape. As such, not what is happening but that *it is happening to young people* marks its stature as a broad social concern and potential panic. Here youth is a condensation point that affords various practices the mercurial capacity to ignite popular distress. A social disturbance is always more deeply felt when youth is a participant.

And the crisis in the "Teens in Crisis" episode of *Oprah* is not that of teens in general, but of youth in "aberrant" family situations. The show documents the stories of "teen victims" who consequently become involved in a broad range of other crimes. This social cycle of transgression is traced back to the family. For youth *always* appears in relation to the social institution of the family. The family acts as guardian and ideological model. When a young person begins to speak, or begins to confess, the activities of the immediate parents are lodged in the subtext and often emerge in a central position. As the runaways indicate, when youth does not figure in the family in the appropriate manner, there are the makings of a social crisis.

The talk shows in question are invariably about social concerns and the identification of threats and crisis. In this way, transgressions and criminal activity are staple preoccupations even when lighter topics are addressed. To illustrate, May 1989 saw such topics as "Mexican Satanic Cult Murders,"[3] "Mothers of Murderers," "Children of Affairs," and "Mother/Daughter Reunions" on *Oprah;* "Babysitters, Baby Killers," "Wild Kids," "Kids Visiting Moms in Prison," "To Mom with Love," and "Execution of Innocence" on *Geraldo;* "I Was Gang-Raped," "Child Stars ... Fame, Fortune Failed," "Siamese Twins," and "Childhood Sweethearts" on *Sally;* and "Children Not Worthy of Kindergarten" on *Donahue.* The programs move among the soft topics ("Mother/Daughter Reunions"), the freakish ("Siamese Twins"), and the criminal ("Babysitters, Baby Killers").

Perhaps most striking is the frequency of the family, and more particularly youth, as an imprecise focal point from which diverse concerns spin out. In this way, these shows seem to point to a "new traditionalism" (see Probyn 1993). And yet this new traditionalism is peculiar because it has gone hand in hand, and perhaps is fundamentally located in, the pathologization of the nuclear family. This is evident in diverse contexts and does not refer solely to the talk show. Yet, most distinctly, everywhere the talk show looks, it finds abhorrent circumstances and responds with alarm. Nothing, no corner of public or private life, is invulnerable to the unsettling changes of contemporary existence. The broad diffusion of this sensibility—a crisis without a single location, mobile and mutable—lends substance to the proposition of a crisis-in-process, one in which an array of events can be articulated. But, most certainly, as an itinerate locus of consternation, the family seems to be particularly susceptible. What is closest and most sacrosanct is also the location of the most terrible violence and horrors. Never has there been more talk of incest, child abuse, wife battery, marital rape, and so on. And though these concerns did not originate there, they have come to roost in the daytime talk show as central preoccupations. Even when they are not the explicit focus, they often surface in various forms during the course of diverse discussion topics and not infrequently as a litany of contemporary concerns. This pathologization engenders a dual effectivity, on one hand, revealing previously hidden violence, particularly against women and children, and, on the other, becoming easily articulated with an agenda of the qualities of the *normal* family.

Equally fundamental is the delighted detailing of the sick and sickening. There is always the promise of "some pretty tough stuff," as Geraldo Rivera states, something unusual with more than a hint of the interdicted. And insomuch as the topics and events covered are slightly out of the realm of the acceptable, there is a tendency toward the inexplicable, toward those baffling incidents that have no inherent sense. The most heinous of crimes, those reveled in by talk shows, are those that are beyond the comprehension of the "normal" mind: "random murder" and crimes in which the only apparent motive is "just for the fun of it."

Nothing threatens and titillates more than the prospect of the insoluble transgression, one that can be debated, reworked, solved, then re-solved endlessly.

In short, the mobile nature of evidence on the daytime talk show, in particular the display value of the confession, guides the articulation of social concerns. Although no representation or ideological position is guaranteed, there is a logic that negotiates the introduction, placement, and response to topics, issues, and events. Thus, we find an environment in which no single concern is given precedence over a myriad of others, though there is a general and diffuse presumption of social crisis and moral panic. An endless host of accidents guides the deployment and cultural work of the texts of a moral panic. Youth, as a key site of scrutiny, is frequently deployed to elicit interest, shock, and fear. The irrefutable evidence, and the affective power, of the performance of confession assures the treatment of youth as that which threatens and as that which is failing.

7

The Body by the River: Youth Movies and the Adult Gaze

When the cultural practices of contemporary American youth are not ignored, they are interpreted as nihilistic and self-destructive. Adults remain ignorant and confused about what kids do and think. This makes them hostile and mistrustful.

—**Donna Gaines,** *Teenage Wasteland*

Six years before Nicholas Ray directed *Rebel Without a Cause* (1955), he made the original "live fast, die young, leave a good-looking corpse" film, *Knock on Any Door* (1949). Humphrey Bogart plays an attorney, Andy, who defends a young punk accused of robbery and of killing a police officer. Even though Nick "Pretty Boy" Romano, played by John Derek, admits that he committed the robbery, he contends that he is innocent of murder. And his lawyer believes him, having also lived in the slums and only just missed leading a life of crime himself. As the lawyer makes his opening statement to the jury, the film uses flashbacks to tell the story of Nick's short life, from his struggling immigrant childhood to the trial. The film suggests that were it not for his absent father and a string of traumatic events, including witnessing the brutal murder of a friend while at reform school, Nick might have avoided the recidivism and the desperate anger that rule his existence. When Nick finally breaks down on the stand and confesses to having killed the cop, his lawyer, utterly devastated, enters a plea of guilty and asks for the mercy of the court. "Keep the boy and civilize the boyhood," he says. "Yes, Nick Romano is guilty. But so are we, and so is society." After all, he argues, "knock on any door" in the poverty-stricken areas of the United States and a story similar to Nick Romano's could be told. Despite Andy's passionate plea, the jury decides to have Nick executed.

By the late 1940s, the "blame the home environment" thesis of delinquency prevalent in films about youths, a thesis that had guided the initial formation of the juvenile delinquency genre, had become quite conventional and was falling out of vogue. Warner Brothers originally popularized this cinematic "environmentalism" in its "Dead End Kids" movies. Other studios, such as Columbia, the producers of *Knock on Any Door,* soon emulated them. Under the moral imperatives of the Motion Picture Production Code, this theme provided a convenient and safely liberal way to describe the causes of juvenile delinquency without pinpointing specific social problems or surrendering the ever-important assumption of the innate "goodness" of the child. Though traces of this continue, *Knock on Any Door* marks a certain exhaustion of the genre's environmentalism. In fact, Peter Biskind (1983) suggests that this was one of the last films to capture this particular vision of juvenile delinquency.[1] He argues that with this film, the portrayal of delinquent teenagers shifted from the criminal to the sick. However, it would be misleading to assume that the environmentalist solution to the origins of youth criminality disappeared. Its substantially appealing perspective, one that demonstrates concern, even alarm, while being a safe and nonthreatening social critique, remains an easy narrative device providing quick and acceptable explanations to complicated situations. Nevertheless, by 1949 a shift was clearly in process, a shift to the more general boredom of the suburbs and an emphasis on generational disjuncture.

The final scene of *Knock on Any Door* portrays an unrepentant Nick, still angry and frustrated, fully cognizant of the inescapable life he has been forced to live, and not fearful that it is about to be put to an end. Andy, despairing the outcome, recognizes that nothing could have been done, either during the trial or at any point in Nick's life. Nick is the tragic product of a rapidly urbanized society, one consisting largely of immigrant families torn from their ancestral home and displaced in the city. Modernity tears families apart, with predictable casualties. Andy makes a final promise to Nick to help boys in similar situations before they become involved in serious crime and waste their lives. The last shot of the film shows Nick walking down a long corridor to the electric chair. We watch this over the shoulder of his lawyer.[2] In the distance, just before the last set of doors through which he will pass, Nick stops and gently shakes his escorts aside. He pulls a comb from his pocket and fixes his hair and then continues down the corridor, pushing open the swinging doors and walking into bright whiteness. Andy turns away.

Embedded in this final shot is a complex recognition of the possessor of the gaze. For with few exceptions, it is always the case with youth films that the point of view is adult; the films concern an adult perception of the lives of the young. Two criteria determine the measure of a youth film's authenticity: the extent to which a film *connects with youth,* being taken up as speaking with some resonance to or for youth; and the manner in which a film *cautions adults about youth.* In both cases, the film remains ultimately an adult perspective. Filmic representations of youth depend upon generic conventions. The prospects of breaking these,

particularly by youths, are remote. Admittedly, the question of the audience's nego-
tiations with film complicates the meaning of film conventions; I am not arguing
that youth films are inauthentic or outside the true experiences of youth. Rather,
what is interesting is how the recognition of certain films as more authentic than
others transpires. The point here is that the apparatus of film is such that when we
begin to speak of youth films, either intended for a young audience or about
young people, we are also speaking of the perspective of the adult as it views the
"not-adult." In short, the youth movie is rife with the gaze of the fully socialized.

In *Knock on Any Door*, the lawyer tells Nick's story. And the final scene seems to
be an overt recognition of this, though not necessarily a critical one. Nick is about
to die; yet he still wants to assure that he is presentable. He combs his hair before
his lawyer. But this is done at a distance, so it is unlikely that he does it for his lawyer specifically and certainly not for his anonymous escorts. Instead, it is a moment of male narcissism and an acknowledgment of a general gaze, an imprecise
observing mechanism that will reach and affect him even in death. Nick, whose
entire life has been recounted for him by others, does something for himself. Even
so, as we watch with Andy over his shoulder, we know that Nick is being watched.
In his situation of complete powerlessness he performs the only action still available to him: He preens and moves in that look. He poses.

Hebdige (1988) reads this impulse in youth's fascination with style. In "posing,"
Hebdige sees particular strategies of resistance available to disenfranchised youth.
The same cannot be said of the representation just described above. Nick moves
in the scopic operations of the adult. This moment speaks of the adult, that is, of
what is seen in the young. This particular instance of posing is not resistance,
though it could be agitated and empowering. It is not oppositional, though it
could be nihilistic. For the adult, it is one more example of wasted energy, narcis-
sistic and purely consumptive. Filmic representation does not lend itself well to
what Hebdige reads as youth's expressive "hiding in the light." Instead, a reading
of similar film moments tells of the "light," of the machinations of the adult-eco-
nomic gaze as it constructs the young as "that which is watched." Unlike
Hebdige's claims, Nick's final pose does not concern the practices of youth; it has
to do with what the adult sees youth doing. And the response to the perceived
abandon and carelessness of youth, the empty rebellion of narcissism, is to turn
away. Another lost one, but, as Andy promises, there are many others to be saved.

This adult gaze engages the double connotative force of youth: that youth is
troubled and needs the knowing guidance of the world of the adult, the world of
economic productivity; and that youth is troubling, harboring the potential to
disrupt the "smooth reproduction of real life," to employ Engels's phrase. Andy
looks on as his fallen client casually strolls to the electric chair, thus furnishing a
clear perspective from the inside looking out. Andy is powerless to affect the situation; Nick's fate had been written long before. The shot speaks of the blameless circumstances that disturb "normal" childhood. Despite the necessary presence of
the concerned adult gaze, something went wrong with Nick. As inconsequential

as his interest ultimately was in this case, Andy assures us that there exists a dutiful necessity to attempt to save the youth. The final shot does not expose the futility or impotence of the disciplinary gaze of the adult. Instead, it sadly chronicles the betrayal of Andy's faith in Nick's innocence, the betrayal of the adult by youth.

This is an example of the operations of that adult gaze and its patriarchal function as it attempts to replicate the qualities of the economic social. Here the underlying logic of how youth acts as a point of conjuncture is partially revealed. Youth movies are an important site at which to discern this quality because at some level they always involve the manner in which the adult sees youth—that is, the disciplinary gaze of the adult. Ultimately, this leads to an understanding of the enticing nature of the spectacle of wasted youth, of youth gone wild. This can be explored through a discussion of youth movies, most specifically Tim Hunter's *River's Edge* (1987).

Discourses of the Adult in Youth Films

Youth films are complexly implicated in the historical constitution of youth in crisis. Even though they are about the problems of the young or about how the young are a problem, motion pictures in general have been seen occasionally as problems themselves. Periodically, there are moments of extensive cultural attention to the potentially detrimental effects of the representations of youth *on* youth. This was evident as early as 1933, when the Payne Fund completed comprehensive research on the effect of movies on young people. In various capacities, and in aspects as diverse as children's sleep (Renshaw et al. 1933) and manners of dress (Blumer 1933), the project found that movies have a profound impact on youth. Of particular interest was the proposed relationship between the content of violent films and juvenile delinquency. Henry James Forman (1933, 195) writes, "Entertainment like gangster and crook pictures in such neighborhoods [of high delinquency] appears as nothing less than an *agent provacatuer*, a treacherous and costly enemy let loose at the public expense." The overarching conclusion is that at some level movies play an educational function, where the "new and strange" life experienced by the adolescent is explained through glimpses of adult behavior in film (Blumer 1933, 194).

Since then, this perspective has governed the perceived relationship between media and young audiences, becoming particularly prevalent in the mid-1950s. One significant example was *Blackboard Jungle* (Richard Brooks, 1955), which, despite its content of concern for contemporary teenagers, was taken to be a threat itself. More recently, this has been expressed rather predictably about the work of African-American filmmakers. Spike Lee's *Do the Right Thing* (1989) and *Malcolm X* (1992), John Singleton's *Boyz N the Hood* (1991) and *Poetic Justice* (1993), and Mario Van Peebles's *New Jack City* (1991) all became the topic of public commentary as to whether these films incited violence in young audiences. With anecdotal evidence at best, and often with none at all, the fact that they were films by African-Americans, that they would appeal to African-Americans, and that they were set in urban African-American communities was sufficient cause for alarm for a predominantly white press. Although the question of the consequences of violent imagery is a topic of ongoing debate, it is instructive to observe when a certain "obviousness" is presumed. Here it is not the imagery per se but the black and young and, interestingly enough, the black cultural producer that strike a note of worry for American moral authorities.

Youth problems in film and youth films as problems weave an intricate discursive pattern that complicates any discussion on the topic; the representation of juvenile delinquency, depicting the consternation of the adult world, becomes the focus of scrutinizing operations for the films' own implication in the very crisis of which they speak. The representation of the deviant becomes deviant representations. And this shift is most often propelled by the popular political context, having less to do with the film than with the discursive conjuncture in which it comes to be located.

The abundance of films specifically for teenagers in the 1950s reflected changes in the demographic makeup of the United States. This is the focus of Thomas Doherty's *Teenagers and Teenpics: The Juvenilization of American Movies in the 1950s* (1988). He indicates four types of "teenpics" that coalesce around 1955: the rock and roll teenpic, the juvenile delinquent movie, the horror teenpic, and the clean teenpic. These categories help capture the scope of concern and the various generic conventions that define these films. But as with any such typology, it misleads as well.[3] Most notable here is that separating, for instance, the juvenile delinquent film from the clean teenpic conceals the congruous elements. There are particular connotative forces that facilitate the filmic conventions of the teenpics and make them cohere to varying degrees. Doherty detours around a debate about what constitutes a genre by defining it simply as "clusters of seemingly similar films" (p. 10).

It is most certainly the case that there has been a thorough juvenilization of American film.[4] In the present context, it is difficult to point to an aspect of American cinema that is not touched by the youth market. The ratings system once was a way to designate the audience, but home videotape easily circumvents that intention. It is quite common for an R-rated film to become popular with young teenagers. Equally, the market demographics of the average moviegoer have decreased in age over the past ten years; audiences are now centrally made up of teenagers on weekends. In fact, not too long ago "adult film" referred to pornography; currently it is employed to designate a film that is not specifically attempting to capture a youth audience. It is now difficult to talk about teenpics as a genre because of the juvenilization of virtually every genre.

Here the analysis concerns the highly abstract notions of adult and youth, but these always have material consequences. As a cogent player in popular discourse, filmic convention at once contains the culturally predominant representations of youth while evoking possible shifts and ruptures. The omnipresence of the adult gaze is the first and founding consistency of youth films. What, then, does the adult gaze see youth doing? To begin with, wherever it resides, the presumed distressed and disturbing qualities of youth taint the representation. Even the cleanest of the clean teenpics still bears this feature; the seeds of the uncontrollable persist. Youth itself indicates dis-ease by its very presence. It ostensibly requires no further explanation; the action and conflict that ensue can always be reliably understood "because the characters are young," though the exigencies of narrative furnish some response.

In films about youth, we see roughly five possible explanations for their contentious nature. First, there are those films that indicate the environment of economic depravity, usually associated with some failure of the nuclear family or cultural displacement, as the central precipitator of delinquency (e.g., *Knock on Any Door*). Second, some films focus on a general social apathy and boredom, usually in the context of the spoils of middle- or upper-class life (e.g., *Less Than Zero* [Marek Kanievska, 1987]). In this way, while continuing to implicate nuclear families, they make it possible to see the abuse of class power as a cause. Third, occasionally, though not frequently, there is the suggestion of genetic causes of delinquency. Here the child is just born bad, and the problem is beyond the influence of anyone (e.g., *The Bad Seed* [Mervyn Le Roy, 1956]). This theme is not prevalent, perhaps because it subverts the cultural faith in the inherent goodness of the child. Fourth, demonic possession has become quite popular, and typically this is where one finds the sickest and most destructive youths (e.g., *The Omen* [Richard Donner, 1976]). Strangely enough, however, even these dark and horrific depictions tend to posit that the young are but empty vessels, innocent and unknowing, taken over and possessed by some malevolent being. In *The Exorcist* (William Friedkin, 1973), poor Regan is but a battleground for the struggles between Satan and the Catholic church. And fifth, there are the films that claim that a contentious youth *is* a normal youth, though most often it is the most banal delinquency that is depicted here (e.g., any of producer-director John Hughes's youth films). These films involve the formation of the "everydayness" of American youth. Not surprisingly, then, the representation becomes that of an overwhelmingly white, heterosexual, middle class.

These five filmic explanations for troubled youth provide the general scope of the representation of youth in American film. A further element of representational specificity is reference to the constitutive gaze of the adult; youth in film always in some manner calls out to the world of the adult. In this respect, youth films rest implicitly upon the discursive composition of the ideal adult viewer. In a documentary feature *James Dean, the First American Teenager* (Ray Connolly, 1975), Dennis Hopper provides a perceptive explanation of Dean's acting style by quoting Dean, "I've got Marlon Brando in one hand screaming, 'Screw you!' and Montgomery Clift in the other saying, 'Help me'" (quoted in Doherty 1988, 140). This is a deft description of two manners of the screen's depiction of youth. Film after film typically reiterates this tension between the anarchic and the misguided, between the angry and the pitiable. Even the true child inside the demon-possessed Regan of *The Exorcist,* in a moment of twisted anguish, manages to write "Help me" on her stomach. A cry to the adult, the plea is for that guiding hand that demonstrates the method of integration back into the realm of the normal youth, which in turn signifies the easy flow toward the adult. The contentious nature of youth, quintessentially depicted by Marlon Brando in *The Wild One* (Laslo Benedek, 1954), equally suggests the Otherness of youth, though here the cry is to repudiate the offerings of the adult. "What have you got?" is Brando's reply to a question concerning what he is rebelling against. This is youth as a danger to the ordered world of the adult, but it is still well within the bound of what is expected of the young, particularly male, white, and young.[5]

Both of these attitudes address the adult. "Screw you" and "Help me" reverberate as cries directed toward the abstract body, usually institutionally constituted, of the adult. Or put differently, the call is equally a recognition of what has the power to affect the lives of the young. And in this orientation, these cries are locked into an ideological dichotomy of age. As a point of antagonism or as a potential source of aid, the adult is the central position of the social order; it connotes the normative, the stable, and the economically productive. In this respect, the adult remains the primary location that defines the positions of Others; it carries the power to constitute the qualities of the limits of the social.

As a case in point, *The Breakfast Club* (1985), the first film of John Hughes that earned him some degree of critical success, begins with Simple Minds singing, "Don't You Forget About Me." A quote from David Bowie's "Changes" appears on screen declaring that "these children that you spit on ... are quite aware of what they are going through." The quote splinters like a breaking window, revealing the high school setting for the action. A group of students must attend a Saturday detention. As they arrive individually, short conversations with parents, the cars, and the clothing set up their character types. A domineering father in a pickup truck drives Andrew, the "jock." A Cadillac drops off Alison, the "basket case," who has no interaction with the driver, presumably one of her parents. The car speeds off abruptly. Bender, the "criminal," walks across the parking lot, arriving alone.

Their assignment for the detention is to write an essay about who they think they are. This request seems ironically cut off by the first moment of the film. The audience recognizes them as stock character types of youth movies: the jock, the juvenile delinquent, the brain, the princess, and the oddball. But during the course of their encounter, trapped in the library for the entire day, the arrangements presented so simply at the beginning of the movie break apart. The demonstration of discomfort with those roles culminates in one character's voicing of the ultimate fear: "My God! Are we going to be like our parents?"

The Breakfast Club was highly successful, finding an abundant teenage audience. Not surprisingly, however, the movie continually addresses the adult, from the opening theme song "Don't You Forget About Me" to the closing "You see in us what you want to see." The adult is embedded in every moment of the film as an absent addressee. The film operates like that autobiographical essay assignment, which in the end a single student writes for everyone. Both the film as a whole and the diegetic essay speak to the ever-present and diffuse authority of the adult. Clothed in the garb of their roles, the characters' conspicuous surfaces become recognizably flat. As the film substitutes itself as that essay, the drama of calling to the adult and the presentation of the incompatibility of those surfaces intrigue the youth audience. The film in this fashion begins to expose this discomfort with the hand-me-down stereotypes—ones constructed by generic conventions of teenpics—claiming that "each one of us is a basket case, a brain, an athlete, a princess, and a criminal." In the conclusion there is the suggestion that by Monday the shattering of those traits and the liberatory sense of release will be forgotten.[6] As Grossberg (1993, 193) writes of the film, the students "are all content to leave such moments of salvation and empowerment behind, to assume that they are unavoidably temporary and even worse, tainted." Even though the film is unambiguously about that struggle, it remains lodged in the gaze of the adult as an explanatory document about that discomfort, pleading for understanding.

Arguably, there are some films that may refer to an antagonistic attitude toward the adult and make a call for help but that reveal a certain *refusal* of the adult. As distinct from repudiation—the "screw you" attitude—which is still a moment constituted in the power of the adult, refusal does not recognize those powers. It carries the potential to evade the adult gaze. By providing the most significantly horrific of films about youth as the utterly unreachable, films of refusal usurp the discursive powers that act to designate a position for the normal youth. Doherty (1988, 237) comments upon the differences between the teenpics of the 1950s and those of the 1980s with the proposal, "If Jim Stark's [James Dean's character in *Rebel Without a Cause*] scream was 'You're tearing me apart!' the cry of the modern teen is 'You're leaving me alone!'" The latter still falls neatly into the "help me" tendency; instead, I suggest that the cry of refusal is "I'm alone, we're all alone, we will always be alone, leave us that way."

It is in this vein that I want to understand perhaps the most powerful youth movie of the 1980s, *River's Edge*. This film, in its depiction of the alienation and Otherness of contemporary American teenagers, is continuous with the history of youth films. It is emblematic of the machinations of adult authority and of the indeterminate grasp on the certainty of that operation. But it also demonstrates the attributes of this historically specific moment, where refusal is the last instance of both community and politics.

The Spectacle of the Living (Dead) Teenager

River's Edge is loosely based upon an event that took place in 1981 in Milpitas, California.[7] The film so disturbed the townspeople that they refused to let it be shown, which only meant that people had to drive to nearby San Jose to see it. In this respect, the film itself was news, with both *Newsweek* and *Variety* printing articles about Milpitas, the townsfolk's response to the film, and the accuracy of the film. For example, "Mark Fowlkes, 23, who was [the murderer, Anthony Jacques] Broussard's best friend and one of the teenagers who kept quiet about the murder, said he is waiting to see the movie on video cassette so that he can 'sit there and think it over' at home" (Abramson 1987, 25). For those from the area in which the original murder occurred, the movie entailed reliving the incident. And the popular response to the film also framed it as a document of the tragedy. For many, *River's Edge* was news not because of the nature of its depiction but because of the fact that the murder was fictionalized in a film at all.

Variety's review of the screening of *River's Edge* at the Montreal Film Festival proposed that "Tim Hunter's *River's Edge* is an unusually downbeat and depressing youth pic. It's peopled with a bunch of thoroughly unlovely characters, and it seems doubtful that many people will fork out money to spend time in their company" ("*River's Edge*: Review" 1986, 16). And it appears that distributors also believed this. After it was made on the relatively low budget of $2 million, with one month of shooting, a distributor could not be found for seven months, at which time Island Pictures picked it up (Barthel 1987, 26). With an advertising campaign that tried to cash in on the success of the unusual and disturbing *Blue Velvet* (1986), even in limited release *River's Edge* did remarkably well at the box office. Within a week of its national release, at only ninety-three screens, it pulled in more than $500,000 (Greenberg 1987, 3). Given this, though the film's initial target market was an art film audience—that is to say, an adult audience—it became particularly popular with teenagers. In short, *River's Edge* reached a strange mix of audiences: art film and mainstream, adult and teenage, popular and elite.

The film tells the story of a young man, Samson (Daniel Roebuck), who for no apparent reason kills a female friend, Jamie (Danyi Deats). He leaves her naked body and invites his friends to come and see what he has done. These teenagers (Figure 7.1) react in a confused and emotionless manner, not being able to grasp the tragedy of their friend's death and the reprehensibility of murder. One, Layne (Crispen Glover), tries to cover it up and help Samson escape, initially by hiding him at the home of a strange recluse, Feck (Dennis Hopper), a one-legged biker from the 1960s who had killed his wife years earlier. Others just ignore the situation but agree tacitly to keep quiet about the killing. This troubles one of the teenagers, Matt (Keanu Reeves), who eventually does report the crime to the police but becomes a suspect for doing so. To complicate things, the fact that Matt breaks this "code of silence" offends his younger brother, Tim (Joshua Miller), who then spends the last half of the movie trying to find and kill him.

By most standards, *River's Edge* is a flawed film with a confused tone and heavy-handed symbolism. Nonetheless, this movie contains some powerful moments of deadening shock. And the performances of the greasy-haired, decidedly unglamorous youths strike a strong chord for the film's realism, in particular that

Figure 7.1   *The spectacle of wasted youth: the cast of* River's Edge. *(© Island Pictures, 1986)*

of Keanu Reeves. The cinematography emphasizes gray and blue, giving a cloudy and slightly depressing ambience to the proceedings. This washed-out look, and the downplay of the potentially gorgeous environs of the Sierra Nevadas, makes for a very drab and oppressive setting and in the end provides a unique visual rendering of the vacancy and the affectlessness of the community. The mannered and hyperactive performances of Hopper and Glover, interestingly, contrast this and lend a large dose of the surreal and the comic to an otherwise naturalistic film.

The popular critical response found the movie to be, for the most part, mediocre at best. However, the film's cry that "the kids aren't alright" was seen to be important (Ansen 1987, 68). Critics from Pauline Kael (1987) to Vincent Canby (1987), virtually without exception, took *River's Edge* to be a significant and accurate document of disaffected and disturbed youth. For example, Canby wrote that the film is "about a society that's reached the absolute end of commitment to—or interest in—anything, set in a time without moral obligations, when the quick and the dead have at long last achieved the same body temperature" (p. 23).

When the film moves into the absurd, critics for the most part condemned it for violating the gripping realism. For instance, Crispin Glover's highly exaggerated performance was widely criticized as inappropriate in the context of the film's overall subdued ambience.[8] As a picture of youths in distress, and of their murderous potential, *River's Edge* was not seen with the same eye to the surreal as *Blue Velvet*, though it contains equally absurd moments and also frequently subverts conventions of realism. Indeed, critics praised *River's Edge* as a vision with the potential to incite adult concern for the seemingly alien youths in our midst.[9]

Some academic scholars assumed a similar stance. For instance, Jon Lewis (1992, 19) supposes that the film was "just a little too real for teenagers themselves." In fact, as a marker of its cultural currency, reports of other murders committed by youths employed *River's Edge* as a metaphoric reference point to describe the amorality and alien qualities of today's teenagers. For example, a front-page *Globe and Mail* article on a murder in British Columbia, in which a "code of silence" among teenagers kept the identity of a killer and the location of the body secret for eight months, drew comparisons not only with the Milpitas murder but also with the film version, (Wilson 1990). And in *The Preppy Murder Trial*, Taubman (1988, 112) suggests that the reactions of friends of Robert Chambers and Jennifer Levin actually predict some of the dialogue of *River's Edge:* "One young woman at Dorrian's declared herself a friend of both. 'We have to fight for Robert's rights,' said the friend, Norah Bray. 'There's nothing we can do now for Jennifer.' It was about a year before the same line would be heard in the film *River's Edge*." One film review made this connection explicit, claiming that *River's Edge* is "inevitably reminding us of the real-life drama of sex and violent death in New York's Central Park a year ago with Jennifer Dawn Levin and Robert Chambers" (Barthel 1987, 26).

My reading of *River's Edge* reveals the contradictions in the critical reception of the film. In the final analysis, the informal consensus in the film's reception could be seen as a way that critics and audiences alike dealt with an anomalous and, at a certain level, incomprehensible film. Despite the difficulty apparent in making sense of the film, possibly part of its appeal, a certain "dominant" reading about the terror of youth became evident.

Central to the structure of the movie, and to the suggestion of a macabre repetition of the events and sentiments depicted, is a formal mirroring or doubling. The opening sequence announces this. As the grainy image of the river behind the credits slowly bleeds into a clear resolution of the brown and gray landscape, the camera pans to look through the bars of a bridge. A child with an earring, Tim, whose gender is momentarily ambiguous, appears in close-up (Figure 7.2). A low angle shot shows this child reaching through the bars and dropping a doll into the river. From the point of view of the child, the doll falls into the water; the current carries it up out of frame. Tim walks across the pedestrian bridge to look at the river from the other direction. He hears a scream and looks through the bars to see Samson in the distance, staring across the river, sitting beside a naked, lifeless woman. Samson howls again. Tim cycles off into the mist, center screen, in an extremely symmetrical shot, the bars of the bridge perfectly balanced on either side. Next a medium shot of Samson shows him looking at the river from the bank. The camera pans to the corpse of the murder victim beside him, which is then

Figure 7.2 *Tim (Joshua Miller) in* River's Edge. *(© Island Pictures, 1986)*

.sectioned by close-up shots of her hands, feet, and face. A scene at a convenience store follows in which Tim tries to earn Samson's respect by stealing beer for him. "I saw you this morning," he says, with little concern. As Samson drives distractedly, appearing unaware of Tim's presence, Tim finds a pair of panties, presumably belonging to the murder victim. "Radical," Tim comments.

This opening sequence introduces two important elements. First, there is an association between the "death" of the doll and the death of the young woman. The introduction of Ellie, Feck's "girlfriend," a blowup sex doll, adds to this theme of the reduction of women to lifeless forms. Ellie, strangely enough, becomes somewhat of a central character who accompanies Samson and Feck and who is found abandoned, or "murdered," in the river at the end of the movie. The presence of "lifeless women" and their association with specific male individuals operate as a structuring principle of the society depicted. In effect, the subdued, silenced, and powerless female forms become forceful emblems of the constitution of patriarchal order. In fact, the film goes so far as to suggest that the presence of the lifeless woman is a necessary requirement for the experience of empowerment in patriarchy—that is, that against which the male characters are able to feel alive. Therefore, it is important that this touches a number of characters; in this respect, instead of being presented as an isolated instance, an aberration, this motif announces the sickening "necessity" of the powerless woman to the constitution of this numbed community. Like the confessions of Pierre Rivière and Robert Chambers, the terms of misogyny constitute the fundamental basis for expressions of masculine power and social stability.

Certainly the murder victim is the most prominent woman in the film. In the depiction of her death, Jamie appears to be almost complicit as she wordlessly, expressionlessly, and complacently looks at Samson as he strangles her. This severe demonstration of an absence of feeling matches Samson's unconcerned and unmotivated murderous actions; Jamie is apathetic about her own life, just as Samson is about his own. The presence of her body by the river acts as a persistent reminder of this. The camera returns to it and studies it, providing at once a cool sense of detachment and an unwavering confrontation with what should not exist, what should not have taken place. The highly stylized cinematography encourages a simultaneous response of repulsion and enticement; the image aestheticizes the body. The suggestion of necrophilia is unavoidably apparent; this play with taboo is assured when we discover that the now-naked body was fully clothed at the time of the murder. And the spectator soon becomes implicated as well; the image of the body lying there begs to be looked at with concern, horror, and desire. It is the ultimate expression of the waste of these young lives. The remains of this young woman that litter the banks of the river, to be joined by other bodies and dolls, remind us metaphorically of the marginal differences between the dead and the living (dead) teens. The aestheticized presence of the corpse is the spectacle of wasted youth, activating both terror and pleasure, danger and desire.

This doll/woman motif initiates a second element: the connection and almost complicity between Samson and Tim and later between Samson and Feck. The connections between the two murderers, Samson and Feck, is obvious; both are killers of women and find immediate affinity in each other. But there are moments in the film where Tim appears to be a miniature version of Samson's shapeless form, with a similarly murderous impulse. When Tim first returns home after "killing" his little sister's doll in the opening sequence, his older brother, Matt, chides him by saying, "You are stupid enough to pull a stunt like that, but then to go and brag about it." This is precisely what Samson does after his murder. Later when Tim feels that Matt has betrayed Samson, he steals a gun and hunts his brother down. Thus, the film presents a bizarre intergenerational continuity of psychotics and misogynists.

In *River's Edge* youth is not just a time of distress; it is a time of death: dead friends, dead families, and seemingly living dead youths. Jane Caputi (1988) provides an intriguing analysis in her reading and comparison of *Night of the Living Dead* (George Romero, 1968) and *River's Edge*. Both, she argues, concern "a 'psychic numbing' [that] prevails as one of the hallmarks of consciousness in the Nuclear Age" (p. 101). In reference to Tim Hunter's unrelenting examination of the murdered corpse, Caputi comments, "If that cold body is the screen emblem of psychic death in life, it is the aimless, unfeeling, and anomic teenagers who— through hyperkineticism (in one case) or generalized dullness—truly embody the emotional state of the undead" (p. 104). Caputi's argument is compelling; in the end, *River's Edge* is a horror film depicting a nightmarish realism, the world of the affectless, of deadened senses and lifeless movements. The teenagers of this film are a product of the fears voiced in films for the last fifty years and in public debate for the last hundred. What if our sons and daughters were so alienated from us that there was no possibility of leading them back into the realm of the normal? What if the promises of the next generation were abruptly cut off with no heirs apparent? The film presents an untenable situation in which the promises of a certain life do not hold or draw young people. That refusal presents an unprecedented challenge, for there is no longer the certainty of the reproducibility of the social order.

Consequently, it makes sense that the film depicts a parallel economy of exchange, trafficking in the usual contraband: beer, guns, drugs, and sex. None of the proceedings appears particularly anarchic; on the contrary, there is almost an ordered and routine manner in which the youths procure drugs; steal cars, guns, and ammunition; and so forth. They are remarkably successful in all their endeavors, and their inverted system seems, in an odd manner, to operate smoothly. But it is clearly a grotesque inversion of the ordered and sanctioned world of the adult. And, of course, those sorts of potentially utopian claims about alternative youth societies are subverted from the very beginning. After all, a young woman has been killed by a young man for no reason. Furthermore, it is significant then that all the youths appear guilty. This is an indictment of an entire generation.

The film ultimately concerns a supreme loss of affect. Most striking about this is the fact that *River's Edge* does not offer alternative, humanistic responses, such as empathy, as a possibility. On the contrary, the film depicts caring as equally futile, equally murderous, and quite possibly the very catalyst to the surrendering of emotion. There are two representatives from the 1960s who code that period as a time, perhaps the final moment, of passion: Feck and the history teacher, nicknamed Berkeley by the students. The teacher reminisces about his hippie days, the protests against the Vietnam War, and the opportunity to fight authority through direct conflict with police officers. When a student responds that "wasting pigs is radical" (referring to the word's 1980s definition as extreme and outrageous entertainment, not to its politically progressive connotation), the teacher sadly murmurs to himself that the class missed the point of the lesson and the rationale for the protests. After the murder, Berkeley is beside himself trying to elicit some response from his students. The best he can get is moral indignation and a sarcastic concern as to whether they will be "tested on this shit." The response of the youths involved is to cut class and wander around the river's edge, the murder scene.

Feck's role is similar, though it is significantly more integral to the film's complicated politics. Though he is introduced as a natural double of Samson, differences between the two emerge; each has an incommensurable psychopathic code of ethics (Figure 7.3). Samson's "you do shit and it is done, then you die" nihilism guides his directionless asocial behavior. He describes the extreme absence of motivation or emotional involvement when he talks of the murder. "She was dead there in front of me and I felt so fucking alive," screams Samson as he recounts the murder to Feck. This is the single moment of empowerment in the film, a terrible and sickening condemnation where the only possibility to feel is in the instance of a woman's death. It is done, and the sense of empowerment dissipates, and Samson is ready to die. "You could fry for this," says Layne. "Yeah," says Samson.

This lack of emotional involvement horrifies even the psychotic Feck. He insists that he killed his wife because he loved her, which gave his action some semblance of a rationale. In a brilliant instance of male hysteria, Feck is disturbed when Samson randomly fires Feck's gun into the night. "It's not something I shoot off without reason," he says. "It's got sentimental value." This sense of intangible value, of emotive and sexual association, eludes Samson. And this absence of affect terrifies Feck to the point where he feels he must kill his new friend, Samson. Feck explains this last murder by saying, "There was no hope for him. There's no hope at all. He didn't love her. He didn't feel a thing. I at least loved her. I cared for her." Affect may allow for a certain sense of meaning, but it does not provide any guarantees against psychosis.

One of the central oversights of critics was that while *River's Edge* depicts a deadened generation of apathetic and detached youths, it also casts off any romance associated with pathos. The film reduces feeling to the logic of a psychopath or to Layne's hyperactive fantasies. Layne's mania seems wildly out of place in the flat ambience of *River's Edge*.[10] But his inauthentic frenzy is a perfect contrast. For instance, the recognition that "it's like some fucking movie" unambiguously fuels Layne's ardor. With references to Chuck Norris, *Starsky and Hutch*, and *Mission Impossible*, Layne constructs a fictitious plot line in which a group of friends have their loyalties tested and must pull together to resolve an adverse situation. During his attempt to "save" the unconcerned and uninterested Samson—something he does unilaterally, having been unable to enlist the others into his fantasy—Layne makes cliché speeches about their situation. Talking to Samson and frustrated by his indifference, Layne says, "It's people like you that are sending this country down the tubes. No sense of pride, no sense of loyalty, no

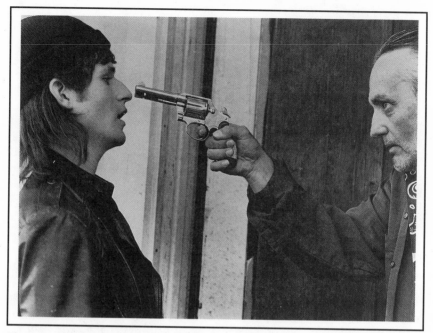

Figure 7.3 *Generational conflict: Feck (Dennis Hopper) confronting Layne (Crispin Glover) in* River's Edge. *(© Island Pictures, 1986)*

sense of nothing, man." Some of the other youths, unable to reiterate Layne's hyperaffective movie fantasy and cognizant of their inability to feel, also employ familiar movie representations to try to understand their numbed state. The fact that *Brian's Song* affected her more than the death of a friend puzzles Clarissa (Iona Skye). They think that maybe they will cry at the funeral. But the closing of the film once again presents the youths as unaffected as they file past the open casket of their friend with blank faces. As Janine Marchessault (1988, 43) puts it, "Death is just another pretty face in a world of images that derive their power from their pretense of reality. As the real is made unreal, the unreal becomes the only point of reference from which to comprehend lived experience." With the amphetamine-saturated Layne as the model, the claims to the experience of passion seem absurd; there is only the dream of emotional involvement, a very thin and dubious reverie. By the end of the film we discover that Layne did not really know Samson.

With a cynical view of pathos and a thesis affectlessness, *River's Edge* depicts a general alienation of youths *and* adults. In this respect, contrary to the popular critical reading, the film is not solely about youth in the age of Ronald Reagan. It concerns the thorough atomization of the post-1960s United States.

River's Edge presents the complete carnage of the traditional family by creating two universes of the young and the adult, each unable to reach the other. The adults in *River's Edge* exist almost exclusively in closed locations: Feck hiding for years in his home, the disembodied voice of Clarissa's mother calling from her bedroom, and Samson's simple aunt, helpless in her living room, wanting to have *Green Eggs and Ham* read to her. The youths peek in at this world through windows, through doorways, bewildered but unmoved. As Matt and Layne look in the window at Tony's house, they see their friend's father sitting alone in the dark, the blue light of the television flashing on him. In an absurd and unmotivated moment that is reminiscent of *Night of the Living Dead*, Tony's father sees the teenagers, gets his shotgun and shoots at them, as though these teenagers truly are the cannibalistic undead.

In this environment of division and isolation, only the youths move. They roam the wasteland of vacant areas, video arcades, and convenience stores. They are in constant movement, only returning to the oppressive environment of their homes to pick up drugs and sleeping bags. The teenagers choose to inhabit the spaces between the locations of the adult. The river's edge, a barren landscape looking more like a potential landfill site than a recreational area, draws them. *This place that is no place is theirs.* Here they can convene, escape, act as they please, and, most significantly, reflect upon the fact that they cannot feel. Once again, this has been an oversight in the film's reception: The teenagers are fully aware of their tragic inability to respond to the death of their friend, or to anything, in an appropriately "human" capacity. Beside the river, Samson screams about his murderous struggle to feel something. Matt and Clarissa discuss their stifled attempts to feel remorse. Clarissa and Maggie (Roxanne Zal) unsuccessfully try to call the police to report the murder, talking about how wrong the situation is but affirming that they have no way to conduct themselves any differently.

River's Edge, continuous with the history of youth films, unsettles the adult with that wily element of youth. But here the centrality of youth in the constitution of the adult issues forth with a certain necrophiliac drive. The scopic operation of the adult gaze, evidenced throughout the film but most pronounced in the cinematographic rendering of the murdered teenager, produces a confrontation with the *unheimlich*. Like Freud's discussion of the automaton in E.T.A. Hoffman's "The Sand-man," this proceeds further with the presence of the two dolls, the one Tim drops into the river in the opening sequence and Ellie, who also ends up in the river at the conclusion of the film.[11] These lifeless objects are mistaken for animate; there is a funeral for the first doll, and the characters address Ellie as though she is no different, no more or less sentient, than the others. And the collapse of the difference between the dead and the living (dead) teenagers is an even more significant rendering of this quality. *River's Edge* is at its most successful when it announces the profoundly ideological element of the desirous and frightening nature of youth in relation to the adult and *the gendering of this relation*. The anxieties that youth in crisis trigger in the adult world are alluring, even while that adult gaze tries to negotiate the reproduction of its economic and social order.

In conclusion, *River's Edge* associates its deadened youth with displacement and alienation, a life with little prospect for change or hope. At best, there is the possibility of a troubled fit in a stifling situation, as represented in different manners by Matt, Clarissa, and Layne. At worst, there is refusal, as embodied in Samson, Feck, and Tim. This is similar to what Jonathan Crane (1988) refers to as an "empowering nihilism," which is seen as a response to a condition of indifference and smothered opportunities. He argues that empowering nihilism is a way to "feel good" about one's powerlessness and disenfranchisement. Although there is a danger of masking the actual discomfort and frustration that are felt, nihilism is most certainly evident in *River's Edge* as a last moment of community for youth. The only thing shared is their concern about their care for nothing. This structure of experience provides a common ground for understanding the associations between youth and the distinctions from the adult. As Grossberg (1993, 196) puts it, "Youth is represented in terms of the experiential and affective consequences of inhabiting a certain place in the social order, of living everyday life according to someone else's maps." The question becomes, What does youth do when frustrated with those secondhand maps that no longer carry the weight they did in the past?

Refusal is one possible response. And this triggers the demonization of the young. However fantastic the representation, there is a general belief that something very serious has gone wrong with contemporary youth. *River's Edge* is a striking text in this vein, a unique depiction of a 1980s youth crime and its aftermath. As a portrait of youth in crisis, heightened by pretenses to telling the story of an actual murder, it voices the extreme anxiety of lost youth as a horror film. It depicts the young as the terrible products of a general disappearance of affect, of an order that rests on social atomization, and of a society whose patriarchal foundation requires the construction of the lifeless woman to assure its power. Despite a troubled and contradictory fit, the abatement of emotion seems to be a reasonable response for the youths. Equally, the film writes the adult as being as thoroughly atomized and zombielike as the young. It is astonishing, then, though perhaps not entirely surprising, that popular critics took *River's Edge* to be about the deadened contemporary youth *only;* even when it depicts the adult world with equal suspicion and concern.

The adult world crowds around the accident scene of contemporary youth, of youth in crisis, jostling and stretching to see the carnage. It is revolted, nauseated, by the casualties and by the young's supreme betrayal: their refusal of the promises of the world of their parents. But the gaze never wavers. Instead, it looks on with increasing precision, calculated to inspect the remains thoroughly. The allure of the young and wayward draws the gaze. There is a terrible intrigue that fuels the scopic desire: a pleasure in the discerned and known and a pleasure in the horrible failure of youth. This is the curiously provocative quality of the outside that *was to become the inside.* The efficacy of the crisis is manifold; in its wake, we see the attraction of ruin and the caution it suggests. Order has a key function: to reproduce itself. Youth in crisis, youth gone wild, is a central site in which this activity of reproducing order takes place. It involves the constitution of the qualities of the normal adult, the normal youth, and the relation between the two. The deviant youth is thus a crucial trope in the fabric of this relationship; it helps patrol the boundaries. And in all this attention, in the investment of such energy in this discursive project, the fetishization of the young, of its troubled and troubling nature, occurs. The psychic charges of the fetish incite that scopic drive. In the end, the least the young can do is leave a good-looking corpse.

8

The Spectacle of Wasted
Youth: A Felt Crisis
in the United States

The spectacle is not a collection of images, but a social relation among people, mediated by images.

— **Guy Debord,** *The Society of the Spectacle*

By 1990, curfews for minors had been established in a number of cities, including Detroit, Newark, and Camden. A court challenge overturned Washington, D.C.'s curfew, but a similar challenge in Iowa upheld the right of a local government to impose such restrictions. Atlanta passed a curfew law in November 1990 that would hold parents responsible if their children were under eighteen and were caught out after 11:00 P.M. on a weekday. The American Civil Liberties Union claimed that the law was a violation of civil rights and that it specifically targeted African-Americans (Smothers 1990).

If the infringement upon the lives of African-Americans specifically and youths in general seemed to be of little importance to those introducing such measures, so, too, was their effectiveness. There is no evidence that curfews have ever been successful instigators of parental responsibility. Nonetheless, the idea of surveillance of the young continued to attract public attention. In 1992, a Canadian company began to market a device that controls television viewing. It allows parents to regulate what and how much their children watch. TV Allowance is a computer that blocks off certain time periods to specified family members and keeps track of each child's viewing time. An individual code allots, say, fifteen hours per week of television viewing to the child. When that time is used up, the access code will no longer turn on the set. This, the company claims, frees up time for more educational activities. The product's marketing combines the popular images of television as monster corrupter, the delinquent child, and the absent parent. The problems of education, assumed a priori to necessitate control of television in the home, are substituted with a stratagem of surveillance. Given the obvious model for TV Allowance, are we to expect that chores will be exchanged for an increased time allotment? And are we to expect that the not-television time will be replaced with more so-called creative or educational activities, such as homework? As the company's president frankly admits, the objective is to "take the hassle away from parents and give the time management to the children" ("Home Unit" 1992, B1). The very idea of convenient surveillance is sufficient evidence of the device's contributions to the modern family.

Youth's complex relationship with popular culture as a lived and expressive domain is menacing because the uses of culture cannot be policed completely. In some instances, those uses are evidence of something greater than individual delinquency: crisis. In a front-page newspaper article (Szymczak and Sjostrom 1988, 1–2) reporting a multiple stabbing in a high school appears a photograph of the suspect's jean jacket. It is emblazoned with the image of a devil. According to the caption, the jacket is displayed by the police. It is more than evidence of musical taste, of subcultural membership, or of youth style. The jacket in its own way implicates the suspects and speaks the truth of youth crime in general.

Evading Ideology

Style as an expression of youth culture becomes one way to identify affiliations with "subcultures" and, by implication, with crime. Just as Jennifer Levin's "provocative attire" suggested her intentions to the popular press, concern has been expressed for the popularity of L.A. Raiders fashion. The links among Raiders gear, black style, and black crime immediately inspire worry that as Raiders gear proliferates, so, too, will the possibilities of youth crime (Goldin 1991). An interesting comparison is the Los Angeles program to help black inner-city youths through organized golf, as described in a *New York Times* article with the headline "Beckoned by the Greens, Not the Gang" (Lipsyte 1992). One wonders if part of the assumption is that the good, white sport can save the troubled teens from the influences of the bad, black sport and if there is a mandatory substitution of oversized football jerseys and Raiders baseball caps with plaid pants and white shoes.

Hebdige (1988, 35) writes, "Since the 1950s, the 'politics of youth' has been played out, first and foremost as spectacle: as the 'politics' of photogenic confrontations, of consumption and 'life style.'" In fact, Hebdige is referring to the ample presence of "American" style and attitude in British youth, that is, to a transatlantic cultural encounter. In the United States, postwar youth culture has been equally defined by its conspicuousness and visibility, though not in the manner of the spectacular subcultures described by Hebdige. At least since the late 1940s, American youth has been under the eye of public concern simultaneously as socially disruptive, consummate consumers, the unfortunate products of mass media, and the successors of advanced capitalism.

"Youth as mass market" has been central in forming postwar encounters with popular culture in the United States in general, often to the point of obscuring the distinctions between "popular" and "youth." The formation and striking vigor of the new mass youth culture had their own spectacular elements, most prominently located in the domain of cultural consumption. The rising market power of youth as consumers of culture meant that youth achieved a certain conspicuous position in popular culture. This involved the abundant visibility of the movements and desires of an entire generation as well as the spectacle of purchasing power and lifestyle consumption.

Youth culture contains all the appeal of that contentious time outside the adult as well as the pleasurable surveillance of "photogenic confrontations." At every turn, the culture demonstrates its fascination with the young and with "youthfulness." The taken-for-granted qualities of youth circulate and inflect the most remote aspects of contemporary existence. Even with increasing attention being placed upon our aging population, the image of youth still surfaces to define what the conditions of the aged should be ideally. Youth has been demonized *and* democratized, as though it is too important, too precious, too much fun, to be left to the young exclusively! Among other reasons, the 1980s manifestation of this democratization was precipitated by baby-boomers who, through their substantial disposable income, successfully defined a mobile and aging youth culture largely dependent upon the culture from their youth. As what has been popularly understood as youth culture itself ages, and as famous 1960s rock and rollers become grandparents, it appears that youth is a state that is openly available to everyone, any age. In this way, "real" youth, the unnameable Generation X, who by the mid-1980s were already no longer teenagers, become marked as doubly deviant: Not only are they young, but they also cannot compare to the youth culture as authenticated by baby-boomer desire.[1]

This image of the democratization of youth has led others to posit the demise of the category itself. One of the more distinct discourses to have arisen from this situation is the notion of a "disappearance of childhood." Its two most prominent pundits are Joshua Meyrowitz (1985) and Neil Postman (1982). Both in similar fashions argue that television in particular constructs a different relationship between the world of the adult and that of the child. They claim that in the past, children were sheltered from certain aspects of the world. Today television as a source of endless information and as a medium, unlike written material, that requires little prior instruction introduces the young to all of those previously hidden topics, including violence, sex, and a variety of other "adult" situations. For Meyrowitz and Postman, childhood means not being privy to certain secrets. With no forms of knowledge separating the child from the adult, the distinction blurs, and *both* realms disappear.

As discussed in Chapter 2, youth and childhood are historically specific creations. Therefore, their eventual demise should only be expected. However, Meyrowitz and Postman are too quick in making this cry. To begin with, to say that the young of the past led more sheltered lives than their contemporaries do is a dubious claim. Indeed, children had ample access to some "adult" knowledge, for instance, the world of employment or exploitation. Furthermore, the suggestion that awareness or exposure to sexuality came at a later age has little, if any, proof. Shakespeare's Romeo and Juliet, after all, were quite young. Nevertheless, the popularity of this discourse of disappearance of the specificity of youth is itself significant. It is yet another illustration of the shifting conception of contemporary American youth.

This shift in the meanings of youth has been linked up with many other developments, including perhaps most centrally the changing constitution of the family. Youth is a socially visible and mobile site. As the discussions on the performance of confession on the daytime talk show and the operations of the adult gaze in youth films show, ideas about crime and youth are spun out in diverse locations. For this reason, as indicated earlier, the politics of youth *is* the politics of spectacle.

Spectacle complicates ideological struggle. Spectacle by its very nature is more than the sum of its meaning effects and textual determinations. And these asignifying aspects of spectacle confound the crystalline bounds of ideology. This, however, is not to say that spectacle only refers to the visceral and the sensational. To say that there is something beyond meaning, something that defies the *precise* determinations of signification, does not suggest the evacuation of the political terrain. Guy Debord (1977) stresses that spectacle is a form of social relation and therefore that it concerns the structures of power. This is similar to Jean Baudrillard (1983), who expresses a certain fascination laced with lament for the loss of significatory difference. He characterizes this postmodern triumph of the image, the precession of the surface, as the confusion of the map with the territory. And the traveling partner of this confusion is an impossibility of politics.

Even though Baudrillard may conclude that the masses have "nothing to say to us" (p. 49) and that their "silence" is the extent of their political import, the popular remains the most significant political, if spectacular, battleground. In the present context, this is crucially important to a situation in which populist politics seems inseparable from a conservative agenda. In recent years, American politics has seen the articulation of a commonsense experience of crisis with a strategic project of social stability. Thus, given that spectacle involves a social relation that cannot be entirely reduced to ideology, a key political question surfaces: What resources are available for expression or contestation in the gap between the ideological and the asignifying aspects of cultural struggle?

In the introduction to the 1980 edition of *Folk Devils and Moral Panics,* Cohen criticizes the project of *Policing the Crisis* (1978) for being too obsessed with ideology: "At too many points ... the Centre's determination to find ideological closure leads them to a premature theoretical closure" (p. xxiv). True, Hall et al. seem in a rush to tie their observations to broad historical structures and end up providing a rather seamless version of a hegemonic crisis. The description of conjuntural relations is precisely the Gramscian project, one that necessitates analysis of specific contexts across levels of abstraction; thus, the authors take the local incident of mugging in the context of the formations of postwar British national hegemony. Yet Cohen is correct in noting the sense in which the *Policing the Crisis* project privileges ideological analysis.

Cohen's concept of moral panic, which primarily indicates the political purchase of public events, demonstrates similar inadequacies. In its traditional configuration, moral panic cannot read the residual consequences of the affect of fear and desire. Panic is visible and apparent. In this respect, moral panic is a form of secondary deviance, as discussed by Lemert (1972). Although Cohen criticizes Hall et al. for their "ideological closure," Cohen is also guilty of begging the question of moral panic by insisting upon its functional consequences. In the end, moral panic, as conceived by Cohen, always provides negative examples that demarcate the frontiers of the social order and little else.

In many ways, a prominent issue in cultural studies today is the indication and writing of what is *not* ideology. After the important project of politicizing everyday life—that is, the labor of uncovering the suffusion of social relations into the mundane and quotidian—the current ambition is to recuperate the possibility of the non-ideological. For instance, Hebdige (1987) describes a man on his street who harbors an intense affection for his car. This white Thunderbird is his only extravagance, one in which he invests time, energy, and money. Hebdige employs this example to demonstrate how such designations as "false consciousness" or "commodity fetish" cannot capture what this man feels. Something escapes and evades these condemnatory references, for they are unable to acknowledge the experience and energies invested in the object, which Hebdige goes so far as to argue actually rework the relations of production. It is this *sublime* consequence that is traceable but never entirely captured, at least in traditionally sociological approaches. For Hebdige, the sublime is similar to Julia Kristeva's *signifiance*, Roland Barthes's "third meaning" and *jouissance*, and Jacques Derrida's *aporia*. Among other things, they are all attempts to describe a moment of self-reflection on the part of the critic who admits that in all the investigations, analyses, and critical explorations into culture and texts, something is still unaccountable, something that confounds interpretation and staves off epistemological certainty.

Colin Mercer (1986) makes similar attempts to grasp the complexity of the appeal of popular culture by theorizing pleasure. Specifically he suggests, "If we now accept that the field of popular culture is important, that, at the base line, its existence has certain determinate political, ideological and economic effects, then it is absolutely crucial that we engage with its currency, with the terms of its persistence, its acceptability and its popularity: crucial, in other words, to engage with the specific ways in which we *consent* to the forms of popular culture" (p. 50).

Grossberg (1988b, 290) initiates such an engagement, seeing a certain "crisis of the very possibility of politics" in the popular realm. In addition to "the very real and continuing construction of ideological, economic, state and libidinal regimes of power" (p. 290), there is an often overlooked, or derided, politics of affect. He posits *affect* as that which "produces systems of *difference* that are *asignifying*" (p. 285). As an "economy of mood," the affective refers to the manner in which people live inside and alongside what could otherwise be described as structures of ideological containment. Importantly, this is not the same as resistance; as a particular dimension of existence that guides our encounters in a myriad of social relations, affect is "ideologically, economically and libidinally neutral except as it is articulated into these systems under specific historical conditions" (p. 286). The work of Meaghan Morris (1988a) has also been instrumental in theorizing the negotiation between the ideological and the affective. Most effectively, she reworks the cultural labor of the critic as a contest to eke out a compromise between the exigencies of theory and the contradictions of everyday life (see Morris 1988b).

The domain of affect seizes the supplementary relations of popular culture; it provides the possibility of a nonideological location at which to understand those aspects of the popular that are outside of reason, outside of "rational communication." This is of primary relevance to the machinations of popular discourse, in the present case, of youth in crisis. There is currently a consensual moment of crisis concerning youth, one that is met with the affective responses of despair, desire, and fear and with the material changes of increased surveillance and discipline. In this respect, there exists a nonnecessary correspondence of youth in crisis to the maneuvers of the American new conservatism, itself over a decade old by the early 1990s. Crudely put, the spectacular aspects of "youth in crisis" assure (1) that there is a powerful presence of the affective qualities of anxiety and desire concerning youth and (2) that the articulation of youth in crisis in certain agendas, or moral panics, is unstable. By way of concluding, I offer another piece of evidence of these articulations of crisis-in-process and the recurring call to the disciplinization of black youth and families.

Growing Up Scared

The cover of *The Atlantic* for June 1990 summons up the imminent perils of contemporary youth (Figure 8.1). It depicts a children's lunchbox adorned with brightly colored images of animals and riddled with bullet holes. The cutline reads "The most pressing 'children's issue' is not day care, health care, or education. It is the control of violent crime." The feature article by Karl Zinsmeister, entitled "Growing Up Scared," discusses precisely this menace to youth and links it to a general societal breakdown. The title's obvious reference to Paul Goodman's classic *Growing Up Absurd* (1960) begs the assessment that the past thirty years have taken American youth from bad to worse. Of principal concern is violent

141

Figure 8.1 *"Growing Up Scared" on the cover of* The Atlantic, *1990.*

crime in the education system, most prevalent in African-American communities. As one teachers' union official is quoted as saying, "If we can't ensure at least inside a school building or a schoolyard that there is still safety from the chaos of the streets ... then I fear for the future of our whole society" (Zinsmeister 1990, 61). And Zinsmeister does present a dismal state of affairs in which rape, assault, theft, and vandalism in the lives of young people are "virtually normal" (p. 61). He associates these crimes with an empirically supported general increase in violent crimes. More specifically, Zinsmeister perceives the current state of juvenile delinquency to be related to the vague but more distressing categories of drug and gang activity.

Ultimately, Zinsmeister only sees those crimes that occur in the public arena. Not surprisingly, he indicates the changing configurations of family relations and composition as what facilitates youth violence: increasing numbers of single parent homes, decreasing parental responsibility for children, and increasing numbers of mothers who work. He ignores the exceptionally high incidence of violence within the home, though he argues that "dysfunctional families" are the main cause of youth violence. Thus, he recommends the reinstallation of the nuclear family through an agenda of policing the home, policing "bad" parents, and encouraging, through various incentive procedures, the development of traditional family units. Parents, he argues, need to be held accountable for the actions of their children; if they cannot live up to their responsibility as parents, they should be punished. "There is no fully adequate substitute, public or private, for intact families" (p. 53).

If the location of the "roots of the problem" is in the decay of the family, Zinsmeister goes on to suggest that the crisis of contemporary youth is associated specifically with the "lack of male direction" (p. 52) in many families. He responds to African-American author Toni Morrison's statement that there is nothing inherently wrong with "a female running a house" by arguing, "So long as thinking like this prevails, there will be no brake on our slide toward family forms that are economically, socially, and emotionally less tenable for children—and that perpetuate themselves over generations" (p. 53). In marvelous hyperbole, Zinsmeister provides a metaphoric case against "aberrant" familial circumstances: "There are children being raised in Beirut today who will turn out fine too; nonetheless, growing up in Beirut is not to be recommended" (p. 52). This strange logic, among other things, uses the foreign and violent to connote the dangers of altering the sanctimonious traditional family unit.

This article, situated in a popular upscale magazine, is a perfect example of the political confusion and the ideological struggles concerning the questions of contemporary youth, families, race, and ethnicity. Marked by an interest in the poor, the nonwhite, the disadvantaged, and "dysfunctional families," Zinsmeister's article articulates a series of contradictory concerns; for the author, this adds up conclusively to an equation that says fear for the health and safety of youth is equally fear of social instability. Thus, the project of law and order in the ranks of the traditional family unit involves implicitly the reproduction of the social order. For instance, Zinsmeister warns, "A child who comes of age under a haze of fear will never know the early assurance that is the only reliable basis for adult competence. Later he will discover that schools dominated by outlaws are no place to acquire job skills. If he is afraid to wait at a bus stop in the evening, he will be no candidate for steady employment" (p. 66). In this patriarchal vision of social order, the "fear" of "outlaws" jeopardizes the acquisition of "job skills." The concern is that this threatened young (male) person "will be no candidate for steady employment." This is also where what has been discussed as a problem in African-American schools is treated as affecting every (employed) individual. Fear *for* the young and black has become fear *of* the young and black.

Zinsmeister's article is premised upon the existence of a taken-for-granted crisis of youth. It presents additional supporting evidence for the claim that the young require increasing guidance as they negotiate their entrance into adulthood. An abstract notion of the "modern woman" lurks in the shadows of this argument as the figure most responsible for the changing American family and hence for the associated decline of American youth. Zinsmeister may be right about one thing: The "next generation of Americans" is not apparent in the way it was previously. For many, the future is increasingly impossible to envision. But for Zinsmeister and other pundits of youth crisis, this becomes an occasion to express distress about feminism having "gone too far," guilt about the 1960s as the root of misguided social change, and disappointment that so many African-American youths seem to be turning their backs on the possibilities of American mainstream culture.

This moral panic concerning youth has reached the level of common sense; it is suffused throughout civil society and, importantly, has become central in the structuring of a particular moment of hegemony. The constitution of this popular sense of crisis comes to pass in the light of a complex and multiply composed national program. Roughly, this agenda of crisis arranges itself around the "decomposition" of the traditional family unit, the increasing demands for support and recognition of those changing relations (as evidenced by the influence of feminist issues such as day care, abortion, and welfare compensation), and the supposedly incomprehensible nature of a generation uncertain of its own future, though seemingly unmoved by the "loss" of the past (or, rather, the disappearance of the promises of the past).

Youth, deviant and straight, refers simultaneously to youth-in-trouble and to troubling-youth—that is, youth's need for guidance as well as its capacity to unsettle. This dual concern/threat forms a certain common sense. The unique aspect is that youth is the outside that is to become the inside; youth is what is alien to the central order of the adult economic, but only temporarily so. It is in the process of transition, of normalization. It follows that wasted youth is a powerful caveat: the outside that *was* to become the inside but is no more. Youth violence, nihilism, and "refusal" are all instances that proclaim the loss of a particular vision of the social and hence are readily available to demonstrate the importance of prudence, tradition, and caution.

The landscape of a moment of hegemonic formation consists of particular logics experienced at a level of popular engagement. The contours of this formation compose the attributes and effectivity of the crisis of youth. Furthermore, the consequences of these domains of sense-making echo in their configuration as a national hegemonic formation. It takes more than a perceived increase in the incidence of crime to constitute a moral panic. Discursive operations beyond the designation of the criminal incite the cultural activity that is spun out from the crisis. This discourse of panic concerns the nature of cultural evidence—that is, how certain elements demonstrate and support specific stories, conclusions, and narratives. In turn, this evidence figures in a crime's correspondence to the broader formation of youth in crisis. I have pointed to a few discursive operations that resonate in the composition of youth in crisis: the historical specificity of youth, the construction of the transgressions of the preppy murder, the display value of representations of deviance, and the centrality of the young criminal subject, in this case Robert Chambers, as grounded in the evidence of confession. Confession-performance works by engaging the qualities of the individual transgressing subject as that piece of evidence that cannot be logically refuted. Its installment on the daytime television talk show amplifies the process further and facilitates links to other crises, other moral panics, establishing a chronology of crisis.

Youth films center on the omnipresent gaze of the adult social as it observes the spectacle of wasted youth. But, in fact, all the evidential procedures discussed embody that same gaze as they establish, define, and demonstrate youth in crisis. The adult gaze as it constitutes the visibility of wayward youth renders youth in crisis symbolically central to the ordering of the social. Not a discrete episode in the history of social hierarchization, the position of youth as such has had an extensive relation to the structuring of social power. Nevertheless, the deployment of youth in crisis in the contemporary United States quite strategically entails a hegemonic project. A specific bearing operates as the discourses circulate; youth in crisis becomes intertwined with other concerns, other interests, all associated with those domains of evidential certainty. In the end, these domains act as determining forces upon the fabric of the popular.

The national-popular in the contemporary United States pertains to a taken-for-granted crisis of shifting relations of power. At the end of the 1980s, the foundation of such a design rested upon youth criminality. Always formed through the vectors of class experience, gender, race, and ethnicity, criminal youth patrols the outside, giving occasions to demonstrate the crisis. Thus, there is a continued struggle over youth, what the term indicates, what it implies of social and familial responsibility, and what characteristics are salient in the identification of deviant and straight youth. Youth is a site of engagement at which the order materializes. Order refers to an ideological construct rather than a particular state of being. In fact, the adult economic order is replete with contradictions; this order is exploitive at best and, paradoxically, chaotic at worst.

The spectacle of wasted youth makes youth fearsome. Fear, panic, and terror are lived responses to a situation involving felt self-implication in powers of coercion—that is, the imagined or real possibility of personal harm. These states all effect restriction and censure in a manner that is experienced bodily. In this respect, such obvious instances of repression can be thought to be the least effective measure of social control. The source, the applicant of those pressures, is always apparent. Youth is dangerous and threatening; and this has specific ideological consequences. If the emotions of fear and terror are paranoic and do not have a specific source, then ideological effects are confounded. This more general panic may in fact be an important contemporary "structure of feeling," one that is not entirely irrational. Paranoia is not grounded to an affective source or location, and it can be made to make sense in a number of ways. Therefore, the extremes of popular paranoia are relatively open for articulation.

The experiential condition of crisis organizes people's daily responses to, and in, the world. There is a taken-for-grantedness to fear, an *un*extraordinary quality—a *heimlich*. Not only do these terrors compel us to return to the familiar; they alaso *are* familiar. Consequently, fear, terror, and a variety of anxieties settle comfortably in hegemony, seeming to straddle the consensual and the coercive. The experience of terror is the foundation for crisis-in-process; like repressive state control, the basis of this experience is a known probability and possibility of threat and bodily harm, one that need not be exercised. But as a hegemonic mechanism, the fear of the Other structures daily existence; it organizes our movements and encounters. This is the case of youth in crisis. Youth sits strangely in hegemony. It is feared, it is desired, it holds promise, it is wasted. Youth is symbolically central to the social order as that which harbors the potential for unbounded successes and for dismal failures. As a consequence of these two connotative tendencies, youth in crisis, invested with anxieties about social transformation, has been possible.

Wild in the Streets?

An early marker of the formation I have been referring to as youth in crisis was Brenda Spencer's 1979 nihilistic cry, "I don't like Mondays." To mark the end of the period of formation and the beginning of its success as part of common sense, I point to the rapid adoption of the term *Generation X* into popular vernacular. Although this adoption is difficult to date, certainly the term's resonance occurred sometime after the 1991 publication of Coupland's novel *Generation X: Tales for an Accelerated Culture*. It is here that the unnameable is named and in so resonant a manner that the term rapidly entered popular vernacular. Coinciding with this generation's cultural absence, even this term has been hijacked by a more attractive and, from most media accounts, a more optimistic demographic. Although Coupland was referring to those born in the early to mid-1960s, Generation X is now used to describe those born in the 1970s. A case in point is the NBC news special "The Lost Generation," broadcast in the summer of 1993. Narrated by Tom Brokaw, the program begins with the post-baby-boomers who are unemployed or underemployed and who have little opportunity for advancement despite their education or their desire to do so. These interviewees are in the late twenties and early thirties. The show ends by demonstrating the areas of hope for this "lost" generation, focusing upon successful apprenticeship programs. The people at the center of this final story are all in their teenage years. This suggests that, while there is the continued moral panic about the failure of youth, there are new ways to deflect the concern. Here what is understood as a single generation is seen to have its "bad" elements, spoiling future prospects for all but a few.

Terrible youth crimes will continue; and popular scrutiny will place them into the context of a now commonsense idea about increasing youth violence. The first week of August 1993, *Time*'s cover story concerned "the deadly love affair between America's youth and firearms" (Hull 1993) and *Newsweek*'s cover story dealt with "teen violence: wild in the streets" (Kantrowitz 1993). The stories and their claims are entirely predictable; they differ little, even in terms of specific examples, from similar stories published in previous years. The generalized fear of youth has a commonplace quality. Consequently, is it any wonder that arrest rates are increasing or that high schools are increasingly calling in police officers for incidents that would have previously been dealt with internally?

If the recent history of youth is one of "deregionalization," as Michael Mitterauer (1992) suggests, in which there now exists an international, metropolitan culture connecting young people across the globe, we could hypothesize that this criminalization will also be transported and shared. The "violent" drive of youth has been naturalized; the contentiousness of youth has become the inherent anomie of youth. Rebellious acts are expected, and when they occur, criminal or not, they are slotted into the appropriate chronology. The late twentieth century has seen the emergence of a new conception of the period between child and adult. Not only has the period we call youth been extended in time, and not only is youth accustomed to its own downward mobility. Where we have had a conception of the essential innocence of childhood, we now have another relation: the essential guilt of youth.

Notes

Chapter One

1. The U.S. Bureau of the Census (1988, 165) states that the number of individuals under eithteen years of age arrested in 1975 was 2,078,000 and that this represented 25.9 percent of all arrests made. By comparison, in 1986 only 1,748,000 of the same age group were arrested, which constituted 16 percent of total arrests.

2. Two superb critique-surveys of the central issues of feminist criminology are Brown (1986) and Cain (1990). A more comprehensive general text is Heidensohn (1985).

3. The *Time* feature article, "Our Violent Kids" puts the toll at 200,000 acts of violence on television seen by the time a youth turns sixteen (Toufexis 1989, 55).

4. For more complete discussions of articulation theory, see Grossberg (1992), Hall (1986a), and Laclau and Mouffe (1985).

Chapter Two

1. Perhaps it is part romance and part sociological misapprehension, but the notion of the unnameable generation is not new. Indeed, sociologist Hamblett (1965) described the British postwar generation as a "generation X." And the late 1970s punk group of the same name was yet another appropriative claim to the title.

2. An influential, later example of this argument of development is Erikson's *Childhood and Society* (1950). Following a Freudian model, Erikson describes sexual development and the formation of identity as irreducible processes. He charts out the "eight ages of man" that lead toward the healthy ego.

3. The encounter between the Birmingham Centre for Contemporary Cultural Studies and the British radical criminologists is often forgotten by the intellectual histories of cultural studies. This was a key moment in which the reading of Althusser and Gramsci came together through a study of deviance and popular culture. Subsequently, the agenda was set for at least the next decade, which saw the productions of influential works, among them *Resistance Through Rituals* (Hall and Jefferson 1976), *Policing the Crisis* (Hall et al. 1978), and *Subculture* (Hebdige 1979).

Chapter Three

1. It has now been about three years since I was able to find any news on this second film. The currency of events like the preppy murder, however concentrated, is eventually transi-

tory. It is probably safe to assume that the capital moment of this crime has past and that these particular film plans have been dropped.

2. Interestingly, although the term *wilding* momentarily designated random black crime, the news media began to employ it to designate violent *youth* crimes, usually involving gang rape or sexual assualt. Soon after the Central Park wilding was the Glen Ridge wilding, which was perpetrated by four "clean-cut" white high school boys against a mentally retarded girl.

The origins of this term are uncertain. However, before the Central Park incident, wilding was not part of black vernacular. It has been suggested that the word was the result of a misinterpretation by a white journalist. When interviewing one of the participants, who may have said something like "We were just doing the wild thing" (a reference to a popular rap tune), the journalist understood him to say "wilding" (Cooper 1989, 28). In any case, the term is certainly the invention of the news media.

3. The idea of wilding as a criminal virus is taken to its extreme by Derber (1992) in his book *Money, Murder, and the American Dream: Wilding from Wall Street to Main Street.* His argument is largely an extension of Lasch's (1978) *The Culture of Narcissism;* Derber notes that the 1980s United States became aggressively self-obsessed to the point of rewarding criminal narcissism. Derber uses wilding to describe any expression of extreme individualism, from murder to junk bonds. Here the Central Park rape is placed alongside the Boston murder of Carol Stuart by her upwardly mobile husband, Charles. The image of the "body" of American society being attacked by the "virus" of wild individualism runs throughout the book, with Derber's use of AIDS metaphors to heighten the panic. Like Lasch's earlier work, Derber's veneer of left-liberal nostalgia is not enough to conceal his conservative longing for a peaceful, democratic United States of the past in which families were safe and intact and schools were effective; in other words, a United States that never existed.

Chapter Four

1. The burglaries refer to other crimes with which Chambers had been separately charged. They were all unassociated with Levin's murder. Later the Levin family was awarded $25 million in damages in a default judgment because Chambers did not contest the claim. In December 1992 Chambers came up for his first parole hearing. The parole board denied his release on the grounds that, with an assault on a prison guard and a possession of marijuana charge, Chambers had not been a model prisoner (Pérez-Peña 1992b). He will be eligible again in 1995.

Chapter Five

1. Since the preppy murder, Detective Mike Sheehan has embarked on a career in film. Before his role in *The Preppy Murder,* Sheehan was hired to transform Tom Berenger into a realistic New York City cop for Ridley Scott's *Someone to Watch over Me* (1987). More recently, Sheehan appeared in *Rocky V* (John Avildsen, 1990).

2. The height and weight discrepancy was one of the principal reasons that any doubt was cast upon Chambers's version of the crime. There is some confusion as to the precision of the figures popularized in the press. During the videotape statement, Chambers insisted that he was 190 pounds and six foot three. Similarly, he overestimated Levin at 135 pounds.

3. In fact, those opposed to the institutionalization of the confessional claimed that it let people off too easily, particularly women (Hepworth and Turner 1982, 47). The counter-argument was that if the telling of one's sins and then the recitation of a few Hail Marys were considered sufficient penance in the eyes of the church, this procedure might very well encourage the sinful activity.

4. Althusser (1971) describes the process of subjectification as one of being "hailed" into an ideological position. He employs the example of responding to a police officer's "hailing"; one turns to face the officer, in effect recognizing oneself in a particular relation of power. The very act of orientation is equally that of "coming into being" in, and through, an ideological relation. This is the moment of *interpellation:* the moment of being situated in the appropriate subject position. Althusser's example is one that captures a visible and immediate instance in which one feels the presence of the ideological apparatus; not all are so crystalline in their manifestation. But the confession is a powerful situation, with the instruments of "enforcement" and their possible effects apparent and tangible. Not only does one turn and face; one also speaks and confesses. In French, *interpeller* refers to an obligation to explain oneself.

Chapter Six

1. The most notorious of the recent talk shows was the now-defunct *Morton Downey, Jr. Show.* Despite its high popular recognition as the "worst of the worst," as the most sensational and "trashy" of this genre, it was only ever a local phenomenon in New York City. In contrast, *Oprah, Geraldo, Donahue,* and *Sally* all achieved national popularity and geographically broad audiences. In addition, *Morton Downey, Jr.* was a late night talk show.

2. Of course, not all live television is actually so. Many shows that continue to suggest live programming, such as the situation comedy and the talk show with their live studio audiences, are in effect "canned live." This is effectively connoted on *Oprah* and *Donahue* where telephone questions suggest an interactive process that includes the home audience. This, of course, is just an illusion because these shows are prerecorded.

3. This show was particularly controversial for allegations made by one guest that some Jewish families practice the sacrificial killing of children. Winfrey was criticized for accepting the assertions without challenge and for encouraging an elaboration from the guest (Gerard 1989). The subsequent protests caught Harpo Productions, Winfrey's studio, in a bind because while attempting to disassociate itself from such anti-Semitic claims, Harpo also needed to attest to the credibility of its guests, upon which the entire program rested.

Chapter Seven

1. McGee and Robertson (1982) point to *City Across the River* (1949), released the same year as *Knock on Any Door,* as a similar pivotal moment in the juvenile delinquency film. They argue that this violent tale of gang life, directed by Maxwell Shane, was the first to shift attention from the adult characters trying to make sense of or save the young delinquents to the rituals and styles of deviant youth.

2. "The End" appears over the action of this final scene and remains on screen for an unusually long time. This lends an almost comic edge to the scene, as though Ray wanted to provide an ironic counterpoint to this tragic closure. "The End" thus announces the conclusion of the film, the end of Andy's involvement with this client, and the end of Nick's life.

3. Films for young people can be typologized in a number of different manners. Jackson (1986) traces historical shifts in the manner in which children are represented. She argues that the pre–World War II period was the child star era, characterized by films as star vehicles for popular child actors such as Shirley Temple and Mickey Rooney. These films tended to portray "fix-it" young people who when faced with problems and complications energetically set to correcting the situation. After World War II, the inherent innocence of childhood remained a fundamental quality, though the stories began to depict a certain disquiet, often having sad endings and failed objectives. By the 1970s, the increasingly challenged sanctimony of childhood culminated in the "child-as-monster" films. Jackson also points to a subgenre of films depicting the child as adult-in-miniature, of which *Paper Moon* (Peter Bogdanovich, 1973) is perhaps the most popular example. She notes in the 1980s the resurgence of some earlier portrayals, particularly as a result of the vast popularity of Steven Spielberg's films.

4. "Juvenilization" is a convenient term to describe a general shift in the focus of American film; the term may carry with it the unfortunately negative connotation that the films are increasingly sophomoric. This association should be suspended. As films come to cater to an audience of young people, they are not necessarily accompanied by a compromised aesthetic or an absence of sophistication, as is often mistakenly suggested. The term marks a particular reconfiguration of filmic convention; it is not a statement of quality.

5. The gendering of male rebellion, and the women the protagonists seduce and victimize, is a strikingly consistent convention of youth pictures. There has been the coding of the female juvenile delinquent as somewhat more unhealthy than her male counterpart. Our culture thoroughly naturalizes the presumption that youth is a time of contentiousness. This ropes in the discomfort and rebelliousness expressed as typical and to be expected. But the female youth has posed a slightly more difficult problem; a plenitude of other cultural demands upon women siphon off the possibility for the same freedom to be rebellious found in young males. Furthermore, this often romanticized myth of male rebelliousness is a particularly white tradition. It appears that the black rebel has been simply too threatening for American cinema.

6. Wood (1986, 63) describes this moment in *The Breakfast Club* as "the ultimate political question: what are you going to *do*" on Monday? The fact that the teenagers answer it ambiguously at best contributes to the film's anti-idealism and sophisticated rendering of teenage angst.

7. The killer in the Milpitas case was African-American. In the movie version, his character is white. One can speculate how the film would have differed if this fact had not been altered. I suggest that race and ethnicity tend to be considered over all else, as though they are the singularly important determining qualities in the crime. This, of course, would significantly change, and patently distort, the representation of the crime.

8. Marchessault (1988, 43) is an exception here who refers to Glover's performance as "the film's most radical component. His overbearing portrayal of a character who believes he is acting in a film takes on Brechtian overtones."

9. Two anomalous examples are worth mentioning. First is Smith's (1987) thoughtful review, which attempts to understand youth's penchant for Hughes-style teen movies over the more "arty" *River's Edge*. Unfortunately, he neglects to recognize that while similar movies, such as *The Boys Next Door* (Penelope Spheeris, 1985) and *Over the Edge* (Jonathan Kaplan, 1982), were not particularly popular with young audiences, *River's Edge* was surprisingly so. A similar error is made by Bruce (1988) in a thorough comparison between the

politically "radical" *Over the Edge* and the "reactionary" *River's Edge*. While I ultimately agree with the tenor of the argument, Bruce's analysis rests upon dichotomies between *Over the Edge* as a "B" exploitation film designed for teens and starring real teens and *River's Edge* as an "A" art film designed for adults and starring teen actors. In a number of instances, this analysis is not only problematic; it is also incorrect.

10. There is a similar contrast in another film of refusal, *Less Than Zero*, from the popular book of the same name. Though more highly stylized than *River's Edge*, the universe of affectless youths and absent adults is the same. In depicting the world of upper-class Los Angeles youth, *Less Than Zero* presents the wooden Clay (Andrew McCarthy) and Blair (Jami Gertz) as the perfect products of this sterile environment. The hyperactive decadence of Julian (Robert Downey, Jr.) threatens, or electrifies, this environment. His overabundant physical and emotional energy is a terrible reminder of the extremes required to incite sensations of existence. Like the comparable character of Layne in *River's Edge*, Julian's excessive behavior signifies an immediate and not unreasonable response to a situation of limited possibility. Importantly, *Less Than Zero* associates Julian's recalcitrance with drug use only and proceeds to present a fairly traditional melodramatic and moralistic narrative concerning his "problem." It is movie fantasies in addition to drugs that energize Layne.

11. Freud ([1919] 1955, 220) writes of "that class of the frightening which leads back to what is known of old and long familiar": the *unheimlich*, which roughly translates as the "uncanny." Importantly, Freud stresses that the *unheimlich* is not just the terrifying and the unknown; it is that which at one time was the *heimlich*. In this manner, the concept refers to the emergence of the repressed; "everything is *unheimlich* that ought to have remained secret and hidden but has come to light" (p. 225). For instance, the animation of an inanimate object—a chair, a dead person, a toy—is not *unheimlich* in and of itself. However, Freud's use of Hoffman's "The Sand-man" illustrates how a man's obsession with a "living doll" brings together certain fears and, more significantly, desires, thus making it *unheimlich*. This desire and disruption elicit the qualities of the *Unheimlich*, that is, that which derives from the illicit wishes lodged in the familiar.

Chapter Eight

1. Without the defining features of "youth" as established by the baby-boomer generation and equally alienated from a new teenage culture, Generation X is sometimes characterized by an absence of distinguishable forms of popular cultural expression. As such, one of the Generation X strategies has been to be cynical about youth culture, to treat it with a certain distance, in effect "to be old." The Generation X fascination with the culture of the 1950s is one appropriative gesture that attempts to mark a distinctive cultural space. I have discussed this elsewhere as ahistorical nostalgia (Acland 1992).

References

Abramson, Pamela. 1987. "Bitter Memories of Murder." *Newsweek,* June 22, p. 25.

Acland, Charles R. 1991. "'Tall, Dark, and Lethal'; The Discourses of Sexual Transgression in the Preppy Murder." *Journal of Communication Inquiry* 15.2 (Summer):140–158.

_____. 1992. "Textual Excess and Articulations of Gender in *Pee Wee's Playhouse*." *Communication* 13:21–38.

Addams, Jane. 1909. *The Spirit of Youth and the City Streets*. Urbana: University of Illinois Press.

Alexander, Shana. 1985. *The Nutcracker: Money, Madness, Murder: A Family Album*. New York: Doubleday.

Allen, Judith. 1989. "Men, Crime and Criminology: Recasting the Questions." *International Journal of the Sociology of Law* 17:19–39.

Althusser, Louis. 1971. *Lenin and Philosophy, and Other Essays*. London: New Left Books.

_____. 1977. *For Marx*. Trans. Ben Brewster. London: Verso.

American Medical Association and National Association of State Boards of Education. 1990. *Code Blue: Uniting for Healthier Youth*. Alexandria, Va.: NASBE Publications.

Ansen, David. 1987. "The Kids Aren't Alright: A Powerful Portrait of Deadly, Disaffected Teens." *Newsweek,* June 1, p. 68.

Ariès, Phillipe. 1962. *Centuries of Childhood: A Social History of Family Life*. Trans. Robert Baldick. New York: Knopf.

Bakan, David. 1971. "Adolescence in America: From Idea to Social Fact." *Daedalus* 100.4 (Fall):979–995.

Barrett, Michael J. 1990. "The Case for More School Days." *Atlantic Monthly* (November):78–106.

Barrett, Michèle and Mary McIntosh. 1991. *The Anti-Social Family*. 2d ed. New York: Verso.

Barthel, Joan. 1987. "*River's Edge:* The Grim Sleeper." *Ms. Magazine* (September):26.

Barthes, Roland. 1972. *Mythologies*. Trans. Annette Lavers. New York: Hill and Wang.

_____. 1977. *Image, Music, Text*. Trans. Stephen Heath. London: Fontana.

_____. 1981. *Camera Lucida: Reflections on Photography*. Trans. Richard Howard. New York: Hill and Wang.

Baudrillard, Jean. 1983. *In the Shadow of the Silent Majorities*. Trans. Paul Foss, John Johnston, and Paul Patton. New York: Semiotext(e).

_____. 1987. *Forget Foucault*. New York: Semiotext(e).

Becker, Howard. 1973. *Outsiders: Studies in the Sociology of Deviance*. 2d ed. New York: Free Press.

Bell, Daniel. 1960. *The End of Ideology: On the Exhaustion of Political Ideas in the Fifties*. New York: Free Press.

Benjamin, Walter. [1935] 1968. "The Work of Art in the Age of Mechanical Reproduction." In *Illuminations*, ed. Hannah Arendt. Trans. Harry Zohn. New York: Schocken Books, pp. 217–251.

Bennett, Tony. 1982a. "Media, 'Reality,' Signification." In *Culture, Society and the Media*, ed. Michael Gurevitch, Tony Bennett, James Curran, and Janet Woollacott. New York: Methuen, pp. 287–308.

——. 1982b. "Theories of the Media, Theories of Society." In *Culture, Society and the Media*, ed. Michael Gurevitch, Tony Bennett, James Curran, and Janet Woollacott. New York: Methuen, pp. 30–55.

——. 1986a. "Introduction: Popular Culture and 'The Turn to Gramsci.'" In *Popular Culture and Social Relations*, ed. Tony Bennett, Colin Mercer, and Janet Woollacott. Milton Keynes, England: Open University Press, pp. xi–xix.

——. 1986b. "The Politics of 'the Popular' and Popular Culture." In *Popular Culture and Social Relations*, ed. Tony Bennett, Colin Mercer, and Janet Woollacott. Milton Keynes, England: Open University Press: pp. 6–21.

Berggren, Erik. 1975. *The Psychology of Confession*. Leiden, Netherlands: E. J. Brill.

Bettelheim, Bruno. 1965. "The Problem of Generations." In *The Challenge of Youth*, ed. Erik H. Erikson. Garden City, N.Y.: Anchor Books, pp. 76–109.

Biskind, Peter. 1983. *Seeing Is Believing: How Hollywood Taught Us to Stop Worrying and Love the Fifties*. New York: Pantheon Books.

Black, Joel. 1991. *The Aesthetics of Murder*. Baltimore: Johns Hopkins University Press.

Blumer, Herbert. 1933. *Movies and Conduct*. New York: Macmillan.

Bordwell, David, Janet Staiger, and Kristen Thompson. 1985. *The Classical Hollywood Cinema: Film Style and Mode of Production to 1960*. New York: Columbia University Press.

Brown, Beverley. 1986. "Women and Crime: The Dark Figures of Criminology." *Economy and Society* 15.3:355–402.

Brown, Peter H. 1989. "'There Was No Sex Diary': Jennifer Levin Wasn't Asking for Trouble." *TV Guide* 23–29 (September):24–27.

Brownmiller, Susan. 1989. *Waverly Place*. New York: Grove Press.

Bruce, Bryan. 1988. "The Edge." *CineAction!* (Spring):32–38.

Cain, Maureen. 1990. "Towards Transgression: New Directions in Feminist Criminology." *International Journal of the Sociology of Law* 18:1–18.

Cameron, Deborah, and Elizabeth Frazer. 1987. *The Lust to Kill: A Feminist Investigation of Sexual Murder*. New York: New York University Press.

Canby, Vincent. 1987. "Into the Dark Heartland." *New York Times*, June 14, pp. H23ff.

Capote, Truman. 1966. *In Cold Blood: A True Account of a Multiple Murder and Its Consequences*. New York: Random House.

Caputi, Jane. 1988. "Films of the Nuclear Age." *Journal of Popular Film and Television* 16.3 (Fall):100–107.

Carr, C. 1987. "Who's on Trial?" *Village Voice*, October 27, p. 22.

Caughie, John. 1986. "Popular Culture: Notes and Revisions." In *High Theory/Low Culture: Analysing Popular Television and Film*, ed. Colin MacCabe. New York: St. Martin's Press, pp. 156–171.

Certeau, Michel de. 1984. *The Practice of Everyday Life*. Trans. Steven Rendall. Berkeley and Los Angeles: University of California Press.

Chambers, Iain. 1986. *Popular Culture: The Metropolitan Experience*. New York: Methuen.

Coburn, Marcia Froelke. 1987. "Rough Sex Gets Real." *Mademoiselle* (May):238ff.

Cohen, Stanley. 1972. (1980, 2d ed.). *Folk Devils and Moral Panics: The Creation of the Mods and Rockers.* London: MacGibbon and Kee.

Cohen, Stanley, and Jack Young, eds. 1973. *The Manufacture of News: Social Problems, Deviance and the Mass Media.* London: Constable.

Coleman, Jonathan. 1985. *At Mother's Request: A True Story of Money, Murder, and Betrayal.* New York: Atheneum.

Colimore, Edward. 1989. "Tragic Trend Among City Youth." *Philadelphia Inquirer,* January 4, pp. A1, A7.

Cooper, Barry Michael. 1989. "Cruel and the Gang." *Village Voice,* May 9, pp. 27ff.

Coupland, Douglas. 1991. *Generation X: Tales for an Accelerated Culture.* New York: St. Martin's Press.

Cousins, Mark. 1980. "Men's *Rea:* A Note on Sexual Difference, Criminology and the Law." In *Radical Issues in Criminology,* ed. Pat Carlen and Mike Collison. Oxford: Martin Robertson, pp. 109–122.

"Crackdown on Underage Drinking Not Working." 1987. *New York Times,* August 26, p. I1.

Crane, Jonathan. 1988. "Terror and Everyday Life." *Communications* 10:367–382.

Curran, James, Michael Gurevitch, and Janet Woollacott. 1982. "The Study of the Media: Theoretical Approaches." In *Culture, Society and the Media,* ed. Michael Gurevitch, Tony Bennett, James Curran, and Janet Woollacott. New York: Methuen, pp. 11–29.

Davis, Mike. 1988. "Los Angeles: Civil Liberties Between the Hammer and the Rock." *New Left Review* 170 (July-August):37–60.

de Lauretis, Teresa. 1987. *Technologies of Gender: Essays on Theory, Film, and Fiction.* Bloomington: Indiana University Press.

Debord, Guy. 1977. *The Society of the Spectacle.* Detroit: Black and Red.

Deleuze, Gilles. 1988. *Foucault.* Trans. and ed. Seàn Hand. Minneapolis: University of Minnesota Press.

Dempsey, John. 1987. "Par's 'Geraldo' Deal Signals Escalating Syndie Competition over Major Market TV Control." *Variety,* April 15, pp. 41ff.

Derber, Charles. 1992. *Money, Murder, and the American Dream: Wilding from Wall Street to Main Street.* Boston: Faber and Faber.

Deutschmann, Alan. 1992. "The Upbeat Generation." *Fortune* 126.1 (July): 42–54.

Doherty, Thomas. 1988. *Teenagers and Teenpics: The Juvenilization of American Movies in the 1950s.* Boston: Unwin Hyman.

Dostoyevsky, Fyodor. 1991. *Crime and Punishment.* Trans. David McDuff. London: Penguin Books.

Dreyfus, Hubert L., and Paul Rabinow. 1982. *Michel Foucault: Beyond Structuralism and Hermeneutics.* Chicago: University of Chicago Press.

Dubin, Steven C. 1992. *Arresting Images: Impolitic Art and Uncivil Actions.* New York: Routledge.

Durkheim, Émile. [1893] 1947. *The Division of Labor in Society.* New York: Free Press.

———. [1897] 1951. *Suicide: A Study in Sociology.* New York: Free Press.

Elliott, Gregory. 1987. *Althusser: The Detour of Theory.* New York: Verso.

Ellis, Bret Easton. 1985. *Less Than Zero.* New York: Penguin Books.

Ellis, John. 1982. *Visible Fictions.* Boston: Routledge and Kegan Paul.

Erikson, Erik H. 1950. *Childhood and Society.* New York: Norton.

Erikson, Kai T. 1966. *Wayward Puritans: A Study in the Sociology of Deviance.* New York: John Wiley and Sons.

Faludi, Susan. 1991. *Backlash: The Undeclared War Against American Women.* New York: Crown.

Farber, M. A. 1986. "Suspect Indicted in Central Park Slaying." *New York Times,* September 11, p. B10.

"Fatal Shootings Among Youths Are Studied." 1989. *New York Times,* October 29, p. A27.

Fine, Benjamin. 1957. *1,000,000 Delinquents.* New York: Signet.

Finestone, Harold. 1976. *Victims of Change: Juvenile Delinquents in American Society.* Westport, Conn.: Greenwood Press.

Fiske, John. 1987. *Television Culture.* New York: Methuen.

Fontana, Alexandre. 1975. "The Intermittences of Rationality." In *I, Pierre Rivière, Having Slaughtered My Mother, My Sister, and My Brother. ...* Ed. Michel Foucault and trans. Frank Jellinek. Lincoln: University of Nebraska Press, pp. 269–288.

Forgacs, David, ed. 1988. *An Antonio Gramsci Reader.* New York: Schocken Books.

Forman, Henry James. 1933. *Our Movie Made Children.* New York: Macmillan.

Foucault, Michel. 1978. *The History of Sexuality: An Introduction.* Vol. 1. Trans. Robert Hurley. New York: Pantheon Books.

———. 1979. *Discipline and Punish: The Birth of the Prison.* Trans. Alan Sheridan. New York: Vintage Books.

———. 1980. "Two Lectures." In *Power/Knowledge: Selected Interviews and Other Writings 1972–1977.* Trans. and ed. Colin Gordon. New York: Pantheon Books, pp. 78–108.

———. 1981. "Questions of Method: An Interview with Michel Foucault." *I&C* 8:3–14.

Foucault, Michel, ed. 1975. *I, Pierre Rivière, Having Slaughtered My Mother, My Sister, and My Brother. ...* Trans. Frank Jellinek. Lincoln: University of Nebraska Press.

"Four at Dorrian's Bar Accused of Serving Alcohol to Minors." 1986. *New York Times,* November 17, p. B2.

Fraser, Matthew. 1990. "Ignored by French Society, Bleak Suburbs Explode in a Violent Rage." *The Gazette* (Montreal), October 22, p. B1.

Freedman, Samuel G. 1986a. "Darkness Beneath the Glitter: Life of Suspect in Park Slaying." *New York Times,* August 28, pp. A1ff.

———. 1986b. "Underage Drinking Sparks Tragedy and Debates." *New York Times,* August 29, p. B3.

———. 1986c. "Weeks Before Slaying, Neighbors Reported Minors Drinking at Bar." *New York Times,* August 30, p. 1.

———. 1986d. "Death in Park: Difficult Questions for Parents." *New York Times,* September 11, pp. B1ff.

Freud, Sigmund. [1919] 1955. "The 'Uncanny.'" In *The Standard Edition of the Complete Psychological Works of Sigmund Freud.* Trans. James Strachey. London: Hogarth Press, pp. 217–252.

Friend, Tim. 1988. "More Teens Are Dying Violently." *USA Today,* December 6, p. 1.

"Fuss in Californian City over *River's Edge* Showing; Site of Original Murder." 1987. *Variety,* May 27, pp. 1ff.

Gaines, Donna. 1991. *Teenage Wasteland: Suburbia's Dead End Kids.* New York: Pantheon Books.

Genet, Jean. 1967. *The Thief's Journal.* New York: Penguin Books.

"Geraldo Rivera's Nose Broken in Scuffle on His Talk Show." 1988. *New York Times,* November 4, p. B3.

Gerard, Jeremy. 1989. "Winfrey Show Evokes Protests." *New York Times,* May 6, p. A50.

Gilbert, James Burkhart. 1986. *A Cycle of Outrage: America's Reaction to the Juvenile Delinquent in the 1950s*. New York: Oxford University Press.

Gillis, John. 1974. *Youth and History: Tradition and Change in European Age Relations, 1770–Present*. New York: Academic Press.

Glynn, Kevin. 1990. "Tabloid Television's Transgressive Aesthetic: *A Current Affair* and the 'Shows That Taste Forgot.'" *Wide Angle* 12.2:22–44.

Glynn, Lenny. 1988. "Sex and Death in Manhattan." *Maclean's*, January 25, p. 46.

Goldberg, Robert. 1988. "Soapbox for Sickos?" *Wall Street Journal*, November 21, p. A14.

Goldin, Tim. 1991. "Raider's Chic: A Style and Sinister Overtones of Crips and Gangs." *New York Times*, February 4, p. A12.

Golding, William. 1954. *Lord of the Flies*. London: Faber and Faber.

Goodman, Paul. 1960. *Growing Up Absurd: Problems of Youth in the Organized System*. New York: Random House.

Gore, Tipper. 1987. *Raising PG Kids in a X-Rated Society*. Nashville, Tenn.: Abingdon Press.

Gramsci, Antonio. 1971. *Selections from the Prison Notebooks*. Ed. and trans. Quintin Hoare and Geoffrey Nowell Smith. New York: International Publishers.

Greenberg, James. 1987. "*Cop II* Still Way Ahead of Pic Field at National Boxoffice." *Variety*, June 3, pp. 3ff.

Greenwood, Victoria. 1981. "The Myth of Female Crime." In *Women and Crime*, ed. A. Morris and L. Gelsthorpe. Cambridge: Cambridge Institute of Criminology.

Gross, Jane. 1986. "At Teen-ager's Funeral, Tears for a Vibrant Life." *New York Times*, August 30, p. A29.

Grossberg, Lawrence. 1988a. *It's a Sin: Essays on Postmodernism, Politics and Culture*. Sydney: Power Publications.

———. 1988b. "Postmodernity and Affect: All Dressed Up with No Place to Go." *Communication* 10:271–293.

———. 1992. *We Gotta Get Out of This Place: Popular Conservatism and Postmodern Culture*. New York: Routledge.

———. 1993. "The Media Economy of Rock Culture: Cinema, Postmodernity, and Authenticity." In *Sound and Vision: The Music Video Reader*, ed. Simon Frith, Andrew Goodwin, and Lawrence Grossberg. New York: Routledge, pp. 185–209.

Hackett, George. 1988. "When the Victim Goes on Trial." *Newsweek*, January 18, p. 31.

Hall, G. Stanley. 1904. *Adolescence and Its Psychology and Its Relations to Physiology, Anthropology, Sociology, Sex, Crime, Religion, and Education*. New York: D. Appleton.

Hall, Stuart. 1971. "Cultural Analysis." *Working Papers in Cultural Studies* 1.

———. 1974. "Deviance, Politics and the Media." In *Deviance and Social Control*, ed. Paul Rock and Mary McIntosh. London: Tavistock, pp. 261–305.

———. 1980a. "Cultural Studies: Two Paradigms." *Media, Culture, and Society* 2:57–72.

———. 1980b. "Popular-Democratic vs. Authoritarian Populism: Two Ways of Taking Democracy Seriously." In *Marxism and Democracy*, ed. Alan Hunt. London: Lawrence and Wishart, pp. 157–185.

———. 1981. "Notes on Deconstructing the Popular." In *People's History and Socialist Theory*, ed. Samuel Raphael. London: Routledge and Kegan Paul, pp. 227–240.

———. 1982. "The Rediscovery of 'Ideology': Return of the Repressed in Media Studies." In *Culture, Society and the Media*, ed. Michael Gurevitch, Tony Bennett, James Curran, and Janet Woollacott. New York: Methuen, pp. 56–90.

———. 1984. "The Narrative Construction of Reality: An Interview with Stuart Hall." *Southern Review* 17.1:3–17.

———. 1985. "Signification, Representation, Ideology: Althusser and the Post-Structuralist Debate." *Critical Studies in Mass Communication* 2.2:91–114.

———. 1986a. "On Postmodernism and Articulation: An Interview." *Journal of Communication Inquiry* 10.2:45–60.

———. 1986b. "Popular Culture and the State." In *Popular Culture and Social Relations*, ed. Tony Bennett, Colin Mercer, and Janet Woollacott. Milton Keynes, England: Open University Press, pp. 22–49.

Hall, Stuart, Chas Critcher, Tony Jefferson, John Clarke, and Brian Roberts. 1978. *Policing the Crisis: Mugging, the State and Law and Order*. New York: Holmes and Meier.

Hall, Stuart, and Tony Jefferson, eds. 1976. *Resistance Through Rituals: Youth Subcultures in Post-War Britain*. London: Hutchinson.

Hamblett, Charles. 1965. *Generation X*. London: Tandem Books.

Hays, Constance L. 1989. "A Film on the Levin Case Is 'Really Creepy.'" *New York Times*, August 9, p. B4.

Hebdige, Dick. 1979. *Subculture: The Meaning of Style*. London: Methuen.

———. 1987. "The Impossible Object: Towards a Sociology of the Sublime." *New Formations* 1 (Spring):47–76.

———. 1988. *Hiding in the Light: On Images and Things*. New York: Comedia.

Heidensohn, Frances M. 1985. *Women and Crime*. London: Macmillan.

Heller, Anne Conover. 1987. "A Walk with Love and Death." *Mademoiselle* (January): 145ff.

Hepworth, Mike, and Bryan S. Turner. 1982. *Confession: Studies in Deviance and Religion*. Boston: Routledge and Kegan Paul.

Hirschi, Travis. 1975. "Labelling Theory and Juvenile Delinquency: An Assessment of the Evidence." In *The Labelling of Deviance: Evaluating a Perspective*, ed. Walter R. Grove. New York: Sage, pp. 181–203.

Hoggart, Richard. 1958. *The Uses of Literacy*. Harmondsworth, England: Penguin Books.

"Home Unit Controls Viewing Time." 1992. *Globe and Mail* (Toronto), August 13, p. C1.

Howe, Neil, and Bill Strauss. 1993. *13th Gen: Abort, Retry, Ignore, Fail?* New York: Vintage Books.

Hull, Jon D. 1993. "A Boy and His Gun." *Time*, August 2, pp. 29–35.

Huyssen, Andreas. 1986. *After the Great Divide: Modernism, Mass Culture, Postmodernism*. Bloomington: Indiana University Press.

Jackson, Kathy Merlock. 1986. *Images of Children in American Film: A Sociocultural Analysis*. Metuchen, N.J.: Scarecrow Press.

Jameson, Fredric. 1979. *Fables of Aggression: Wyndham Lewis, the Modernist as Fascist*. Berkeley and Los Angeles: University of California Press.

———. 1981. *The Political Unconscious: Narrative as a Socially Symbolic Act*. Ithaca: Cornell University Press.

"Jennifer Levin's Mother Plans Book on Slaying." 1989. *New York Times*, June 1, p. C20.

Johnson, Kirk. 1987. "Chambers Loses Ruling on Statements: Judge Allows 3 Versions of Levin's Death in Park." *New York Times*, October 17, p. A33.

Kael, Pauline. 1987. "*River's Edge*: Review." *New Yorker*, June 15, pp. 77–79.

Kantrowitz, Barbara. 1993. "Wild in the Streets." *Newsweek*, August 2, pp. 40–47.

Kass, John. 1989a. "Consumer Information Is Out There, But Can Be Hard to Find." *Chicago Tribune*, May 28, p. 18.

_____. 1989b. "Youth Psychiatry: What's the Bottom Line?" *Chicago Tribune*, May 28, pp. 1ff.

Keniston, Kenneth. 1971. *Youth and Dissent: The Rise of a New Opposition*. New York: Harcourt Brace Jovanovich.

Kitsuse, John I. 1975. "The 'New Conception of Deviance' and Its Critics." In *The Labelling of Deviance: Evaluating a Perspective*, ed. Walter R. Grove. New York: Sage, pp. 273–284.

Kunen, James S. 1988. "Blaming His Victim, a Killer Cops a Plea." *People Weekly*, April 11, pp. 24ff.

_____. 1989. "Madness in the Heart of the City." *People Weekly*, May 22, pp. 106–111.

Lacayo, Richard. 1988. "The Rough-Sex Defense." *Time*, May 23, p. 44.

Laclau, Ernesto, and Chantal Mouffe. 1985. *Hegemony and Socialist Strategy: Towards a Radical Democratic Politics*. Trans. Winston Moore and Paul Cammack. London: Verso.

Lambert, Bruce. 1986. "Citywide Crackdown to Begin Against Under-age Drinking." *New York Times*, September 3, p. A1.

Lasch, Christopher. 1978. *The Culture of Narcissism: American Life in an Age of Diminishing Expectations*. New York: Norton.

Leary, Warren E. 1990. "Gloomy Report on the Health of Teenagers." *New York Times*, June 9, p. A24.

Lemert, Edwin M. 1972. *Human Deviance, Social Problems, and Social Control*. 2d ed. Englewood Cliffs, N.J.: Prentice-Hall.

Lewis, Anthony. 1990. "Where Kids Are Poor But Billionaires Abound." *Globe and Mail* (Toronto), July 9, p. A21.

Lewis, Jon. 1992. *The Road to Romance and Ruin: Teen Films and Youth Culture*. New York: Routledge.

Leyton, Elliott. 1986. *Compulsive Killers*. Toronto: McClelland and Stewart.

"License Is Suspended at Dorrian's Red Hand." 1987. *New York Times*, November 25, p. B5.

Lipsyte, Robert. 1992. "Beckoned by the Greens, Not the Gang." *New York Times*, June 28, pp. H1ff.

Macdonald, Dwight. 1957. "A Theory of Mass Culture." In *Mass Culture: The Popular Arts in America*, ed. Bernard Rosenberg and David Manning White. New York: Free Press, pp. 59–73.

Marchessault, Janine. 1988. "Your Life Is a Film." *CineAction!* (Spring):39–43.

Marx, Karl, and Friedrich Engels. 1978. *The Marx-Engels Reader*. Ed. Robert C. Tucker. 2d ed. New York: Norton.

May, Clifford. 1986. "Rape and Murder Scar Innocence of Potsdam." *New York Times*, September 5, p. B1.

McGee, Mark Thomas, and R. J. Robertson. 1982. *The J.D. Films: Juvenile Delinquency in the Movies*. Jefferson, N.C.: McFarland.

McGinniss, Joe. 1983. *Fatal Vision*. New York: Putnam.

McInerney, Jay. 1984. *Bright Lights, Big City*. New York: Vintage Books.

McLuhan, Marshall. 1964. *Understanding Media: The Extensions of Man*. New York: McGraw-Hill.

McRobbie, Angela. 1980. "Settling Accounts with Subcultures: A Feminist Critique." *Screen Education* 34:37–49.

_____. 1991. *Feminism and Youth Culture: From "Jackie" to "Just Seventeen."* Boston: Unwin Hyman.

Mercer, Colin. 1986. "Complicit Pleasures." In *Popular Culture and Social Relations,* ed. Tony Bennett, Colin Mercer, and Janet Woollacott. Milton Keynes, England: Open University Press, pp. 50–69.

Merton, Robert K. 1957. *Social Theory and Social Structure.* New York: John Wiley and Sons.

Meyer, Peter. 1986. *Death of Innocence: The True Story of an Unspeakable Teenage Crime.* New York: Berkley.

Meyrowitz, Joshua. 1985. *No Sense of Place: The Impact of Electronic Media on Social Behavior.* New York: Oxford University Press.

Mitterauer, Michael. 1992. *A History of Youth.* Trans. Graeme Dunphy. Oxford: Basil Blackwell.

Morris, Meaghan. 1988a. "At Henry Parkes Motel." *Cultural Studies* 2.1:1–47.

———. 1988b. "Banality in Cultural Studies." *Discourse* 10.2 (Spring-Summer):3–29.

Morse, Margaret. 1985. "Talk, Talk, Talk." *Screen* 26.2:2–15.

Musgrove, Frank. 1964. *Youth and the Social Order.* London: Routledge and Kegan Paul.

Nix, Crystal. 1986. "Slain Woman Found in Park: Suspect Seized." *New York Times,* August 27, p. B1.

Packard, Vance. 1957. *The Hidden Persuaders.* New York: D. McKay.

Park, Robert, E. Burgess, and R. D. McKenzie. 1925. *The City.* Chicago: University of Chicago Press.

Pérez-Peña, Richard. 1992a. "Board to Hear Bid for Parole from a Central Park Killer." *New York Times,* December 15, p. B4.

———. 1992b. "Parole Denies Release of Chambers for Two More Years." *New York Times,* December 18, p. B1ff.

"Playing with Dolls." 1988. *U.S. News & World Report,* May 30, p. 9.

Postman, Neil. 1982. *The Disappearance of Childhood.* New York: Delacorte.

Probyn, Elspeth. 1989. "TV's Local: The Exigency of Gender in Media Research." *Canadian Journal of Communication* 14.3:29–41.

———. 1993. "TV's *Unheimlich* Home." In *The Politics of Everyday Fear,* ed. Brian Massumi. Minneapolis: University of Minnesota Press, pp. 269–283.

Quinney, Richard. 1970. *The Social Reality of Crime.* Boston: Little, Brown.

Raab, Selwyn. 1986. "Lawyer Weighs Plea of Insanity in Park Slaying." *New York Times,* August 30, p. A29.

Reik, Theodor. 1966. *The Compulsion to Confess: On the Psychoanalysis of Crime and Punishment.* New York: John Wiley and Sons.

Renshaw, Samuel, Vernon A. Miller, and Dorothy Marquis. 1933. *Children's Sleep.* New York: Macmillian.

Riot, Philippe. 1975. "The Parallel Lives of Pierre Rivière." In *I, Pierre Rivière, Having Slaughtered My Mother, My Sister, and My Brother. ...* Ed. Michel Foucault and trans. Frank Jellinek. Lincoln: University of Nebraska Press: pp. 229–250.

Rivera, Geraldo. 1988. "Interview." *Broadcasting* 19 (December):43–48.

"*River's Edge:* Review." 1986. *Variety,* September 3, p. 16.

Rock, Paul, and Mary McIntosh, eds. 1974. *Deviance and Social Control.* London: Tavistock.

Ross, Andrew. 1989. *No Respect: Intellectuals and Popular Culture.* New York: Routledge.

Rubin, Gayle. 1984. "Thinking Sex: Notes for a Radical Theory of the Politics of Sexuality." In *Pleasure and Danger: Exploring Female Sexuality,* ed. Carole S. Vance. Boston: Routledge and Kegan Paul, pp. 267–319.

Rule, Ann. 1987. *Small Sacrifices: A True Story of Passion and Murder.* New York: New American Library.

Russo, Mary. 1986. "Female Grotesques: Carnival and Theory." In *Feminist Studies/Critical Studies,* ed. Teresa de Lauretis. Bloomington: Indiana University Press, pp. 213–229.

Salisbury, Harrison E. 1958. *The Shook-Up Generation.* New York: Harper.

Saussure, Ferdinand de. 1966. *Course in General Linguistics.* New York: McGraw-Hill.

Schickel, Richard. 1987. "*River's Edge*: Review." *Time,* June 1, p. 73.

Smart, Carol. 1976. *Women, Crime and Criminology: A Feminist Critique.* Boston: Routledge and Kegan Paul.

Smith, Gavin. 1987. "Pretty Vacant in Pink." *Film Comment* 23.4(July-August): 70–71.

Smothers, Roland. 1990. "Atlanta Sets a Curfew for Youths, Prompting Concern on Race Bias." *New York Times,* November 21, pp. A1ff.

Soothill, Keith, and Sylvia Walby. 1991. *Sex Crime in the News.* New York: Routledge.

Sorkin, Michael. 1986. "Simulations: Faking It." In *Watching Television,* ed. Todd Gitlin. New York: Pantheon Books, pp. 162–182.

Spigel, Lynn. 1988. "Installing the Television Set: Popular Discourses on Television and Domestic Space, 1948–1955." *Camera Obscura* 16:11–46.

Spitzack, Carole. 1990. *Confessing Excess: Women and the Politics of Body Reduction.* Albany: State University of New York Press.

Stallybrass, Peter, and Allon White. 1986. *The Politics and Poetics of Transgression.* Ithaca: Cornell University Press.

Steedman, Carolyn Kay. 1987. *Landscape for a Good Woman: A Story of Two Lives.* New Brunswick, N.J.: Rutgers University Press.

Stokes, Geoffrey. 1986. "Bubblehead Slut Dies, Deserves It." *Village Voice,* September 9, p. 8.

Stone, Michael. 1986. "East Side Story." *New York,* November 10, pp. 42ff.

Szymczak, Patricia M., and Joseph Sjostrom. 1988. "3 Teenagers Stabbed in Suburb High School." *Chicago Tribune,* December 8, pp. 1ff.

Tannenbaum, Frank. 1938. *Crime and the Community.* Boston: Ginn.

Taubman, Bryna. 1988. *The Preppy Murder Trial.* New York: St. Martin's Press.

Theriot, Nancy. 1983. *Nostalgia on the Right: Historical Roots of the Idealized Family.* Chicago: Midwest Research.

"Three Store Employees Accused of Selling Fake Identification." 1986. *New York Times,* September 12, p. B6.

Tolson, Andrew. 1990. "Social Surveillance and Subjectification: The Emergence of 'Subculture' in the Work of Henry Mayhew." *Cultural Studies* 4.2 (May):113–127.

Toufexis, Anastasia. 1989. "Our Violent Kids." *Time,* June 12, pp. 52–58.

UNESCO. 1981. *Youth in the 1980s.* Paris: UNESCO Press.

U.S. Bureau of the Census. 1988, 1989. *Statistical Abstracts of the United States.* Washington, D.C.: U.S. Department of Commerce.

U.S. Congress, Office of Technology Assessment. 1991. *Adolescent Health: Background and the Effectiveness of Selected Prevention and Treatment Services.* Vol. 2. Washington, D.C.: GPO, November.

Van Biema, David. 1986. "The Violent Death of Young Jennifer Levin Sobers the Preppy Elite of New York." *People Weekly,* September 15, pp. 56ff.

Voloshinov, Valentin. 1973. *Marxism and the Philosophy of Language.* Trans. Ladislav Matejka and I. R. Titunik. New York: Seminar Press.

Waters, Harry F. 1988. "Trash TV." *Newsweek,* November 14, pp. 72–78.

Webster, Duncan. 1988. *Looka Yonder!: The Imaginary America of Populist Culture.* New York: Routledge.

Weedon, Chris. 1987. *Feminist Practice and Poststructuralist Theory.* New York: Basil Blackwell.

Wertham, Fredric. 1954. *Seductions of the Innocent.* Port Washington, N.Y.: Kennikat Press.

West, Cornel. 1988. "Interview with Cornel West." In *Universal Abandon?: The Politics of Postmodernism,* ed. Andrew Ross. Minneapolis: University of Minnesota Press, pp. 269–286.

Whyte, William Foote. 1943. *Street Corner Society.* Chicago: University of Chicago Press.

Williams, Raymond. 1961. *The Long Revolution.* New York: Columbia University Press.

Williamson, Judith. 1986. "The Problem of Being Popular." *New Socialist* (September):14–15.

Willis, Paul. 1977. *Learning to Labor: How Working Class Kids Get Working Class Jobs.* New York: Columbia University Press.

Wilson, Deborah. 1990. "Breaking the Adolescent Code of Silence." *Globe and Mail* (Toronto), July 16, pp. A1ff.

Wolfe, Linda. 1987. "The People Versus Robert Chambers: The 'Preppy Killing' Case Comes to Trial." *New York,* October 26, pp. 92–108.

———. 1989. *Wasted: The Preppy Murder.* New York: Simon and Schuster.

Wood, Dennis. 1986. "Seeing and Being." *Film Quarterly* 39 (Spring):62–65.

Woollacott, Janet. 1982. "Messages and Meanings." In *Culture, Society and the Media,* ed. Michael Gurevitch, Tony Bennett, James Curran, and Janet Woollacott. New York: Methuen, pp. 91–111.

Worrall, Anne. 1990. *Offending Women: Female Lawbreakers and the Criminal Justice System.* New York: Routledge.

Zinsmeister, Karl. 1990. "Growing Up Scared." *The Atlantic* (June): 49–66.

About the Book and Author

In this book, Charles R. Acland examines the culture that has produced both our heightened state of awareness and the bedrock reality of youth violence in the United States. Beginning with a critique of statistical evidence of youth violence, Acland compares and juxtaposes a variety of popular cultural representations of what has come to be a perceived crisis of American youth.

After examining the dominant paradigms for scholarly research into youth deviance, Acland explores the ideas circulating in the popular media about a sensational crime known as the "preppy murder" and the confession to that crime. Arguing that the meaning of crime is never inherent in the event itself, he evaluates other sites of representation, including newspaper photographs (with a comparison to the Central Park "wilding"), daytime television talk shows (*Oprah*, *Geraldo*, and *Donahue*), and Hollywood youth films (in particular *River's Edge*).

Through a cultural studies analysis of historical context, Acland blurs the center of our preconceptions and exposes the complex social forces at work upon this issue in the late 1980s and early 1990s. Acland asks of the social critic, "How do we know that we are measuring what we say we are measuring, and how do we know what the numbers are saying? Arguments must be made to interpret findings, which suggests that conclusions are provisional and, to various degrees, sites of contestation." He launches into this gratifying book to show that beyond the problematic category of "actual" crime, the United States has seen the construction of a new "spectacle of wasted youth" that will have specific consequences for the daily lives of the next generation.

Charles R. Acland teaches cultural and media studies in the Faculty of General Studies at the University of Calgary, where he is an assistant professor. His articles have appeared in *Communication*, the *Journal of Communication Inquiry*, *Wide Angle*, and *Substance*, among other scholarly and popular publications. He is currently writing about the historical tensions between popular taste and national culture, with specific emphasis upon Canadian cultural history.

Index

historical perspective of concept of, 26, 137–138
ideology of protection and, 25
institutions associated with, 26
macrolevel analysis of, 20
market for, 36, 119, 137
microlevel analysis of, 20
middle class and, 27
minimum-age requirements and, 20
myths of inherent traits of, 21
"The Other" and, 19, 28, 41, 121, 122
preparing for the world and, 21, 26
as problem, 28–29, 36, 38. *See also* "Youth in crisis"
sexuality and, 91
as social category, 10, 20, 28, 29, 36, 137–138

as spectacle, 135–146
structural crisis of, 4, 5
style and, 36–38, 117, 136
surveillance of, 23, 24–25, 28, 41, 71, 135–136
symbolic centrality and, 19, 41
underage drinking and, 70–71
See also Crime; Crisis
"Youth in crisis," 5, 18, 19, 111, 118, 132, 140, 144, 145
Youth movies, 115–133
explanations for troubled youth in, 120
perspective of adults and, 116–117, 131–132
refusal vs. repudiation of adults, 122
teenpics, 119–120

Zinsmeister, Karl, 140–145